Grade Aid

for

Baron, Byrne, and Branscombe

Social Psychology

Eleventh Edition

prepared by

Melinda Blackman
California State University, Fullerton

PEARSON

Boston New York San Francisco
Mexico City Montreal Toronto London Madrid Munich Paris
Hong Kong Singapore Tokyo Cape Town Sydney

ISBN 0-205-45754-1

Printed in the United States of America

10 9 8 7 6 5 4 3 2 10 09 08 07 06 05

TABLE OF CONTENTS

PREFACE

USING YOUR STUDY GUIDE

Your instructor has chosen a classic, internationally-respected social psychology text. Most social psychologists regard the Baron and Byrne *Social Psychology* text as one of the best—if not *the best*—in the field. And the new co-author (Nyla Branscombe) has certainly helped to strengthen the book still further. This text will inform you about the exciting and important field of social psychology. I am also confident that you'll find it quite helpful in years to come with respect to your future academic and career endeavors.

This study guide has been designed to help you get the most out of your text. Let me stress a very important point *before* you begin your use of this study aid: ***This study guide is not a substitute for reading your text.*** It also should be said that this study guide cannot cover every single detail covered in your text. Now, with that behind us, let me say that I truly believe that this study guide will aid your study efforts considerably—and make that "A" a more plausible reality for you. Here is an overview about how you should use this study guide...

You will find that there are *four* self-explanatory, distinct sections for each of your twelve text chapters and two modules. The "Before You Read..." section should literally be reviewed prior to your text reading for that specific chapter. This section highlights the key learning objectives and summarizes the basic issues that the chapter discusses.

Now, the "As You Read..." section will be most effective while you're reading your text chapters. Here you'll first encounter several dozen key terms from the chapter; I would recommend that you know these words very well. You'll also find a medley of exercises and questions. You should *not* be using these questions as a final test of your knowledge for that chapter. These exercises were designed so that you could complete them as you go along with your readings. In other words, they're meant to reinforce and solidify your understanding of what you've just read. *It is important to know that you will not find the answers to these exercises contained in this study guide.* In case you're wondering why—this decision was made because the purpose of these exercises are for you to search for the responses. By doing this, you'll be actively engaged with the material, so, when test time comes around, you should know this material quite well.

Next, check out the "After You Read..." section for four exams and 3-6 short essay questions. The first three exams contain ten multiple-choice questions. Each of these three practice tests covers a subset of the chapter. When you're done with these, complete the comprehensive exam: This twenty-three item (fifteen multiple choice, eight true-false) exam covers material from the entire chapter. Whether you choose to complete all four exams at once or take them one at a time is up to you, of course. However, I'd probably recommend the latter suggestion. After the true/false questions you will find 3-6 short essay questions to solidify your understanding of the material. The answers to all of these short answer/essay questions, as well as the questions contained in the "After You Read..." section, can be found in an Appendix at the end of this study guide.

The last section is referred to as the "When You Have Finished... section." There are three basic elements to this last section. For each chapter, you'll find an "Applications of Social Psychology to Your Life" section, suggesting how the material contained in each respective chapter is relevant for ***your*** life. I also suggest some interesting exercises that you might consider doing either for a class project or for your own personal enjoyment. Next you will find a list of relevant internet sites if you would like to pursue more knowledge about any of the topics in the chapter. And finally, as a fun exercise I have included a crossword puzzle containing clues to key terms in the chapter. Again, the answers to the puzzle can be found in the Appendix section of this study guide.

After reading these sections, I hope you'll share not only my passion for social psychology, but also my strong belief that it is relevant for ***all*** of our lives. One more thing to note, if you still need MORE questions and exercises, check out the Web site for this text www.ablongman.com/baronbyrne. I think you'll find it to be another valuable resource too.

I wish you well in your studies and I sincerely hope that this study aid will be of help to you.

Melinda C. Blackman, Ph.D.
Associate Professor of Psychology
California State University, Fullerton

1 THE FIELD OF SOCIAL PSYCHOLOGY: HOW WE THINK ABOUT AND INTERACT WITH OTHERS

Before You Read . . .

This chapter introduces you to the field of social psychology, which is the scientific study of the nature and causes of individual behavior and thought in social situations. Through a personal example of joining the high school track team, author Robert Baron will show you how virtually everything we do, feel, or think is related in some way to the social side of life. Through this example, you will receive an overview of the types of issues that are studied by social psychologists. Next, the text will give you an explanation of why social psychology is considered a science. Afterward, you'll have a good understanding of the general types of factors and variables that can influence social thought and behavior. You should also be on the lookout for an interesting discussion of some of the hottest contemporary trends in social psychology research. Following that, you'll have a very detailed exposure to the methods of social psychology research; here some of the mystery and intrigue that surrounds such studies will be explained. As part of this discussion, particular emphasis will be placed on a comparison of correlational and experimental studies. After a brief and user-friendly overview of the role of statistics and theories in social psychology research, the chapter concludes with a discussion of the importance of ethics when conducting social psychology research.

Chapter Objectives

After reading this chapter, you should be able to:

- Offer a definition of social psychology and discuss the types of issues this field considers.
- State the four core values to a science.
- Explain why social psychology is based upon the scientific approach rather than common sense.
- State and briefly discuss the five major headings that characterize the variables of interest to most social psychologists.
- Discuss some of the major contemporary research trends in social psychology.
- Describe the difference between social thought and social behavior and the complex interplay between the two.
- Give a general definition of the growing field of social neuroscience.

- Consider the advantages and limitations to systematic observations and the survey method.
- Describe the correlational method including the meaning of correlational coefficients and the key drawback to this method.
- Outline the nature of the experimental method, including all of the key components to this methodology.
- Explain the basic purpose of inferential statistics and meta-analysis.
- Define the term, "theory," and describe the procedure involved in building theories.
- Consider when and how deception is used in social psychological research.
- Discuss the importance of informed consent and debriefing in social psychological research.

As You Read . . .

Important Terms to Know. Below are a list of some of the key terms and concepts from this chapter. Make flashcards in order to enhance your recall ability of these terms. Refer to the definitions that are either in boldface or in the margins of this chapter for help. You may also want to include additional terms from this chapter as you deem necessary.

Social psychology	Accuracy	Objectivity
Skepticism	Open-mindedness	The scientific approach
Cognitive processes	Evolutionary psychology	Common sense
Environmental variables	Cultural context	Biological factors
Social neuroscience	Social categorization	Implicit nonconscious processes
Social diversity	Systematic/Naturalistic observation	Survey method
Multicultural perspective	Representativeness	Hypothesis
Sampling	Correlational method	Cause and effect relationship
Experimental method	Independent variable	Dependent variable
External validity	Inferential statistics	Statistically significant
Meta-analysis	Theories	Confounding variable
Informed consent	Debriefing	Deception
Significant results	Random assignment	

Social Psychology: A Working Definition

➢ Social Psychology is Scientific in Nature

1. In your own words, offer a definition of social psychology.

2. List four possible social settings where a social psychologist could go to observe "helping behavior."

3. Listed below are a variety of research questions. Place a star next to the ones that appear to have definite relevance to the field of social psychology.

_________ Why does schizophrenia develop?

_________ How do people fall in love?

_________ How do children acquire the ability to comprehend language?

_________ Under what conditions might we comply with a request from a person?

_________ Have gender stereotypes changed over the past few decades?

_________ When people help others, do they expect some sort of reward in return?

_________ What part of the brain is responsible for positive emotions?

4. Calling all debaters! Listed below are a few points that a person could make about the nature of science. Your job is to offer a "counterpart" that refutes the point made.

Point: *Science simply refers to fields like biology, chemistry, and physics.*

Counterpoint:

Point: *Science doesn't really have core values.*

Counterpoint:

Point: *Social psychology is nothing but good old-fashioned common sense.*

Counterpoint:

➢ Social Psychology Seeks to Understand the Causes of Social Behavior and Social Thought

1. Listed below are a variety of variables that can influence social behavior and thought. Place these variables under the correct heading in the chart below.

memories of past behavior

behaviors toward elderly vs. young people

the appropriateness of giving gifts to college professors

passing genetic variations onto future generations

how we act when the weather is hot

what is considered by most to be "sexy"

whether we are more helpful when exposed to a pleasant smell

the role of construals

The Actions and Characteristics of Other Persons	Cognitive Processes	Environmental Variables	Cultural Context	Biological Factors

➢ Social Psychology: Summing Up

1. Social behavior and thought are influenced by a wide range of ________________,

   ________________, ________________, ________________, and ________________

   factors.

Social Psychology: Its Cutting Edge

➢ Social Behavior and Social Thought: Two Sides of the Same Social Coin

1. State the two *most* important ways that the cognitive perspective is reflected in social psychological research.

➢ Social Neuroscience: Where Social Psychology and Neuroscience Meet

1. Explain the practical importance of including the area of social neuroscience to the field of social psychology.

2. Develop a question related to social neuroscience that you would like to know the answer to.

➢ The Role of Implicit (Nonconscious) Processes

1. Give an example of how *implicit egotism* affects your everyday interactions and choices of behaviors.

➢ Taking Full Account of Social Diversity

1. Define what is meant by a "multicultural perspective." Why wasn't such a perspective largely adopted until fairly recently by social psychologists? To put it another way, how did most social psychologists address and conceptualize the issue of diversity in the 1960s and 1970s?

Answering Questions About Social Behavior and Social Thought: Research Methods in Social Psychology

➢ Systematic Observation: Describing the World Around Us

1. Systematic observation involves ____

   ____.

2. Define what is meant by a naturalistic observation and denote how such an investigation occurs.

3. *Applying Your Knowledge:* Devise an observational study to determine if "chivalry" is still alive. More specifically, do men still hold the doors open for women to pass through? Where would your study be conducted? How would you obtain the data? Who would you use to observe the participants' behavior?

4. Identify the advantages of the survey method and note the two main issues that *must* be carefully addressed when undertaking such a method.

➢ Correlation: The Search for Relationships

1. Underline the words in parentheses that will make the following statement correct:

   The term correlation refers to a tendency for one event to (cause another event, change as the other changes). When a correlation exists, it is possible to (predict, explain) one variable from information about one or more variables. So, the correlational method tells us (whether only, whether and to what extent) two variables are related to each other. Correlations can range from (0 to 100, 0 to –1.00 or 0 to +1.00), whereby the (greater, less) departure from 0, the stronger the correlation. (Positive, Negative) numbers mean that as one variable increases, the other variable increases; (positive, negative) numbers show that as one variable increases, the other decreases.

2. ***Rank it!*** Rank order the following correlation coefficient values such that a "1" indicates the strongest correlation and a "5" indicates the weakest.

   ______ +.01 ______ -.56 ______ +.17 ______ -.81 ______ +.33

3. Suppose a researcher finds that the average amount of time that a person exercises per week and the number of sweets they have per week is -.72. Briefly state what this correlation tells us about the relationship between these two variables.

4. ***Applying Your Knowledge*:** Suppose a study has found that there is a strong positive correlation between an increase in ice cream sales and rioting in the streets. A layperson might assume that consuming ice cream causes people to be more likely to riot in the streets. What is wrong with this individual's conclusion? What could be a possible third variable that might explain this relationship?

➤ The Experimental Method: Knowledge Through Systematic Intervention

1. ***Match it!*** Match each phrase, word, or sentence on the left side of the page with an identifying concept on the right side of the page. Note that each item on the right should be used *only once*.

__1. Situations where researchers aren't informed of a study's hypothesis.	A. experimentation
__2. The extent to which findings generalize to real life.	B. independent variable
__3. Allowing for an equal chance of exposure to each of the levels in the study.	C. dependent variable
__4. The variable that's measured.	D. random assignment
__5. A method that allows for understanding causality.	E. experimenter effects
__6. Unintended effects on subjects' behavior caused by researchers.	F. double-blind procedure
__7. The variable that's systematically varied.	G. external validity

2. Suppose Professor Green randomly assigns research participants to one of the following conditions: They are instructed to ride an exercise bike for either zero, fifteen, or thirty minutes. Afterward, she asks subjects to rate their positive mood.

   a.) What is the independent variable?

   b.) What is the dependent variable?

   c.) How many levels does this experimental study have?

3. Discuss the disadvantage a study would have if the participants were not randomly assigned to the experimental and control conditions of the study.

Interpreting Research Results: The Use of Statistics and Social Psychologists as Perennial Skeptics

1. What are inferential statistics and why do social psychologists use them?

2. A "significant result" is____

____

3. What is a meta-analysis and why do social psychologists use this technique?

4. ***On the road again***....It definitely is a long road from the moment a theory is tested to when it ultimately is decided as to whether the confidence in the theory will be increased or decreased. In the chart below, outline the steps needed in order for us to make a judgment as to whether the confidence in the theory will increase or decrease.

Confidence in the theory is INCREASED	Confidence in the theory is REDUCED

The Quest for Knowledge and Rights of Individuals: Seeking An Appropriate Balance

1. Why is deception sometimes used in social psychological research? What do research participants tend to think about its use in research?

2. "Informed consent" is____

3. "Debriefing" is ____

4. ***Applying Your Knowledge:*** Suppose a researcher wanted to study the cognitive effects of victims who have been trapped in a burning building. Obviously the researcher for ethical reasons cannot put victims in a harmful situation to obtain data. What would be two alternative research designs in which the researcher could utilize to conduct her study? What would be some disadvantages to these designs?

Alternative Research Design	Disadvantages
1.	**1.**
2.	**2.**

After You Read...

Practice Test 1

1. A scientific field is different from a non-scientific field in terms of
   a. the applied nature of the issues that are studied.
   b. the values and methods that are adopted and used.
   c. whether the investigators hold advanced degrees.
   d. whether a physical or social phenomenon is studied.

2. Representative sampling and wording of questions are particularly important when conducting a(n)
   a. survey.
   b. correlational study.
   c. experiment.
   d. naturalistic observation.

3. All of the following represent core values in the field of science, *except*
   a. open-mindedness.
   b. subjectivity.
   c. skepticism.
   d. accuracy.

4. An experimenter exposed subjects to systematically varied levels of temperature to determine its effect on aggression. The temperature level is the ____ variable.
   a. independent
   b. dependent
   c. control
   d. theoretical

5. When the results of an experiment can be generalized to real-life social situations, the experiment has
   a. external validity.
   b. statistical significance.
   c. theoretical relevance.
   d. random assignment.

6. A sophisticated statistical technique for combing results from many experiments in order to reach an overall conclusion regarding the topic in question is called
   a. replication.
   b. a correlational coefficient.
   c. meta-analysis.
   d. converging operations.

7. A primary goal of social psychological theories is to provide
   a. a description of social behavior.
   b. an explanation of social behavior.
   c. ethical guidelines for researchers.
   d. a summary of previous research in social psychology.

8. A key reason why a social psychologist may use deception in a study is to
   a. protect subjects from the harmful effects of learning negative aspects about themselves.
   b. illustrate that causal relationships between independent and dependent variables cannot be established without the use of deception.
   c. simply obtain useful knowledge that otherwise might not be possible if subjects knew the true purpose of the study.
   d. satisfy the wishes of research participants who routinely enjoy experiments where deception is involved.

9. A research participant gives their ____ once they are told about what a particular study will involve. Once the study is completed, the research participant is given a(n) ____, or a full description about the nature of the research.
   a. deceptive cues; debriefing
   b. safeguarding; informed consent
   c. debriefing; informed consent
   d. informed consent; debriefing

10. The reaction of most research participants to temporary deception appears to be
    a. overwhelmingly negative.
    b. a feeling of concern followed by intrigue.
    c. not negative provided that its purpose and necessity are clear.
    d. overwhelmingly positive.

Practice Test 2

1. The scientific field that seeks to understand the nature and causes of individual behavior and thought in social situations is called
   a. social science.
   b. social psychology.
   c. sociology.
   d. personality psychology.

2. Research involving whether people react differently to the elderly than younger persons primarily involves the study of variables pertaining to
   a. the actions and characteristics of other people.
   b. cognitive processes.
   c. the cultural context.
   d. environmental variables.

3. Biological processes and genetic factors
   a. are unrelated to social behavior.
   b. completely predict social behavior.
   c. affect social behavior to some extent.
   d. might influence social behavior, but this issue hasn't been studied yet.

4. The cognitive perspective reflects basic knowledge about all of the following areas, *except*
   a. memory.
   b. psychopathology.
   c. reasoning.
   d. decision making.

5. An unconscious tendency toward self-enhancement is referred to as________.
   a. implicit self-esteem
   b. nonconscious self-esteem
   c. implicit egotism
   d. explicit self-enhancement

6. A research technique that is often included under the heading of systematic observation is the ____ method.
   a. correlational
   b. survey
   c. experimental
   d. meta-analysis

7. Which of the following correlation coefficients is impossible to have?
   a. -1
   b. 1
   c. 0
   d. 10

8. Variables that occur in a study that are <u>not</u> under systematic investigation are referred to as
   a. explicit factors
   b. extraneous inputs
   c. subjective variables
   d. confounds

9. When two variables are correlated, we can assume that there is a causal link between these
   a. only if the result is statistically significant.
   b. only when the correlation coefficient value is close to –1 or +1.
   c. under no conditions.
   d. under any conditions.

10. Professor Green and Professor White are conducting research studies in social psychology. Professor Green wants to randomly assign subjects to his two conditions by alternating order (e.g., the first subject goes in the first condition, the second subject goes in the second condition, the third subject goes in the first condition, etc.) whereas Professor White wants to randomly assign subjects on the basis of their sex (e.g., men go in the first condition and women go in the second condition). Which of the following statements *best* summarizes whether random assignment has been followed?
    a. Both professors have randomly assigned their subjects.
    b. Neither professor has randomly assigned their subjects.
    c. Professor Green has randomly assigned his subjects, but Professor White has not.
    d. Professor White has randomly assigned his subjects, but Professor Green has not.

Practice Test 3

1. Experimenter effects can often be avoided if ____ is used.
    a. double-blind procedure
    b. random assignment
    c. external validity
    d. the correlational method

2. A research result is considered to be "significant" when
    a. a majority of social psychologists claim it to be so.
    b. it has applied relevance.
    c. the likelihood of obtaining the observed findings by chance is low.
    d. the result appears to be important in some way.

3. Suppose a theory supported by Dr. Williams has ultimately been accepted. What are the implications of this decision?
    a. No further research on this theory is necessary.
    b. The theory still remains open to further refinement.
    c. Outside reviews should question whether Dr. Williams' decision was ethical.
    d. We can assume that Dr. Williams noted many instances where his results were inconsistent with the theory.

4. Right before Professor Peterson is about to begin her study, she tells her research participants that they will be sampling a variety of cookies. This is consistent with
    a. truth-telling.
    b. informed consent.
    c. deception.
    d. debriefing.

5. The view that social psychology should apply to all humans regardless of where they live or their cultural identity is
    a. generally considered to be racist.
    b. consistent with the multicultural perspective.
    c. no longer dominant within the field.
    d. fairly accurate and accepted by most social psychologists.

6. During a naturalistic observation, the experimenter
   a. tries to ask prospective research participants as many questions as possible.
   b. absolutely must make use of random assignment.
   c. should be very concerned about the wording of questions used during the study.
   d. attempts to avoid influencing the persons observed.

7. Which of the following correlation coefficient orders represent values ranging from the weakest to the strongest?
   a. -.66; 0; +.33
   b. +.54; -.61; -.49
   c. -.80; -.22; 0
   d. +.18; -.27; -.41

8. When an independent variable is confounded with another variable,
   a. the results of an experiment may be meaningless.
   b. this suggests that the experimenter failed to use random assignment.
   c. we can assume that the experiment is a success since this should occur in an experimental study.
   d. this offers evidence that we should reject the given theory.

9. Meta-analysis is considered to be a(n) ____ procedure.
   a. correlational
   b. experimental
   c. mathematical
   d. theoretical

10. Suppose you learn that a certain researcher has claimed to have "proven a theory of social behavior." How should you respond to the researcher's statement?
    a. You should ask the researcher to explain the methods of his or her study.
    b. You should ask the researcher to state how he or she has proven the theory.
    c. You should tell the researcher that we can never prove a theory in any absolute way.
    d. You should congratulate the researcher on proving the theory, given how difficult it is to "prove" any theory.

Comprehensive Test

(NOTE: Items 1-15 are multiple-choice questions and items 16-23 are true-false questions.)

1. Which of the following is considered to be a component of the definition of social psychology?
   a. It is a science.
   b. It focuses on large groups of persons.
   c. It is used to understand the nature of social situations only.
   d. It primarily examines individual behavior.

2. When Dr. Williamson discovers that a certain result hasn't been replicated in a study, she grows wary of initial claims made by a certain researcher. This example *best* illustrates the importance of ____ in scientific research.
   a. accuracy
   b. objectivity
   c. skepticism
   d. open-mindedness

3. The fact that many people believe that "opposites attract" and "birds of a feather flock together" suggests that
   a. the scientific method has very limited applications.
   b. most people have a good understanding of human behavior irrespective of whether they are psychologists.
   c. common sense often portrays a confusing, inconsistent picture of human behavior.
   d. it is very difficult to even begin to understand the dynamics of interpersonal attraction.

4. All of the following issues would be illustrative of environmental variables, *except*
   a. whether we act more aggressive when it is hot.
   b. whether we are more likely to help others after smelling a pleasant odor.
   c. what is considered to be attractive in a given country or culture.
   d. the impact of a full moon on social behavior.

5. The crucial, concrete outcome of evolution is ____.
   a. variation
   b. inheritance
   c. selection
   d. attraction

6. ______occurs at the beginning of a study and _______at the end of a research study.
   a. Debriefing, informed consent
   b. Informed consent, debriefing
   c. Debriefing, external validity
   d. Confounds, external validity

7. The issue of sampling in survey research suggests the importance of
   a. random assignment.
   b. systematic manipulation of a certain variable.
   c. making sure the researcher isn't noticed by the research participants.
   d. having participants who are representative of the larger population.

8. A correlation coefficient value of ____ is greater than a correlation coefficient value of ____.
   a. +.80; -.90
   b. -.31; +.21
   c. 0; -.52
   d. +.44; -.44

9. The greatest flaw of a correlational study is generally considered to be its inability to
   a. be used in natural settings.
   b. gather a large amount of information in a short period of time.
   c. highly efficient.
   d. draw conclusive causal relationships.

10. Suppose Dr. Kern devises an experimental study where her research participants either watch zero, five, or fifteen minutes of very violent television and then she takes their pulse. In this study, there would be ____ levels of the independent variable.
    a. two
    b. three
    c. four
    d. twenty

11. Another major area in social psychology is _______, which relates activity in the brain and other biological events to key aspects of social thought and behavior.
    a. psychological neuroscience
    b. biological sociology
    c. social neuroscience
    d. neurobiology

12. A key reason why social psychological research often yields inconsistent findings is due to
    a. a poor understanding of statistical methods used in research.
    b. the fact that social psychology can never explain human behavior "across the board."
    c. the use of different methods by different researchers.
    d. a general dependence on outdated theories of social thought and behavior.

13. For the confidence in a theory to be reduced,
    a. its predictions must have been disconfirmed.
    b. the theory must be rejected.
    c. the research designed to test its predictions must be faulty.
    d. the theory must be worthless.

14. The use of deception in social psychological research
    a. is no longer permitted.
    b. usually causes great harm to those exposed to it.
    c. is typically not tolerated by research participants.
    d. must never be used to persuade people to participate in a study.

15. All of the following are guiding principles for researchers in social psychology, *except*
    a. use deception only when it is absolutely essential to do so.
    b. always proceed with caution.
    c. make certain that all possible precautions are taken to safeguard the protection and well-being of subjects.
    d. try to avoid telling the research participant about the true nature of the study once they have completed it.

16. Your text asserts that highly advanced fields, such as physics, chemistry, and biology, are scientific in nature, whereas social psychology does *not* meet the criteria of being a "science."

17. Our judgments about persons we meet are likely to be influenced by the mood we are in when we meet them.

18. Social psychology focuses its study on groups of persons or society as a whole.

19. The role of construals in determining social behavior is primarily studied by evolutionary social psychologists.

20. Strong findings in correlational studies provide conclusive evidence that the variables being measured have a causal relationship with each other.

21. The preferred method of research by social psychologists has generally been the experimental method.

22. The goal of social psychological research is to prove that a particular theory of social behavior is true.

23. Social psychologists typically believe that it is permissible to use deception without informed consent and debriefing.

Short Answer/Essay Questions

1. **Social Psychology as a Science**
   State the four most important core values to a scientific field.

2. **Social Behavior and Other Causes of Social Behavior and Thought**
   State and briefly define at least three causes that social psychologists examine when studying social behavior and thought.

3. **Correlational Studies**
Suppose Professor Stone conducts a correlational study in which he asks individuals how many times (on average) they get into an argument with a friend or close other and the number of colds (on average) they get per year. If he records a correlation coefficient value of -.43, what does this value specifically tell us about the relationship between these two variables?

4. **Experimental Studies**
Suppose Dr. Wheeler conducts an experimental study in which research participants who are in a romantic relationship are asked to write about the benefits of their relationships, the drawbacks to the relationships, or to write about what they ate for breakfast that morning. Then, she measures and records each of the subject's blood pressure. Identify the independent and dependent variables in this study.

5. **The Role of Deception in Social Psychology Research**
Provide a brief overview of why deception is sometimes used in social psychological research, the problems that can result after using it, and how to minimize such problems.

When You Have Finished . . .

APPLICATIONS OF SOCIAL PSYCHOLOGY TO YOUR LIFE

At this point, perhaps you may be thinking, "OK, this stuff is interesting, but what does it have to do with *my* life?" That's certainly a very fair question. Remember that social psychologists typically try to apply many of their theories and empirical findings to "real" people in the "real" world—lest we forget Kurt Lewin's (the "founding father" of social psychology) famous maxim, "There's nothing as practical as a good theory." Let us try to specifically list how the study of social psychology truly has meaningful relevance for our lives on an everyday basis. Here is a list of relevant applications.

1. Since we all truly are 'social animals' who are interacting with others on a regular basis, *life itself* represents a study of social psychology!

2. We are consumers of information. By understanding scientific methods and what is considered to be "scientific," we are better equipped to carefully and critically analyze such information.

3. If we are aware of all of the possible major factors that influence social thought and behavior, then we will be more apt to pinpoint the possible causes of these thoughts or behaviors.

4. Since many social psychologists are concerned with applying their research findings in order to better the lives of people in the "real world," in some way you may have already benefited from the work of social psychologists (perhaps without even knowing it)!

5. If *you* are considering a career in psychology or other scientific fields, understanding the basic dynamics of research methodology will help further your career.

For each of the following chapters, you will be presented with different "Applications of Social Psychology to Your Life" lists. Be advised that this (and the others) represents the (Study Guide) author's subjective view as to how these items should be ranked. A fun exercise might be for *you* to come up with your own "Applications List" for each of the chapters. Additionally, I would encourage you—whether it be for paper assignments, class presentations, or general personal enrichment—to try to extend any or all of these points (from each of these lists) into a related exercise or project. To this end, I will suggest some possible exercises. For instance, with respect to point #5, design an experimental and/or correlational study examining some area of interest to you in social psychology. After you've outlined your design and questions, ask a few of your friends or family members to complete your "study" just for fun. Try to get a sense for whether your predictions were validated from your findings. Above all, be creative and have fun doing these exercises!

Here are some web links to provide you with additional information about the topics covered in this chapter:

Internet Resources:

http://www.spsp.org/index.htm: From the website of the Society for Personality and Social Psychology. This page provides some basic information on what social psychology is, what careers one can pursue with a degree in social psychology, what sort of training is necessary, and how one can obtain more information about social psychology.

http://psych.hanover.edu/Research/exponnet.html: Contains links to known experiments on the Internet that are psychologically related. Maintained by Dr. John H. Krantz at Hanover College.

http://www.socialpsychology.org: Social Psychology Network. The largest social psychology database on the Internet, developed and maintained by Scott Plous of Wesleyan University. Contains more than 5,000 links to social psychology related resources, including a directory of social psychologists and of research groups, information about professional journals, an extensive directory of teaching resources, information about social psychology textbooks and about graduate programs, and access to online studies.

http://www.socialpsychology.org/siteweek.htm: A website developed by Scott Plous and his social psychology classes over the years, based on the best web illustrations that students submitted.

http://www.sesp.org: The homepage of the Society of Experimental Social Psychology. It contains information about membership to this organization and upcoming conferences.

Crossword Puzzle

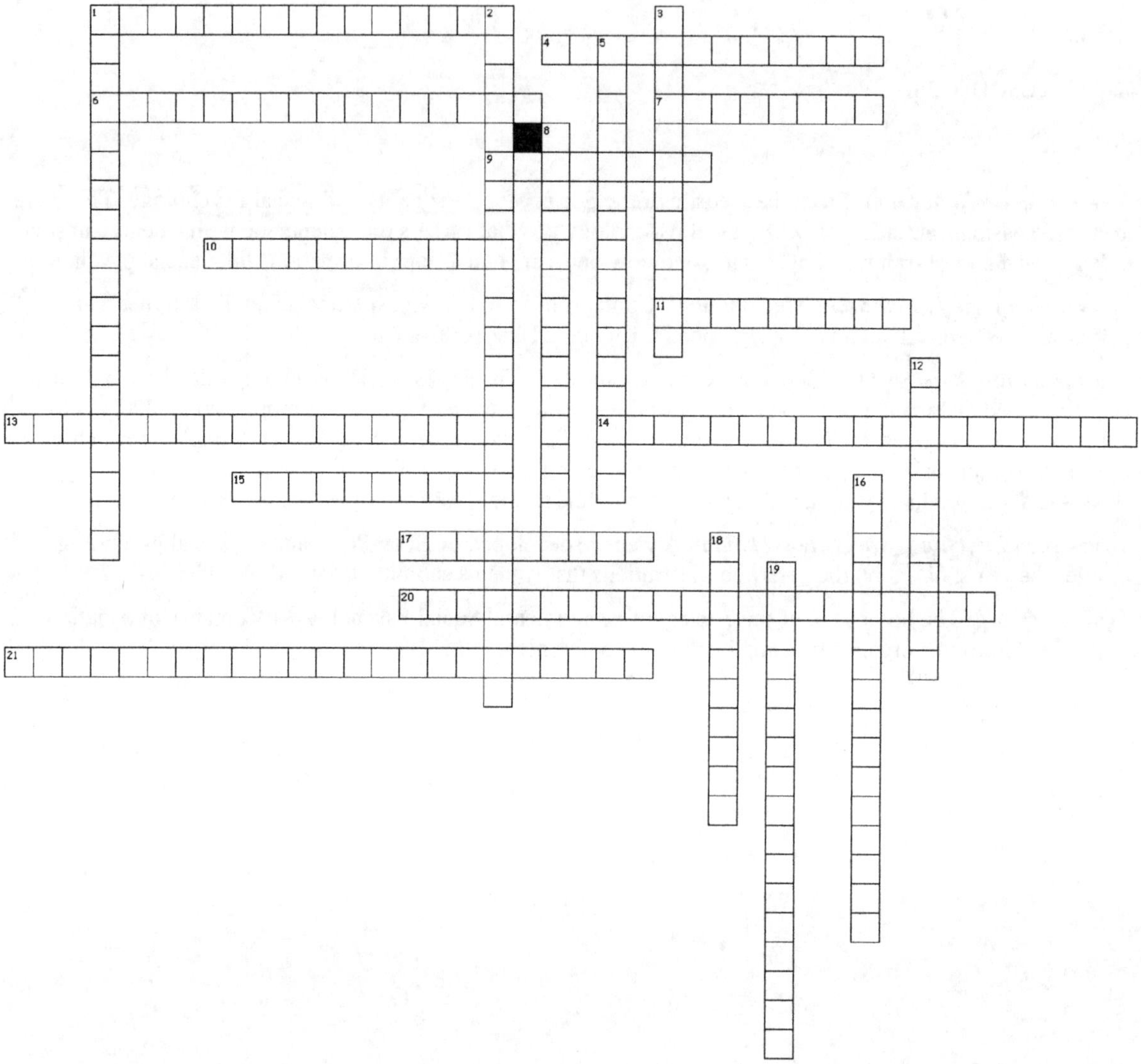

Across

1. unconscious self-enhancement
4. asking a large number of questions
6. generalizing findings
7. core value of the field
9. extraneous variable
10. likelihood of obtaining the observed findings by chance
11. a mental picture of who we would like to be
13. area in social psychology that studies biological bases of social processes
14. unintended researcher effects
15. unverified prediction
17. withholding information

20. technique for studying social behavior
21. observing behavior in natural settings

Down

1. factor systematically varied
2. understanding cultural and ethnic factors that influence social behavior
3. many combined studies
5. equal chance of being exposed
8. giving participants information prior to the study
12. two related variables
16. behavior of others in social settings
18. full description of purpose of study
19. aspect of behavior studied

2 SOCIAL COGNITION: THINKING ABOUT THE SOCIAL WORLD

Before You Read . . .

In this chapter, you'll be provided with an introduction to the study of social cognition; this field considers how we interpret, analyze, remember, and use information about the social world. After reading this chapter, you'll have a good understanding of why we often make many errors and mental short cuts when thinking about social information. This is especially highlighted in the "**Beyond the Headlines**" section which will reveal the possible cognitive bases of the false belief that S.U.V.'s are safer than other vehicles. You will then be introduced to a discussion about the neural bases of our distinct systems for evaluating various aspects of the social world--automatic and controlled. By this time, you will also have a better appreciation for why total rationality in social cognition is not that common in light of such phenomena as heuristics, negativity and optimistic biases, counterfactual and magical thinking, and thought suppression. Despite all of these potential forms of cognitive bias, you'll also have an appreciation for why we still do a fairly good job of processing social information. The last segment of this chapter explores the two-way relationship between affect and cognition. In other words, as you can imagine, our feelings can influence our thoughts and our thoughts can influence our feelings.

Chapter Objectives

After reading this chapter, you should be able to:

- Discuss what is meant by "social cognition" and list the basic assumptions that most social psychologists have with respect to cognitive processes.
- State the basic purpose and function of schemas as well as the three basic processes that they influence.
- Consider how our schemas may (or may not) be altered in the face of new information.
- Discuss how the self-fulfilling prophecy may operate in certain applied settings, such as classroom environments.
- Explain why we often use heuristics and the consequences of their use. Contrast two different types of heuristics.

SOCIAL COGNITION

- Apply your knowledge of heuristics to understand why so many consumers feel S.U.V.s are safer than smaller size cars.

- Discuss the nature of automatic processing in social thought.

- Understand the neural processes that are responsible for making simple good-bad judgments in a rapid manner.

- Examine why we tend to show a negativity bias—particularly from an evolutionary or biological perspective.

- Consider the prevalence of the optimistic bias, its consequences, and when this bias typically is *not* shown.

- Understand why sometimes our tendency to do a minimal amount of cognitive work may be justified.

- Identify the effects that counterfactual thinking may have on our moods and general well-being.

- State the meaning of "magical thinking" as well as the three principles that pertain to this pattern of cognition. Give an example of when we fail to take into account moderating variables into the judgment process.

- Explain what thought suppression is, why it can be—but often is *not*—effective, and identify the individual difference characteristic that is particularly susceptible to the negative effects of thought suppression.

- Provide a rationale for why we actually do a fairly good job in processing social information.

- Consider how affect can influence cognition by discussing mood-dependent memory, mood congruence effects, mental contamination, and the effects of being in a good mood on social behavior.

- List the three ways that cognition can influence affect.

- Understand that there can be social and cognitive disadvantages to being in a good mood.

As You Read . . .

Important Terms to Remember: Below are a list of some of the key terms and concepts from this chapter. Make flashcards in order to enhance your recall ability of these terms. Refer to the definitions that are either in boldface or in the margins of this chapter for help. You may also want to include additional terms from this chapter as you deem necessary.

Social cognition	Affect	Schemas
Attention	Encoding	Retrieval
Perseverance effect	Self-fulfilling prophecy	Information overload
Heuristics	Representativeness heuristic	Availability heuristic
Anchoring	Adjustment heuristic	Affect Infusion model
(Automatic) Priming	Automatic processing	Negativity bias
Optimistic bias	Planning fallacy	Brace for loss effect
Counterfactual thinking	Mood congruence effect	Magical thinking
Rocky past	Golden future	Moderating variables
Two-factor theory of emotion	Thought suppression	Reactance
Mood-dependent memory		

Schemas: Mental Frameworks for Organizing and Using Social Information

➢ The Impact of Schemas on Social Cognition: Attention, Encoding, Retrieval

1. In your own words, what is meant by "social cognition?" Also, what are the two basic assumptions that most social psychologists tend to have about cognition?

2. Look at the picture below. It should activate a certain schema for you. Identify and describe that schema and, how your description further helps you to understand precisely what a schema is.

3. Schemas exert effects on three basic processes. State and define these three processes below.

Process	Definition

4. What do we do with information that is inconsistent with our schemas? Is this information remembered better than information that is consistent with our schemas? How is the perseverance effect relevant to these two questions?

➢ The Self-Confirming Nature of Schemas: When and Why Beliefs Shape Reality

1. Describe the nature of self-fulfilling prophecies by considering how this effect may operate in classroom situations.

2. Name the historical event that may have been caused, in part, due to the nature of self-fulfilling prophecies.

Heuristics and Automatic Processing: How We Reduce Our Effort in Social Cognition

➢ Representativeness: Judging by Resemblance

1. When do we experience information overload?

2. Why do we use heuristics?

3. Suppose Tom starts work at a new business and while setting up his office, he places a U.S. flag and a picture of U.S. President George W. Bush on his desk. Tom's co-workers are trying to "figure out" his personality—will they be more likely to say that he's "patriotic" or "patriotic and conservative" based on how the representativeness heuristic operates? Explain your response. Also, would such a judgment be accurate?

➢ Availability: "If I Can Think of It, It Must Be Important"

1. Even though statistically airplane flying is far safer than automobile driving many people claim a great fear of flying. How does the availability heuristic help to explain this apparent paradox?

2. How does priming help to explain the "medical student syndrome?"

➢ Beyond the Headlines: As Social Psychologists See it—Unsafe at Any Size?

1. Explain why so many people are purchasing S.U.V.'s and the faulty reasoning process that they are using to make judgments about the safety of these vehicles.

2. What heuristic are these purchasers relying on to make their conclusion about the safety of an S.U.V.?

➢ Automatic Processing in Social Thought: Saving Effort--But at a Cost!

1. What is difference between automatic and controlled processing?

2. *Let me be BLUNT: You're RUDE and IMPOLITE!* Okay, not really—I'm sure you're a nice person. However, when you read that sentence, what thoughts came to your mind? In thinking about your response, refer to the study done by Bargh, Chen, and Burrows (1996) that's described in the chapter.

Potential Sources of Error in Social Cognition: Why Total Rationality is Rarer Than You Think

➢ Negativity Bias: The Tendency to Pay Extra Attention to Negative Information

1. *I'm sure you're doing well in school. Perhaps you're even on your school's honor roll? But I bet you're going to fail your social psychology course.* (Okay, there I go again! I really don't have a sadistic streak, honest! And, of course, I'm sure you'll do just fine in your social psychology course.) But, think about it, what aspect of those three sentences in italics "stood out" for you? Even though there were two flattering statements made, I'm sure it was the last sentence. Explain how the nature of the negativity bias may might to shed some light on this matter. Also, summarize the evidence that suggests that the negativity bias has a biological component.

➢ The Optimistic Bias: Our Tendency to See the World Through Rose-Colored Glasses

1. Do you remember that old song from the 1980s, *Don't Worry, Be Happy?* Discuss how the optimistic bias tends to make us to do just that—not to worry and to be happy.

2. When you're planning your work for an assignment, you may give an overly optimistic prediction as to how long it will take you to complete your work. Name the effect that is *most* closely associated with this behavior and briefly note why this effect occurs.

3. Describe what the authors mean when they refer to the concepts of "rocky past" and "golden future" with regard to the perceptions of our own lives.

4. In your own words, what is the "bracing for loss" effect? Why does it occur?

➢ Counterfactual Thinking: The Effects of Considering "What Might Have Been"

1. *Going up...going down.* Listed below are three different scenarios. For each scenario, note whether it illustrates an *upward* or *downward* counterfactual and whether its net effect on the individual will be positive or negative.

   a.) After dating Rachael for almost a year, Isaac told her that "he wasn't sure" if he loved her. Five years later, he still thinks about his statement.

   b.) Oliver, an ice skating Olympic athlete, has just won a silver medal after imagining winning a gold one.

   c.) Seth, an entrepreneur, was reflecting on his decision to not merge his business with another company a year ago.

➢ Thought Suppression: Why Efforts to Avoid Certain Thinking Certain Thoughts Sometimes Backfire

1. *Think about your first romantic "crush." Now, try* ***not*** *thinking about your first romantic "crush" whatsoever.* Given the nature of thought suppression, why might such an exercise be extremely difficult to do?

2. Individuals who are ______________________________ tend to be a particular risk for the negative effects associated with being unable to suppress one's thoughts.

➢ Limits On Our Ability to Reason About The Social World: Magical Thinking and Ignoring Moderating Variables?

1. a.) Magical thinking involves assumptions that ______________________________.

   b.) For each of the following examples, denote the principle of magical thinking that is being depicted:

   1.) Ken is reluctant to rent an apartment where an AIDS patient formerly lived.

   2.) Professor Jones has brought a jello mold in the shape of a brain to class for her biology students to eat. She's surprised when very few students seem interested in having some.

   3.) Jon couldn't believe it when another terrorist attack occurred after he thought that another such attack was inevitable.

➢ Social Cognition: Some Words of Optimism

1. Despite our tendency to make many errors in social thought, your text authors maintain that there is reason to believe that we can often successfully process information. Why do they believe this? Do you agree?

Affect and Cognition: How Feelings Shape Thought and Thought Shapes Feelings

➢ The Influence of Affect on Cognition

1. *I second that emotion!* Emotions and affect obviously can impact people in many ways. Three such ways involve mood-dependent memory, mood congruence effects, and mental contamination. For each of the scenarios below, denote which of these three processes is being illustrated:

   a.) Suzy is in a good mood and, as such, she vividly recalls a compliment that someone made to her.

b.) Ed, a juror in a criminal case, realizes that he shouldn't allow a certain aspect of the defendant's testimony to influence his decision (as instructed by the judge), but he can't help but think about it.

c.) Carl remembers learning some very favorable news on the day he learned about the Civil War in his American history class. On the day of his history exam, he finds himself in a good mood since his parents are taking him on a ski trip later that day; consequently, he gets all of the questions on his exam about the Civil War correct.

d.) Barbara is in a foul mood since she had a big fight with her friend. When one of her co-workers mentioned that she looked "tired," she paid particular attention to this comment.

➢ The Science of Social Psychology: Making Sense of Common Sense

1. Research has shown us that there are both social and cognitive advantages and disadvantages to being in a good mood. List the advantages and disadvantages to this phenomenon.

Advantages	Disadvantages

➢ The Influence of Cognition on Affect

1. Complete the sentences below in order to the make these true:

   There are three ways by which cognition can influence affect. First, the ________________-factor theory of emotion suggests that we often don't know our own feelings or attitudes directly; because these internal reactions tend to ambiguous, we infer their nature from __________________.

   Another way is through the activation of _______________ containing a strong affective component. A third way in which thoughts can influence feelings involves our efforts to _____________________ our emotions.

After You Read...

Practice Test 1

1. According to the textbook, social cognition involves the way we _____information. All of the following answers are correct EXCEPT:
   a. interpret
   b. analyze
   c. eliminate
   d. remember

2. In making a judgment about a specific event, people often fail to take into account how likely the event occurs by ignoring
   a. suppressed thoughts.
   b. base-rates.
   c. priming effects.
   d. heuristics.

3. Suppose a professor asks his students "how long is the Mississippi River, greater or shorter than 1,000 miles?" The majority of the students then give estimates very close to 1,000 miles. Which heuristic are these students relying on?
   a. the representativeness heuristic
   b. the stereotype heuristic
   c. the anchoring heuristic
   d. the availability heuristic

4. When planting certain ideas in people's minds causes them to use these ideas to interpret subsequent events, this illustrates
   a. priming.
   b. the representativeness heuristic.
   c. the availability heuristic.
   d. an optimistic bias.

5. Suppose John received a B in his class—just barely missing an A; John's friend, Art, just barely received a B. As such, John will probably engage in ____ counterfactual thinking and be relatively ____.
   a. downward; satisfied
   b. upward; dissatisfied
   c. downward; dissatisfied
   d. upward; satisfied

6. A computer that Mary really wanted was on sale at 50% off, but she was too busy to get to the store. Now, it's on sale again at 25% off. Consistent with counterfactual thinking research, Mary will likely
   a. not buy it since it will remind her of when it was 50% off.
   b. buy it so she won't feel bad when it goes off sale again.
   c. question her judgment and, in doing so, will not show action inertia.
   d. wait to see whether any of her friends purchase the computer before she decides whether to purchase one.

7. Even though Joan loves chocolate, she refuses to eat a piece of chocolate shaped like a spider. This illustrates
   a. the representativeness heuristic.
   b. the negativity bias.
   c. counterfactual thinking.
   d. magical thinking.

8. A rebound effect typically occurs when we
   a. finish appraising our emotions.
   b. try to recover from a negative mood.
   c. have suppressed an intrusive thought.
   d. have been presented with information that contradicts our schema.

9. Unwanted intrusive thoughts occur most often for
   a. low reactance persons allowed to express their thoughts in writing.
   b. high reactance persons allowed to express their thoughts in writing.
   c. low reactance persons instructed to suppress intrusive thoughts.
   d. high reactance persons instructed to suppress intrusive thoughts.

10. Tim, a juror in a court case, will be highly impacted (in terms of his views of a defendant) when information is
    a. neutral and said to be admissible.
    b. neutral and was to be ignored.
    c. emotion-provoking and said to be admissible.
    d. emotion-provoking and to be ignored.

Practice Test 2

1. The **Beyond the Headlines** section in the text attributes the incorrect belief held by many people that S.U.V.s are safer than smaller cars to
    a. the representativeness heuristic.
    b. the availability heuristic.
    c. counterfactual thinking.
    d. the perseverance effect.

2. According to the textbook, the region in the brain that is responsible for automatic evaluative reactions such as good-bad judgments.
    a. front temporal lobe
    b. amygdala
    c. cerebellum
    d. frontal cortex

3. Mary feels very strongly that there is just one way to be a mother and she finds that she will not and cannot change her view even when presented with contradictory information. This illustrates the
    a. perseverance effect.
    b. availability heuristic.
    c. representativeness heuristic.
    d. self-fulfilling prophecy.

4. According to your text, an historical example of the negative effects of a self-fulfilling prophecy would relate to the events of the
    a. Holocaust.
    b. Great Depression.
    c. Watergate scandal.
    d. Vietnam War.

5. We often adopt and use heuristics due to the reality of
    a. the perseverance effect.
    b. cognitive laziness.
    c. information overload.
    d. schema-consistent information.

6. Suppose that on every September eleventh, you think about the September 11, 2001 terrorist attacks on America—in large part due to the high amount of media focus. The key reason for this intense recollection would be due to
   a. the availability heuristic.
   b. priming.
   c. automatic processing.
   d. the negativity effect.

7. According to research by Newby-Clark and Ross (2003) we tend to characterize our past as ____ and our future as _______.
   a. having ups and downs; very optimistic
   b. having ups and downs; very negative
   c. very negative; unclear what is to come
   d. very negative; very optimistic

8. Suppose a group of city developers in Chicago outline a very ambitious building plan and are stunned when, a year later, they only accomplished a quarter of what they had hoped to do up to this point. This illustrates the
   a. bracing for loss effect.
   b. optimistic bias.
   c. negativity bias.
   d. planning fallacy.

9. An important implication and application of the Wilson and Schooler (1991) study in which individuals were asked to rate the quality of certain jams is that
   a. thinking systematically and rationally is always critical.
   b. careful thought can be overdone.
   c. it is impossible to engage in "too much" careful thought when evaluating an issue.
   d. seemingly trivial issues should require more systematic thought than we might think is needed otherwise.

10. An example of a profession where it is *not* common for counterfactual thinking to regularly occur is with respect to
   a. entrepreneurship.
   b. the medical community.
   c. the legal community.
   d. teaching professionals.

Practice Test 3

1. ________________is a tendency to be highly sensitive to negative stimuli or information.
   a. The negativity heuristic
   b. The selective stimuli bias
   c. The negativity bias
   d. Pessimistic sensitivity

2. Suppose Bob doesn't want to rent an apartment that previously housed an AIDS patient and Jill doesn't want to drink a liquid that looks like human blood (even though it's fruit punch). Which of the following statements *best* summarizes Bob and Jill's behaviors as these pertain to magical thinking?
   a. Bob and Jill are demonstrating the law of contagion.
   b. Bob and Jill are demonstrating the law of similarity.
   c. Bob is demonstrating the law of contagion and Jill is demonstrating the law of similarity.
   d. Jill is demonstrating the law of contagion and Bob is demonstrating the law of similarity.

3. Mackie & Worth (1989) have found that being in a ____mood ____our reliance on heuristics.
   a. bad; increases
   b. bad; decreases
   c. good; increases
   d. good; decreases

4. The fact that the criminal justice system hasn't adopted changes in terms of how eyewitnesses examine a police lineup is consistent with the point that
   a. the criminal justice system has purposely chosen to reject social psychological research in this area.
   b. those in the criminal justice system are operating on various social cognitive biases of their own.
   c. those in the criminal justice system are incapable of changing the system—even if they wanted to.
   d. traditional police lineups typically yield extremely accurate identifications from eyewitnesses.

5. Which of the following statements regarding affect and cognition is *true*?
   a. Our feelings influence our cognitions only.
   b. Our cognitions influence our feelings only.
   c. Our cognitions and feelings influence one another.
   d. There is no relationship between our feelings and cognitions.

6. Consistent with ____, when we are in a bad mood, we tend to notice and remember ____ information.
   a. mood-dependent memory; positive
   b. mood-dependent memory; negative
   c. mood congruence effects; positive
   d. mood congruence effects; negative

7. Mental contamination is a type of mental processing that tends to be
   a. conscious and controllable.
   b. unconscious and controllable.
   c. conscious and uncontrollable.
   d. unconscious and uncontrollable.

8. Which of the following statements *best* summarizes the relationship between being in a good mood and helping behavior?
   a. Being in a good mood always increases helpfulness.
   b. Those in a good mood are no more likely to help others than those in a bad mood.
   c. Even though being in good mood makes one more likely to help others, this factor does not always increase helpfulness.
   d. There is a curvilinear relationship between mood and helping.

9. When we yield to temptation and engage in "forbidden pleasures," this is usually done
   a. in an unconscious matter.
   b. to stabilize negative feelings of distress.
   c. in a strategic fashion.
   d. because it does not involve high costs to our well-being.

10. According to the textbook, if you believe that if two objects are in contact with one another, properties can pass from one to the other, we are engaging in
   a. counterfactual thinking
   b. magical thinking
   c. attributional biases
   d. planning fallacy

Comprehensive Test

(NOTE: Items 1-15 are multiple-choice questions and items 16-23 are true-false questions.)

1. Suppose you are told about a fictitious woman named Linda who is shy and likes to read and garden in her spare time. You are then asked to guess her occupation. If you conclude that she must be a librarian, then you are relying on _____ to make your judgment.
   a. the availability heuristic
   b. priming
   c. the anchoring heuristic
   d. the representativeness heuristic

2. A "restaurant schema" would likely describe
   a. how one generally acts and is treated in a dining situation.
   b. how culture influences the eating habits of others.
   c. when it is appropriate to think about the rules of proper etiquette.
   d. why an individual decides to dine in a particular restaurant.

3. ____ refers to what information we notice.
   a. Retrieval
   b. Attention
   c. Encoding
   d. Decoding

4. Jamie tries to go on a diet but feels that she is doomed to fail—and she does. This is consistent with a
   a. perseverance effect.
   b. negativity bias.
   c. self-fulfilling prophecy.
   d. controlled processing effect.

5. ____ helps to explain why many people fear flying, even though driving an automobile is statistically more dangerous.
   a. Automatic priming
   b. The representativeness heuristic
   c. The availability heuristic
   d. The planning fallacy

6. Automatic is to controlled as
   a. conscious is to effortful.
   b. nonconscious is to effortless.
   c. nonconscious is to effortful.
   d. conscious is to effortless.

7. We tend to pay particular attention to a facial expression depicting
   a. sadness.
   b. happiness.
   c. threatening anger.
   d. a neutral emotion.

8. The planning fallacy is an example of the
   a. optimistic bias.
   b. negativity bias.
   c. bracing for loss effect.
   d. mental contamination effect.

9. Suppose a professor is incorrectly told that one of her students is hard of hearing. The professor inadvertently finds herself talking to just that student in a loud voice. By the end of the class the student is asking the professor to speak louder. What phenomenon has just occurred?
   a. a self-fulfilling prophecy
   b. magical thinking
   c. thought suppression
   d. automatic processing

10. The act of suppressing one's thoughts
    a. is rarely successful.
    b. can be successful if information overload or fatigue is not present.
    c. can be successful if information overload or fatigue is present.
    d. appears to be unrelated to individual difference characteristics.

11. The authors of your text conclude that our ability to make sense of social information is
    a. hopelessly flawed.
    b. can be improved in such a way that we will not make too many errors.
    c. rarely subject to potential sources of bias.
    d. fairly impressive, despite errors.

12. Consistent with ____, those in a good mood tend to notice and remember ____ information.
    a. mood congruence effects; positive
    b. mood congruence effects; negative
    c. mood-dependent memory; positive
    d. mood-dependent memory; negative

13. A process where our judgments, emotions, or behaviors are influenced by unconscious, uncontrollable mental processing is called ____.
    a. automatic contamination
    b. mental contamination
    c. reactance processing
    d. emotional contamination

14. Polly is in a good mood, but her friend Anna is in a bad mood. As such, which of the following statements is *true*?
    a. Polly and Anna will show an increase in their likelihood of using mental shortcuts.
    b. Only Polly will show an increase in her likelihood of using mental shortcuts.
    c. Only Anna will show an increase her likelihood of using mental shortcuts.
    d. Polly and Anna will show a decrease in their likelihood of using mental shortcuts.

15. The ____-factor theory of emotion suggests that we don't know our feelings or attitudes directly.
    a. one
    b. two
    c. three
    d. four

Questions 16-23 are True/False Questions

16. After watching a frightening movie, many people are more easily frightened by unexpected sights and sounds. This phenomena is due to the concept of priming.

17. Not eating a candy shaped as a spider illustrates the law of dissimilarity.

18. Raters who carefully analyzed the reasons for their ratings of various strawberry jams more closely matched the ratings of experts than those who simply rated the jams.

19. Efforts to prevent certain thoughts from entering consciousness are referred to as thought repression.

20. To determine whether someone is a coach, I compare his traits to the "average" coach." In doing so, I am using the availability heuristic.

21. An AIDS patient's sweater will be rated less favorably even if it is kept in a sealed plastic bag and never touched by its owner.

22. The tendency to underestimate the time needed to complete a major project is known as the planning fallacy.

23. On the day that Darla learned certain facts about Abraham Lincoln in school, she had a headache. On the day of her school's quiz bowl, she also has a headache—but is surprised when she is able to correctly answer certain facts about Abraham Lincoln. This illustrates mood-dependent memory.

Short Answer/Essay Questions

1. **The Nature of Schemas**
   Briefly offer the most accurate understanding of whether we remember information consistent or inconsistent with our schemas.

2. **Heuristics**
   Contrast how the representativeness heuristic differs from the availability heuristic.

3. **Applying Heuristics**
   Give an example from your life of a time when the concept of "priming" affected your cognitions.

4. **Biases in Cognition**
Suppose you are candidate for a job where four individuals are conducting an interview. You notice that each of these individuals shows a distinct facial expression: one is smiling, one appears to be sad, another appears to have a threatening expression, and the fourth person doesn't appear to be showing any emotional expression. For which of these expressions will you be *most* apt to quickly recognize the emotion in question? Why?

5. **Magical Thinking**
Provide a brief overview of the three principles of magical thinking.

6. **Affect and Cognition**
Detail at least three ways that affect can influence cognition by explaining how these processes operate.

When You Have Finished . . .

Applications of Social Cognition to Your Life

1. By understanding our cognitions' limitations and tendencies to make related errors, we may be in a better position to try and avoid such cognitive pitfalls.

2. We often try to *not* think about something when we don't want to deal with it. For instance, if you're on a diet, you may be trying very hard to avoid thinking about food. By understanding the limits of thought suppression, we may be better equipped to cope with unpleasant or unproductive thoughts.

3. Since we are prone to making the planning fallacy, we should try and reason our limitations in a realistic fashion so that we won't disappoint others—or ourselves.

4. By understanding how affect can influence memory and cognition, we are in a better position to maximize our memory skills and capabilities.

5. Given the prevalence of social cognition errors, we shouldn't be overly self-critical when and if we make such errors.

6. Also, we should be cautious when in a good mood to realize that we may not always be as accurate with our social cognitions.

Consider the following exercise that relates to point #2: Pick a day where you have made a conscious decision to *not* think about a certain friend or acquaintance of yours. Then keep track of how many times during that day you actually think of that person. Contrast the number of thoughts you've had about this person with how often (on average) you thought about this person prior to conducting this exercise.

Here are some web links to provide you with additional information about the topics covered in this chapter:

Internet Sites:

http://www.has.vcu.edu/psy/faculty/fors/psy321/h.htm: An interactive online demonstration of heuristics or rules of thumb.

http://magic.trendy.org/interactivemagic.html: and click on "The Original Mysterious Rabbit." An interactive online magic trick—the bunny will guess your card, every time. A very compelling illusion—until you figure out how it is done! To figure out how the trick is done, write down the list of the original six cards, then compare this to the five cards that pop up on the screen the next time. Demonstrates the power of our schemas and expectations in guiding perceptions.

http://www.psy.ed.ac.uk/psychexps/Exps/experiments.html: A Web lab on the Internet, includes over 20 online experiments, several of which are relevant to automatic processing—for example, a covert attention study, a lexical decision task, and so forth.

http://teach.psy.uga.edu/CogPsychTutor/inductiv/represnt/default.htm: The WWW Cognitive Psychology Tutor. Contains a Web tutorial on the representativeness heuristic (more appropriate for students who have already had statistics).

http://cygnus-group.com/CIDM/risk.html: An article, "Thinking about Risk," by the Center for Informed Decision Making, which discusses the role of availability, representativeness, anchoring and adjustment, and overconfidence in perception of risk in the context of real-life situations. Good examples.

http://www.sfu.ca/counterfactual/:. Counterfactual Research News website, maintained by Neal Roese of Simon Fraser University. Contains a basic description of the concept as well as a bibliography of counterfactual publications in social psychology, and also Web links to the home pages of psychologists active in this area.

Crossword Puzzle

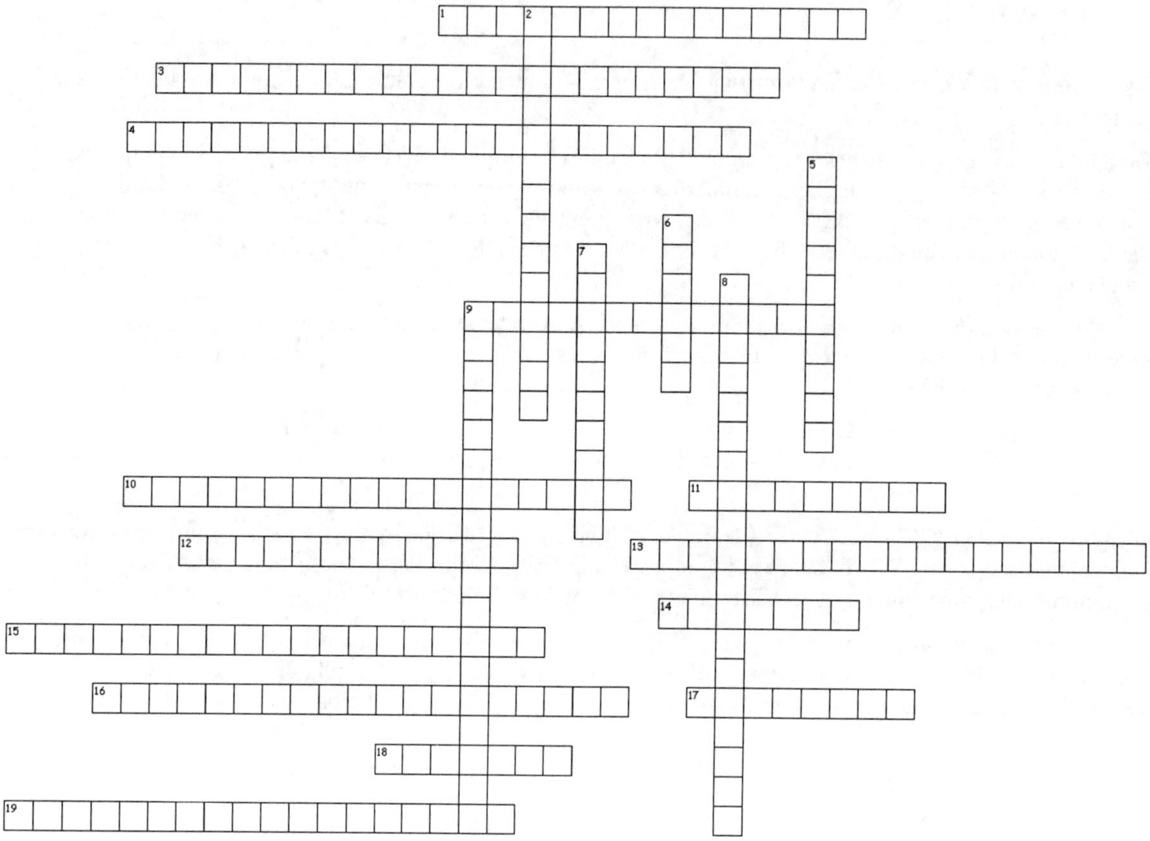

Across

1. optimistic predictions
3. predictions that make themselves come true
4. what might have been
9. unwanted thoughts returning
10. schemas remain unchanged
11. using numbers as a starting point
12. heuristic relying on ease of instance brought to mind
13. preventing thoughts
14. increased availability of information
15. automatic thought
16. ability to process is exceeded
17. brain part responsible for evaluative judgments
18. mental frameworks
19. trepidation

Down
2. sensitivity toward negative information
5. anchoring
6. feelings and mood
7. simple rules
8. how affect influences social thought
9. current stimuli resemble other stimuli

Created by Puzzlemaker at DiscoverySchool.com
http://school.discovery.com/

3 SOCIAL PERCEPTION: PERCEIVING AND UNDERSTANDING OTHERS

Before You Read . . .

This chapter introduces you to the study of social perception, which is a series of sometimes complex processes that attempt to understand other persons. You will first consider why nonverbal communication allows us to express our own and interpret others' emotions, attitudes, and feelings. You will also read about how you may determine whether a person is lying based on their nonverbal cues. The chapter will then specifically examine gender differences in decoding nonverbal behavior. Afterward, you will be looking at how we attempt to understand the causes of our own and others' behavior through the study of attributions. As part of this discussion, you will discover how and why our attributions are often incorrect and how these are often applied in the "real world." Following that, you'll learn about the functions of impression formation and impression management. You will learn about a very well-known study by a famous social psychologist, Solomon Asch, which considers how we combine and use social information. The many ways by which we try to look good to others will also be reviewed. This chapter concludes with an example of "speed dating" and leaves us to consider whether social perception truly allows us to gather accurate information.

Chapter Objectives

After reading this chapter, you should be able to:

- Describe the major purpose and functions of social perception.
- Understand why the process of social perception is so complex.
- Define what is meant by nonverbal communication and how it is related to the concepts and terms, "irrepressible," "deception," and "emotional contagion."
- Describe the six (or perhaps seven) basic emotions expressed in unique facial expressions. Does this mean we are limited to only a small number of facial expressions?
- Describe how body language, including gestures, posture, and movements, can communicate emotion, including such examples as ballet and various emblems.

SOCIAL PERCEPTION

- Identify and describe the key nonverbal cues that may allow us to recognize deception.
- Discuss gender differences with regard to decoding nonverbal behavior.
- Compare and contrast the key elements of Jones and Davis' theory of correspondent inference with Kelley's theory of attribution.
- Explain the difference between internal and external causes and controllable versus uncontrollable factors.
- Contrast the discounting and augmenting principles.
- Describe and contrast the major attributional errors: the correspondence bias, the actor-observer effect, and the self-serving bias. Consider cultural differences with respect to these biases.
- Discuss how attribution theory has been applied to the study of depression and prejudice.
- Understand how attributions can protect a victim of prejudice's self-esteem.
- Discuss how Asch's research on central and peripheral traits support his view that forming impressions involves more than simply adding together individual traits.
- Contrast older models of how we combine diverse information about others into unified impressions of them with more contemporary perspectives.
- Describe the role played by exemplars and abstractions when we make judgments about others.
- List self-enhancement tactics and other-enhancement tactics used in impression management, and describe research results on whether these tactics "pay off" for persons using them.
- Describe how "speed dating" relates to the process of social perception and first impressions.

As You Read . . .

Important Terms to know... Below are a list of some of the key terms and concepts from this chapter. Make flashcards in order to enhance your recall ability of these terms. Refer to the definitions that are either in boldface or in the margins of this chapter for help. Be advised that you may also want to include additional terms from this chapter as you deem necessary.

Social perception	Nonverbal behavior	Irrepressible
Emotional contagion	Basic channels	The "basic" emotions
Gazes and stares	Microexpressions/deception	Body language
Correspondent inference theory	Attribution	Noncommon effects
Theory of causal attributions	Social desirability	Internal/external causes
Consensus	Consistency	Distinctiveness
Stable vs. controllable factors	Discounting	Augmenting
Regulatory focus theory	Promotion vs. prevention focus	Reasons
Causal history of reason	Fundamental attribution error	Correspondence bias
Salient/Perceptual salience	Individualistic vs. collectivistic culture	Attributions and prejudice/depression
Self-serving bias	Actor-observer effect	Gestalt psychology
Central/peripheral traits	Impression formation	Negativity effect
Exemplars	Abstractions	Categorical judgments
Impression management	Self-enhancement tactics	Other-enhancement tactics
Linguistic style	Emotional expressiveness	Speed dating
Slime effect	Cognitive load	Women's intuition

Nonverbal Communication: The Language of Expressions, Gazes, and Gestures

➢ Nonverbal Communication: The Basic Channels

1. Complete the following statement by filling in the blanks:

   We pay careful attention to ________________ provided by changes in people's facial expressions, eye contact, posture, body movements, and other expressive actions. These behaviors are often called ________________ because these are difficult to control.

2. Name that number! How many "basic channels" of communication are there?

3. Listed below are several common emotions. Circle the six basic emotions that are represented clearly on the human face and from a very early age. Underline the other emotion that is thought to be quite basic.

happiness	surprise
love	anger
contempt	desire
jealousy	fear
disgust	relief
anger	sadness
disappointment	worry

4. "The *eyes* have it!" Give at least one example of how eye contact may suggest that a person likes us and at least one example of how eye contact may indicate that a person dislikes us.

5. Name that emotion! For each of the following expressions, state the emotion that is likely being conveyed:

   a. Large number of movements where one part of the body does something to another part: ___________

   b. Rounded postures: _____________

   c. Firm handshakes: _____________

➢ Recognizing Deception: The Role of Nonverbal Cues

1. *"I cannot tell a lie..."* Just in case you're wondering whether someone really did cut down a cherry tree—or are being truthful about a more serious matter—you may want to pay attention to their nonverbal cues. Listed below are five nonverbal expressions. Determine whether the expressions below would indicate whether the person is telling a lie or being honest:

   a. Seeing one facial expression quickly followed by another: _____________

   b. Observing a person who manages their facial expressions, well but cannot look you in the eye as he or she talks to you: _____________

   c. Observing a person who is speaking very clearly and whose pitch of voice does not rise: _____________

   d. Observing an individual who has very dilated pupils: _____________

   e. Showing very exaggerated facial expressions: _____________

2. Underline the words in the parentheses that will make each of the following two statements correct:

   a.) When we are trying to determine if someone is deceiving us, we tend to pay more attention to their (words, nonverbal cues) because we have (unlimited, limited) cognitive capacity. As result of this, we tend to be (more, less) effective at detecting deception.

   b.) People tend to be (more, less, just as) accurate at recognizing lies within their own cultures than another culture. Overall, people tend to be fairly (good, poor) at recognizing lies told by persons from a different culture.

The Science of Social Psychology: Making Sense of Common Sense

➢ Is There Such a Thing as Women's Intuition?

1. Research has found that women are better than men at _____________________ and _______________. However, they lose their edge when _________________________.

2. Give two explanations that could account for women's superior skills at handling nonverbal behavior.

Attribution: Understanding the Causes of Others' Behavior

➢ Theories of Attribution: Frameworks for Understanding How We Attempt to Make Sense of the Social World

1. a. Jones and Davis' (1965) theory of ________________ asks how we use information about others' behavior as a basis for inferring that they possess various traits.

   b. List the three factors that will typically lead us to conclude that others' behavior reflects their stable traits:

2. Let's make a…chart! Listed below is an incomplete chart that details the three main components of Kelley's theory of causal attributions. Your job is to complete the chart by: (a) defining the three terms and (b) on the basis of the information given, determine whether we would ultimately make an internal or external attribution regarding the hypothetical cause.

Component	Definition	High or Low?	Internal or External Cause?
Consensus		Low	
Distinctiveness		Low	
Consistency		High	

Suppose consensus, distinctiveness, and consistency were *all high*. Would we attribute behavior in this case to internal or external causes?

3. Match it! Match each phrase, word, or sentence on the left side of the page with an identifying concept on the right side of the page. Note that each item on the right should be used *only once*.

___1. Whether an individual can change behavior if they want to.	A. reasons
___2. Viewing the first possible cause as less likely due to other causes.	B. promotion focus
___3. Adding weight to a factor when we aren't expecting it to to make a difference.	C. augmenting
___4. Emphasizing the presence and absence of positive outcomes.	D. controllable factors
___5. Emphasizing negative outcomes.	E. prevention focus
___6. Conscious desires, values, or beliefs.	F. causal history of reason
___7. Factors that shape behavior in a way that the persons involved are unaware of.	G. discounting

➢ Attribution: Some Basic Sources of Error

1. Indicate whether the following three statements about the correspondence bias are true or false:

   a.) The correspondence bias is a tendency to explain other's actions as stemming from situational causes and not their dispositions.

   b.) The correspondence bias is often referred to as the fundamental attribution error.

   c.) The correspondence bias is more common in collectivistic cultures than individualistic cultures.

2. According to the actor-observer effect, when you fail at something you will likely attribute it to __________________ causes. However, if one of your classmates fails at something, you will likely attribute this to __________________ causes. When we succeed at something though, we tend to attribute it to internal causes. This is known as the __________________.

➢ Applications of Attribution Theory: Insights and Interventions

1. Define it!

   a.) What are self-defeating attributions? Who are the individuals most likely to express these patterns of attributions?

   b.) What does it mean to be labeled as a "chronic complainer?"

2. Suppose you were not promoted for a position in which you were very qualified for and you suspect that your supervisor harbored prejudice feelings toward you. Explain how you could use the attribution process to maintain your self-esteem level.

Impression Formation and Impression Management: How We Integrate Social Information

➢ Asch's Research on Central and Peripheral Traits

1. Solomon Asch was greatly influenced by the work of ________________ psychologists.

2. In one of Asch's famous studies on impression formation, he showed his research participants two lists of words. Name the two words that were classified as "central traits."

3. Define an implicit personality theory.

4. Explain how the concept of implicit personality theories relates to your impression of meeting someone for the first time.

➢ Impression Formation: A Cognitive Perspective

1. The study of impression formation examines ______________________________ ______________________________.

2. Most social psychologists now agree that impressions of others involve two major components: List these two components.

➢ Other Aspects of Impression Formation: The Nature of First Impressions and Our Motives for Forming Them

1. Exemplar or Abstraction: You Be The Judge! State whether the following events are exemplars or abstractions:

Event	Exemplar or Abstraction?
Our first impression of someone.	
Our belief about someone's personality solely on the basis of his or her profession.	
Our belief that a person is kind on the basis of previous interactions.	
Our impression of a co-worker that we've known for many years.	

➢ Impression Management: The Fine Art of Looking Good

1. The study of impression management examines ________________________________

____.

2. *You look (or you make me look) marvelous!* Listed in the table below are a variety of impression management techniques. Complete the table by stating for each technique: a.) whether it is a self-enhancement or an other-enhancement tactic, and b) whether it is likely to be successful.

Tactic	Self-enhancement or other-enhancement?	Will it be successful?
Describing oneself in positive terms.		
Boosting one's physical appearance.		
Offering excessively flattering statements.		
Showing a high degree of interest in another person.		
Exhibiting behavior that is characterized as "licking upward but kicking downward."		

3. For each of the following three hypothetical individuals, state whether cognitive load would likely increase or decrease their abilities to present themselves favorably.

Individual	Increase or decrease?
A professor interviewing for a job at a university.	
A person on a first date who is trying to find the way to a new restaurant.	
An introvert who is trying to act like an extravert while performing another task.	

Beyond the Headlines: As Social Psychologists See It

➢ First Impressions on the Run: Speed Dating

Apply your knowledge...

1. Discuss how "speed dating" can compromise the accuracy of our judgments of others.

2. Give an example of when meeting people at a quick pace would have its advantages.

After You Read...

Practice Test 1

1. Facial expressions, eye contact, body movements, posture, and touching are the basic channels for
   a. nonverbal communication.
   b. attributions.
   c. impression management.
   d. impression formation.

2. Neumann and Strack refer to a mechanism through which feelings are transferred in a seemingly automatic way from one person to another as
   a. cognitive load.
   b. the slime effect.
   c. emotional contagion.
   d. implicit personality theory.

3. Body movements that carry a specific meaning in a given culture are called
   a. irrepressible.
   b. emblems.
   c. emotional contagions.
   d. the six basic emotions.

4. ____ tend to have higher handshake index ratings than ____.
   a. Men; women
   b. Women; men
   c. Extraverts; introverts
   d. Introverts; Extraverts

5. The following cues are helpful in detecting whether someone is lying EXCEPT:
   a. posture
   b. interchannel discrepancies
   c. microexpressions
   d. eye contact

6. According to Kelley's theory, the basic task we face in making a causal attribution is determining whether a behavior is caused by ____ or ____causes.
   a. internal; external
   b. augmenting; discounting
   c. prevention; promotion
   d. noncommon; common

7. We tend to see our own behavior as stemming largely from ____; we tend to see the behavior of others as stemming from ____. This type of attributional bias is known as the ____.
   a. internal traits; situational factors; actor-observer effect
   b. situational factors; internal traits; actor-observer effect
   c. situational factors; internal traits; self-serving bias
   d. internal traits; situation factors; correspondence bias

8. Minorities often do not challenge discrimination when they encounter it for fear that others will attribute and label them as ____.
   a. having low consistency
   b. showing the fundamental attribution error
   c. having a self-defeating pattern of attributions
   d. being a chronic complainer

9. The fact that persons described as "warm" are perceived quite differently than those described as "cold," illustrates the impact of ____ on overall impressions.
   a. causal history of reason explanations
   b. regulatory focus theory
   c. central traits
   d. flattery

10. Overall, there is ______that women are better than men at <u>all</u> aspects of social perception.
    a. conclusive evidence.
    b. no clear evidence.
    c. overwhelming evidence.
    d. some evidence.

Practice Test 2

1. If you were to study the processes used in order understand other persons, then you would *most* likely be studying the field of
   a. social recognition.
   b. social cognition.
   c. social intelligence.
   d. social perception.

2. When exhibiting the fundamental attribution error we tend to ________internal causes to a person's behavior and ________external causes.
   a. overestimate; overestimate
   b. underestimate; underestimate
   c. underestimate; overestimate
   d. overestimate; underestimate

3. Which of the following behaviors or processes is the *least* likely to be exhibited in "road rage" drivers?
   a. They are in a highly excitable state.
   b. They will show gestures that most people will not find familiar to them.
   c. They will interpret anything approaching a stare from another driver as an aggressive act.
   d. They are very likely to act aggressively toward another driver.

4. "The extent to which the person I am considering reacts in the same way when I change the stimulus or event to which he's reacting." This defines the attributional dimension of
   a. distinctiveness.
   b. consensus.
   c. consistency.
   d. controllability.

5. When you view an initial possible cause of behavior as less likely because other possible causes for a certain action exists, your behavior is consistent with ____.
   a. augmenting
   b. discounting
   c. the correspondence bias
   d. the actor-observer effect

6. The Fundamental attribution error appears to be more ______in cultures that emphasize individual freedom.
   a. common
   b. stronger
   c. weaker
   d. both a and b

7. Complete the following analogy: Individualistic cultures are to collectivistic cultures as
   a. China is to the United States.
   b. external is to internal.
   c. group membership is to conformity.
   d. individual freedom is to interdependence.

8. Models that stress the role of abstractions are sometimes referred to as
   a. exemplars.
   b. categorical judgments.
   c. the negativity effect.
   d. central traits.

9. Efforts to present ourselves in ways that produce favorable first opinions are referred to as
   a. impression management.
   b. impression formation.
   c. impression expressions.
   d. impression presentations.

10. The example in the text "You fell, I was pushed," represents
   a. the slime effect
   b. cognitive overload
   c. the actor-observer effect
   d. impression management

Practice Test 3

1. Of the following research questions, the one that is *least* related to the study of social perception is
   a. How do we form first impressions of others?
   b. How do we attempt to understand the reasons behind others' behavior?
   c. How do we communicate with others using "unspoken" language?
   d. How likely is a person to help someone when others are present?

2. According to Kelley's Covariation Theory, all of the following are pieces of information that we use when making an attribution EXCEPT:
   a. distinctiveness
   b. consensus
   c. awareness
   d. consistency

3. Research has shown that depressed people tend to consistently use ________.
   a. a correspondent bias
   b. the fundamental attribution error
   c. a self-defeating pattern of attributions
   d. an implicit theory of personality attributions

4. We are likely to infer that someone's behavior reflects their actual characteristics when their behavior was
   a. high in social desirability and was freely chosen.
   b. low in social desirability and was freely chosen.
   c. high in social desirability and occurred without choice.
   d. low in social desirability and occurred without choice.

5. We are likely to attribute another person's behavior to internal causes when consensus is ____, consistency is ____, and distinctiveness is ____.
   a. high; high; high
   b. low; low; low
   c. low; high; low
   d. high; low; high

6. If a woman was promoted in an organization that is against affirmative action, she will probably be rated
   a. especially qualified, due to discounting.
   b. especially qualified, due to augmenting.
   c. poorly qualified, due to discounting.
   d. poorly qualified, due to augmenting.

7. Dispositional causes are easier to notice than situational causes. This explains the
   a. self-serving bias.
   b. depressive attribution style.
   c. actor-observer effect.
   d. correspondence bias.

8. The self-serving bias refers to our tendency to
   a. use situational attributions for our own behavior.
   b. use internal attributions for our own behavior.
   c. use internal attributions for our good outcomes, and external attributions for our bad outcomes.
   d. use internal attributions for our bad outcomes, and external attributions for our good outcomes.

9. The fact that Solomon Asch ____ believe that we form impressions about others in an additive fashion highlights his agreement with the ____ psychological perspective.
   a. did; Gestalt
   b. did not; Gestalt
   c. did; clinical
   d. did not; clinical

10. The effect of cognitive load is *least* likely to be negative when
   a. we are able to engage in cognitive distraction.
   b. we are being evaluated in a high-pressure, highly intellectual setting.
   c. we concentrate on the importance of making a positive impression.
   d. we hope for a miracle since it is very difficult to not have the effect of cognitive load be negative.

Comprehensive Test

(NOTE: Items 1-15 are multiple-choice questions and items 16-23 are true-false questions.)

1. Depressed individuals tend to attribute negative outcomes to ______causes and positive outcomes to _____causes.
   a. dispositional; internal
   b. situational; internal
   c. external; internal
   d. internal; external

2. How many basic emotions are represented by a distinct facial expression?
   a. none
   b. only one
   c. six or seven
   d. the number is limitless

3. A high level of eye contact is usually interpreted as a sign of ____, avoiding eye contact as a sign of ____, and staring as a sign of ____.
   a. friendliness; unfriendliness; hostility
   b. unfriendliness; friendliness; hostility
   c. friendliness; hostility; unfriendliness
   d. hostility; friendliness; unfriendliness

4. Aronoff, Woike, and Hyman (1992) studied body postures displayed in classical ballet and found that threatening postures were ____, while warm postures were ____.
   a. ambiguous; more easily defined
   b. easy to display; ambiguous
   c. rounded; angular
   d. angular; rounded

5. When we consciously are trying to detect deception, we tend to pay more attention to ____ cues.which usually cause us to make ____ judgments as to whether the individual in question is lying.
   a. verbal; correct
   b. verbal; incorrect
   c. nonverbal; correct
   d. nonverbal; incorrect

6. The use of fragrance, which tends to be ____ nowadays, ____ a type of nonverbal cue.
   a. increasing; is
   b. increasing; is not
   c. decreasing; is
   d. decreasing; is not

7. Assume your friend is marrying someone who has a single positive trait (he`s very rich), but several negative traits. Apparently your friend is marrying this person for the money. This is an example of how ____ influence(s) our attributions.
   a. noncommon effects
   b. high social desirability
   c. low social desirability
   d. noncorrespondent inferences

8. We are likely to attribute another person's behavior to external causes when consensus is ____, consistency is ____, and distinctiveness is ____.
   a. high; high; high
   b. low; low; low
   c. low; high; low
   d. high; low; high

9. You are less likely to think a mother is mean-tempered if you learn she was shouting at her son because he just ran out in front of traffic. This illustrates
   a. the augmenting principle.
   b. the discounting principle.
   c. the fundamental attribution error.
   d. self-serving bias.

10. Those with a ____ focus tend to be more interested in making ____, whereas those with a ____ focus tend to be more concerned about ____.
    a. promotion; hits; prevention; avoiding misses
    b. promotion; false alarms; prevention; hits
    c. prevention; hits; promotion; correct rejections
    d. promotion; hits; prevention; correct rejections

11. One way to protect your self-esteem after experiencing prejudice behavior towards you would be to make a(n)_____attribution for the prejudice behavior.
    a. implicit
    b. external
    c. dispositional
    d. internal

12. The correspondence bias refers to our tendency to
    a. explain others' actions in terms of traits.
    b. explain others' actions in terms of situations.
    c. give ourselves more credit for our own success than we really deserve.
    d. overestimate the role of situations in causing our own behavior.

13. The actor-observer effect suggests we perceive our own behavior stems largely from ____ causes, whereas we perceive the behavior of other persons stems largely from ____ causes.
    a. situational; internal
    b. internal; situational
    c. dispositional; internal
    d. external; situational

14. Depressives tend to show patterns of attributions ____ to those found with respect to ____.
    a. opposite; correspondence bias
    b. identical; self-serving bias
    c. opposite; self-serving bias
    d. identical; actor-observer effect

15. All of the following are examples of self-enhancement techniques of impression management, *except*
    a. wearing perfume.
    b. dressing in particular clothes.
    c. developing a suntan to improve personal appearance.
    d. directing flattering remarks to your target.

Questions 16-23 are True/False Questions

16. Speed dating has been found to lead to totally accurate first impressions of others.

17. Facial expressions are totally universal around the world.

18. Asch's research was mainly influenced by behaviorist psychologists.

19. Impression management is also referred to as self-presentation.

20. We are likely to attribute another person's behavior to external causes when consensus, consistency, and distinctiveness are all high.

21. Western European countries are usually characterized as collectivistic cultures.

22. Persons who are depressed tend to use the self-serving bias more than nondepressed persons.

23. An individual's linguistic style can be cue that he or she is lying.

Short Answer/Essay Questions

1. **Nonverbal Behavior**
   Briefly state three factors that might allow us to determine whether a person is lying on the basis of his or her nonverbal behavior.

2. **Gender Differences in Nonverbal Behavior**
   Describe two situations in which females would perform better than males with regard to handling nonverbal behavior.

3. **Attributions** Imagine an individual in a theater talked very loudly throughout an entire movie. According to Jones and Davis' model, what would this information tell us about this person? Why?

4. **Impression Management**
   Briefly state three factors that will usually foster other-enhancement.

When You Have Finished . . .

Applications of Social Perception to Your Life

1. We are always trying to figure out other persons in terms of their motives, thinking, and their attitudes toward us. This is what social perception is all about!

2. We typically try to make the "best" impression—through impression management techniques--we can when we are interacting with others, particularly with respect to our initial encounters (such as job interviews, blind dates, etc.).

3. We are often in a position where we are trying to determine whether a person is being truthful to us; one of the best ways to determine this is by using nonverbal cues as a means of recognizing deception.

4. Whenever we are evaluating a person we have just met—particularly whether we "like" them—we tend to place great importance to various contextual and situational cues when describing their traits. Obviously this point suggests the relevance of Asch's classic research on central and peripheral traits.

5. Whenever we are trying to understand someone's actions, we ultimately try to ascertain whether it is due to the individual's unique characteristics or situational influences. We often use Jones and Davis' and Kelley's models of attributions on a regular basis (often without consciously realizing it!).

6. We have learned that by making external attributions for others' harmful behavior toward us can help us protect our self-esteem.

Here are some web links to provide you with additional information about the topics covered in this chapter:

Internet Sites:

http://nonverbal.ucsc.edu: Dane Archer's website. Introduces the topic, and has a sample of exercises in which the viewer can attempt to guess the meaning of depicted nonverbal behaviors.

http://mambo.ucsc.edu/psl/fanl.html: Links to sites of researchers (including Ekman) who analyze facial expressions of emotion.

http://www.marketingprofs.com/Ivorytower/attriberror.asp: Why You're Always Right, and Customers Are Always Wrong. An article that explains the fundamental attribution error to businesspeople and their understanding of customer relationships.

http://euphrates.wpunj.edu/faculty/wagnerk/webagogy/hecht.htm: The Nonverbal Communication Research Page. A very thorough link with regard to research on nonverbal behavior and linking colleagues in the field together.

http://www3.usal.es/~nonverbal/introduction.htm: Another great online page of relevant links for nonverbal behavior research.

Crossword Puzzle

Across

3. a central trait
5. understanding others
7. transferred feelings
10. others' behavior due to dispositions
11. nonspoken language
16. influenced Asch's work
17. aspects of speech
18. lick upward but kick downward
19. situational attribution
20. dispositional attribution
21. attribute our behavior to the situation

22. attributions researcher

Down

1. nonverbal researcher
2. producing favorable impressions
4. beliefs about traits
6. fleeting facial expressions
8. first cause as unlikely
9. steadily gazing
12. effects caused by one factor but not others
13. a piece of information that Kelley says we use
14. cause of others' behavior
15. cues provided by others' bodies

Created by Puzzlemaker at DiscoverySchool.com
http://school.discovery.com/

4 ATTITUDES: EVALUATING THE SOCIAL WORLD

Before You Read . . .

This chapter discusses an issue in which you have had much exposure even before taking your social psychology course—the study of attitudes, or evaluations of various aspects of the social world. We'll begin our consideration of this topic with a discussion of how attitudes develop and the general purposes that these often serve. You will also read about when and how attitudes can influence behavior. Afterward, you will find out about ways to persuade others and why, under certain conditions, such attempts may fail. In particular, the "Making Sense of Common Sense" portion of the chapter will show you the conditions in which fear appear is not effective in changing our attitudes. You'll also be introduced to the study of cognitive dissonance or what happens when we show inconsistent attitudes or a gap between our attitudes and behavior. As part of this discussion, you'll consider why cognitive dissonance often produces attitude change and how it can actually be used to produce benefits for individuals.

Chapter Objectives

After reading this chapter, you should be able to:

- Describe what attitudes are and why these are of interest to social psychologists.
- Give an overview of the learning processes through which we acquire our attitudes, (e.g., social learning, classical conditioning, subliminal conditioning, observational learning and instrumental learning).
- Discuss the basic functions that attitudes may serve.
- Explain the role that attitudes play in enhancing or maintaining our level of self-esteem.
- Outline when and how attitudes may affect behavior from a historical and contemporary social psychological perspective.
- Elaborate on the situational constraints that affect the expression of our attitudes.
- Summarize how the theories of reasoned action and planned behavior and the attitude-to-behavior process model try to understand the attitude-behavior link.

- State the key factors that social psychologists have historically believed lead to successful persuasion.
- Explain why fear appeal is not always effective in changing our attitudes.
- Contrast systematic and heuristic processing in terms of how these relate to persuasion.
- Describe why and how we may resist persuasion by discussing reactance, forewarning, selective avoidance, biased assimilation, and attitude polarization.
- Consider when we experience cognitive dissonance, how we can reduce it, and whether it is unpleasant for most individuals.
- Understand the less-leads-to-more effect by paying particular attention to the famous Festinger and Carlsmith (1959) study.
- Explain how hypocrisy can be used in a manner that produces beneficial effects for an individual.

As You Read . . .

Important Terms to Know... Below are a list of some of the key terms and concepts from this chapter. Make flashcards in order to enhance your recall ability of these terms. Refer to the definitions that are either in boldface or in the margins of this chapter for help. You may also want to include additional terms from this chapter as you deem necessary.

Attitudes	Attitude ambivalence	Social learning
Classical conditioning	Subliminal conditioning	Instrumental conditioning
Observational learning	Social comparison	The functions of attitudes
Attitude origins	Attitude strength and its components	Attitude specificity
Theory of reasoned action	Theory of planned behavior	Behavioral intentions
Subjective norms	Perceived behavioral control	Attitude-to-behavior process model
Persuasion	One- vs. two-sided approach	Systematic vs. heuristic processing
Central vs. peripheral route	Elaboration likelihood model	Reactance
Forewarning	Selective avoidance	Biased assimilation
Less-leads-to-more effect	Hostile media bias	Cognitive dissonance
Third person effect	Attitude accessibility	Hypocrisy
Self-esteem function	Fear appeals	Social norms
Knowledge function	Mere exposure effect	Pluralistic ignorance
Ego-Defensive Function	Impression motivation function	Induced or forced compliance
Trivialization	Spreading of alternatives effect	

Attitude Formation: How Attitudes Develop

➢ Social Learning: Acquiring Attitudes from Others

1. In your own words, what is an "attitude?" Also, what does it mean when we show "attitude ambivalence?"

2. List three attitudes that you hold that are important to you.
   a.
   b.
   c.

3. Match it! Match each phrase, word, or sentence on the left side of the page with an identifying concept on the right side of the page. Note that each item on the right should be used ONLY ONCE.

____1. Strengthening outcomes with rewards	A. social learning
____2. Learning by viewing others' actions	B. classical conditioning
____3. Carried out in order to determine the correctness of our views of social reality.	C. subliminal conditioning
____4. Involves exposure to a stimulus below a person's threshold of conscious awareness.	D. instrumental conditioning
____5. The process through which we acquire new information from others.	E. observational learning
____6. Conscious learning in which a neutral stimulus becomes a signal for the presentation of another stimulus.	F. social comparison

➢ Attitude Functions: Why We Form Attitudes in the First Place

1. Attitudes serve several different functions. These functions are:

   a. ______________________________

   b. ______________________________

   c. ______________________________

   d. ______________________________

   e. ______________________________

2. *Guess who's coming to dinner?* Imagine that you're at a dinner party and you overhear the statements below from different people. Identify the apparent function of each of these attitudes and explain your reasoning.

He told you I was racist! Oh no, I've never even thought a single racial slur in my life!

____

____

____

Oh, so you say that you work for a law firm—I think lawyers do an incredible service to society!

I am proud to call myself a liberal!

______________________________ ______________________________

______________________________ ______________________________

______________________________ ______________________________

➢ Role of the Social Context in the Link Between Attitudes and Behavior- When and Why Do Attitudes Influence Behavior?

1. Describe the study conducted by Richard LaPiere in 1934, and his main findings.

2. In considering the attitude-behavior link, social psychologists now focus on the question, __________ ____, and no longer the question, ____.

➢ When and Why Do Attitudes Influence Behavior?

1. Word scramble! Who said studying can't be fun? Unscramble the following six words below. Use the hints if you're having trouble unscrambling the words. When you unscramble the six words, unscramble the letters contained in the brackets to reveal the "bonus" word. Have fun!

a. RMNETCAIO ___ ___ ___ [___] ___ ___ ___ ___ ___ ___

b. TENTSHRG ___ ___ [___] ___ ___ ___ ___ ___

c. CITYCIEFPS ___ ___ ___ ___ [___] ___ ___ ___ ___ ___ ___

d. WODEKENG ___ ___ ___ ___ ___ ___ ___ [___] ___

e. SEYNITTIN [___] ___ ___ ___ ___ ___ ___ ___ ___

f. TONCTRSINA ___ ___ [___] ___ ___ ___ ___ ___ ___ ___

*BONUS WORD: ____________________________________

Hints:
a. How much a person cares about an issue.
b. This term incorporates many factors.
c. An attitude that's isn't too general, yet it greatly predicts behavior.
d. One's awareness of the attitude object.
e. The level of emotional reaction caused by the attitude object.
f. A situational _____ can moderate the relationship between attitudes and behavior.
BONUS: Pertains to how attitudes are formed.

2. Define the concept of "pluralistic ignorance" and state how this concept affects the expression of our attitudes in public.

➢ How Do Attitudes Guide Behavior?

1. Identify the components of the theories of reasoned action and planned behavior. Which components are unique to each theory?

2. State below the factors that predict the intention to use versus the actual use of the drug ecstasy.

Intention to use	Actual Use

3. In the attitude-to-behavior process model, some event activates an attitude that, in turn, influences

________________________________. At the same time, ___________________________

________________________________ is also activated. Together, ______________________

____ shape our definitions of the

event. Ultimately, this perception influences our ______________________

The Fine Art of Persuasion: How Attitudes are Changed

➢ Persuasion: Communicators and Audiences

1. In your own words, what is meant by "persuasion?"

2. Complete the table below by indicating whether the factor will likely lead to persuasion.

Factor	Persuasive?
Communicators who are credible	
Physically attractive communicators	
Messages that appear designed to change our attitudes	
Being distracted by an extraneous event while paying full attention to a communicator	
Offering a one-sided approach when the audience holds views that are different than yours	
Speaking slowly	
Messages that arouse strong emotions	

➢ The Science of Social Psychology: Making Sense of Common Sense-Can We Be Scared Into Changing Our Attitudes?

Give examples of how the media uses "fear appeal" to change the public's health habits.

1."Fear appeal" is most effective when ____________________________________.

2. "Fear appeal" is least effective when ____________________________________.

➤ The Cognitive Processes Underlying Persuasion

1. Word association time! For each of the terms below, write the word (or phrase) that best describes its meaning.

    a. Systematic processing →

    b. Heuristic processing →

    c. Central route →

    d. Peripheral route →

    e. Elaboration likelihood model →

Resisting Persuasion Attempts

➤ Reactance: Protecting Our Personal Freedom

1. In your own words, define "reactance" and note its implications.

➤ Forewarning: Prior Knowledge of Persuasive Intent

1. In your own words, define "forewarning" and note its implications.

➤ Selective Avoidance of Persuasion Attempts

1. In your own words, define "selective avoidance" and note its implications.

➢ Actively Defending our Attitudes: Counterarguing Against the Competition

1. We're so good at resisting persuasion, not only since we tend to ignore information that's inconsistent with our own views, but we also ____

____.

➢ Inoculation Against "Bad Ideas"

1. Inoculation toward persuasion is____.

We engage in this process by ____.

➢ Cognitive Dissonance: What It Is and How Do We Reduce It?

1. In your own words, describe what is meant by "cognitive dissonance."

2. Complete the chart below by listing the various direct and indirect approaches to dissonance reduction.

Direct Approaches	Indirect Approaches

3. Describe the evidence that suggests that dissonance really is, in fact, an unpleasant state.

4. Summarize the evidence that considers whether dissonance is a universal human experience.

➢ **Beyond The Headlines: As Social Psychologists See It--How television affects attitudes toward same-sex marriage: The "Will & Grace" Effect.**

1. The "Will & Grace" Effect is ______________________________.

2. Explain how watching "Will & Grace" can create cognitive dissonance in some viewers.

3. What will viewers who watch the show and experience dissonance do to relieve this state?

➢ Dissonance and Attitude Change: The Effects of Induced Compliance

1. Suppose an American is kidnapped by a group of terrorists and subsequently releases a statement whereby he denounces America. Why should we *not* really believe that the hostage holds these views?

2. Describe the dynamics of the famous Festinger and Carlsmith (1959) study and, in doing so, discuss the relevance of the less-leads-to-more effect.

➢ When Dissonance is a Tool for Beneficial Changes in Behavior

1. Outline the three elements that need to be in place if one is to successfully use dissonance in order to generate hypocrisy to bring about positive changes.

After You Read...

Practice Test 1

1. Compared to attitudes acquired through indirect experience, attitudes acquired through direct experience
   a. are the basis for slower, more deliberate responses.
   b. exert stronger effects on behavior.
   c. are held with less confidence.
   d. are weaker.

2. Attitudes refer to
   a. aspects of the social world that are controversial.
   b. aspects of the social world that require a lot of thought.
   c. virtually any aspect of the social world.
   d. aspects of the social world that are important to the individual.

3. Which of the following statements about the relationship between attitudes and behaviors is *true*?
   a. Accurate predictions of overt behavior can often be derived from people's specific attitudes.
   b. Attitudes formed as a result of direct experience with the attitude object are poor predictors of behavior.
   c. The more general one's attitudes, the greater the accuracy in predicting specific behaviors.
   d. Attitudes do not predict behavior.

4. Whether a student will actually undergo body piercing to wear a nose ring is best predicted by the ____ and how one reacts to a panhandler who approached them on the street is best predicted by the ____.
   a. theory of planned behavior; attitude-to-behavior process model
   b. attitude-to-behavior process model; theory of planned behavior
   c. theory of planned behavior; theory of planned behavior also
   d. attitude-to-behavior process model; attitude-to-behavior process model also

5. Which of the following statements about persuasion is *false*?
   a. Experts are more persuasive than non-experts.
   b. People who speak slowly are more persuasive than those who speak rapidly.
   c. Persuasion can be enhanced by fear-arousing messages.
   d. It is sometimes easier to persuade a person who's distracted from a message than one paying full attention.

6. The ____ route is used when attitudes are changed without careful thought about the issue or arguments being used.
   a. peripheral
   b. central
   c. elaborative
   d. heuristic

7. According to the elaboration likelihood model, a persuader with strong, convincing arguments should use the ____ route.
   a. peripheral
   b. central
   c. elaborative
   d. heuristic

8. An attitude serves a ____ function when it helps a person to organize and interpret diverse information.
   a. self-identity
   b. self-esteem
   c. knowledge
   d. self-expression

9. Due to ____, a person may resist persuasion attempts since it directs their attention away from information that challenges their existing attitudes.
   a. reactance
   b. forewarning
   c. biased assimilation
   d. selective avoidance

10. When stimuli we are presented with are evaluated in terms of our attitudes, ____________ brain wave activity results compared to when the same stimuli are responded to in nonevaluative terms.
   a. same
   b. different
   c. comparable
   d. little

Practice Test 2

1. Learning based on association is referred to as
   a. instrumental conditioning
   b. classical conditioning
   c. observational learning
   d. associative learning

2. Mary asks her friend about her views on the crisis in the Middle East in order to evaluate her own feelings on the matter. This example illustrates ____.
   a. observational learning
   b. social comparison
   c. instrumental conditioning
   d. classical conditioning

3. The third person effect of media exposure is where the impact of others' attitudes and behavior is ____and the impact on the self is ________.
   a. underestimated; underestimated
   b. underestimated; overestimated
   c. overestimated; overestimated
   d. overestimated; underestimated

4. Attitudes are usually conceptualized as serving all of the following functions, *except*
   a. impression motivation.
   b. depression barrier.
   c. self-identity.
   d. ego-defensive.

5. Even though Bob isn't pleased with the quality of his hamburger, he decides to not complain about it to his waitress for fear of spoiling the festive time he is having with his friends. This example illustrates that ____ often moderate the relationship between attitudes and behavior.
   a. complex genetic factors
   b. attitude origins
   c. individual differences
   d. situational constraints

6. Attitude strength incorporates all of the following elements, *except*
   a. reliability.
   b. accessibility.
   c. intensity.
   d. knowledge.

7. The extent to which attitudes are focused on particular objects or situations is known as
   a. attitude strength.
   b. attitude origin.
   c. attitude specificity.
   d. attitude reasonability.

8. The component(s) that comprise the theories of reasoned action and planned behavior is (are)
   a. attitudes toward a given behavior and subjective norms about it.
   b. subjective norms about a given behavior and perceived behavioral control.
   c. attitudes toward a given behavior and perceived behavioral control.
   d. attitudes toward a given behavior.

9. The importance of social norms tends to be particularly emphasized in the
   a. theory of planned behavior.
   b. theory of reasoned action.
   c. attitude-to-behavior process model.
   d. central route to persuasion.

10. Suppose Josh is about to give a speech to an audience whose views are fairly contrary to his own. In order to be *most* persuasive, he should adopt a ____ approach.
    a. one-sided
    b. two-sided
    c. muddled
    d. non-emotional

Practice Test 3

1. To know whether our attitudes are correct or not we rely on the process of
    a. systematic processing.
    b. heuristic processing.
    c. social comparison.
    d. the third person effect.

2. Of the following professions, the one that is *most* associated with the use of heuristic processing is a
    a. doctor.
    b. salesperson.
    c. professor.
    d. newspaper reporter.

3. ____ is defined as a negative reaction to threats to one's personal freedom.
    a. Forewarning
    b. Selective avoidance
    c. Reactance
    d. Biased assimilation

4. Paul is attending a town meeting. When he hears a speaker with whom he disagrees, he decided to leave the room. This example illustrates
    a. forewarning.
    b. selective avoidance.
    c. reactance.
    d. biased assimilation.

5. Which of the following cognitions by a television news viewer *best* illustrates the hostile media bias?
    a. "TV news today just can't get the story right!"
    b. "You can't believe anything that's said on television—that's why I read the newspaper."
    c. "I sure love how those TV news hosts duke it out when debating issues!"
    d. "Since that channel is so out of line with my views, it must be biased!"

6. Cognitive dissonance typically occurs when
    a. we have inconsistent attitudes.
    b. there is a discrepancy between our attitudes and behaviors.
    c. either we have inconsistent attitudes or there is a discrepancy between our attitudes and behaviors.
    d. we are unsure of how we think about some issue.

7. The process of trivialization is a(n) ____ approach that tends to ____ dissonance.
   a. direct; reduce
   b. direct; increase
   c. indirect; reduce
   d. indirect; increase

8. Induced compliance tends to
   a. create a feeling of dissonance.
   b. not cause dissonance since such statements were made under duress.
   c. cause a person to solidify their own beliefs.
   d. reduce any previous feelings of dissonance.

9. The famous Festinger and Carlsmith (1959) study found that college students reported that they enjoyed a boring task
   a. regardless of how much they were paid.
   b. regardless of whether they were paid.
   c. when they were paid a large amount of money.
   d. when they were paid a small amount of money.

10. Which of the following statements about hypocrisy is *false*?
   a. It can be used as a tool to change other's behaviors in desirable ways.
   b. It involves publicly advocating some attitude or behavior that's inconsistent with one's own attitudes or behaviors.
   c. If hypocrisy is used to try to change others' behaviors, then the individual in question must be made to feel an overwhelming sense of shame.
   d. People often show a great gap between their health-related attitudes and behaviors.

Comprehensive Test

(NOTE: Items 1-15 are multiple-choice questions and items 16-23 are true-false questions.)

1. Fear appeals appear to be most effective when the symptoms of a potential illness are _____.
   a. trivial
   b. highly serious
   c. vague
   d. contagious

2. Since most people feel better after they take an aspirin for a headache, this increases the likelihood that they will take aspirins again for future headaches. Thus, consistent with ____ conditioning, aspirin functions as a ____.
   a. classical; reward
   b. instrumental; reward
   c. classical; punishment
   d. instrumental; punishment

3. The attitudes of identical twins ____ correlate more highly than those of nonidentical twins ____ the identical twins where separated at birth.
   a. do; even if
   b. do; only if
   c. do; unless
   d. do not; regardless

4. Murray doesn't want to confront the fact that he's been cheating on his wife, so he develops a strong belief that adultery is "sinful." This example shows how attitudes often have a(n) ____ function.
   a. delusional
   b. self-esteem
   c. impression motivation
   d. ego-defensive

5. When an audience holds attitudes contrary to those of a would-be persuader, it is often more effective for the communicator to adopt a
   a. one-sided approach.
   b. two-sided approach.
   c. a low pressure sales pitch.
   d. a high pressure sales pitch.

6. A very significant determinant of attitude importance is one's
   a. attitude ambivalence.
   b. parental influence.
   c. general interest.
   d. vested interest.

7. The importance of subjective norms is highlighted in the
   a. theory of planned behavior only.
   b. theory of reasoned action only.
   c. theories of planned behavior and reasoned action.
   d. theory of attitude-behavior reasons only.

8. In order to increase the likelihood that one will be successful at his or her attempts at persuasion, an individual should
   a. not present a message that makes it clear that one is trying to change others' attitudes.
   b. ensure that the audience will not be distracted by an extraneous event.
   c. speak as slowly as possible.
   d. avoid arousing strong emotions.

9. When we believe a message is important, it is quite likely that we'll engage in ____ processing via the ____ route.
   a. systematic; central
   b. systematic; peripheral
   c. heuristic; central
   d. heuristic; peripheral

10. ____, which tends to ____ resistance to persuasion, is defined as advance knowledge that one is about to become the target of an attempt at persuasion.
    a. Reactance; decrease
    b. Reactance; increase
    c. Forewarning; decrease
    d. Forewarning; increase

11. Upon learning of some news that was contrary to her opinions, Shelley viewed this information as unreliable and unconvincing. This example best depicts
    a. biased assimilation.
    b. attitude polarization.
    c. selective avoidance.
    d. cognitive dissonance.

12. Self-affirmation is to trivialization as
    a. indirect is to direct.
    b. direct is to indirect.
    c. helpful is to harmful.
    d. cognitive dissonance is to less-leads-to-more effect.

13. In terms of its impact on the operation of dissonance, cultural factors appear to be
    a. not terribly important.
    b. instrumental in determining whether someone feels uneasy about inconsistent thoughts.
    c. important in ascertaining the precise conditions under which these occur.
    d. irrelevant.

14. The term used to describe the fact that fewer reasons or rewards lead to more attitude change is called the
    a. more-leads-to-less-effect.
    b. less-leads-to-more-effect.
    c. fewer-leads-to-greater-effect.
    d. greater-leads-to-fewer effect.

15. In order to use hypocrisy in an effective way that promotes beneficial changes, all of the following elements must be present, *except*
    a. the person in question must publicly advocate the desired behavior.
    b. the person in question must be given access to direct means for reducing his or her dissonance.
    c. the person in question needs to acknowledge his or her shortcomings as a person.
    d. the person in question must think about his or her own failures to show the beneficial behaviors in the past.

Questions 16-23 are True/False Questions

16. Cognitive dissonance has been shown to primarily generate anxious, but positive, affect.

17. Inconsistent with the openly-expressed prejudice of the 1930s, a study conducted during this time period showed that most U.S. restaurants and hotels did not refuse service to a young Chinese couple.

18. Attitudes tend to predict behavior when these are specific, rather than general.

19. A speaker who is trying to persuade someone should present both sides of the issue if the target is already in agreement with the message.

20. People who speak slowly tend to be less persuasive than those who speak rapidly.

21. Heuristic cues tend to be associated with the peripheral, rather than the central, route.

22. ELM stands for the elaboration likelihood model.

23. In the famous Festinger and Carlsmith (1959) experiment, the more money subjects were paid to tell another person how interesting a boring experiment was, the more the subjects believed what they had said.

Short Answer/Essay Questions

1. **Attitude Formation**
   What is the key difference between classical and subliminal conditioning?

2. **Attitude Functions**
   List and briefly discuss the main functions that attitudes serve.

3. **How Attitudes Influence Behavior**
   Discuss how Fazio's attitude-to-behavior model operates.

4. **Persuasion**
   Suppose you are giving a talk to a group of individuals who may hold views different than your own. What is an effective way to make your talk?

5. **Cognitive Dissonance and Hypocrisy**
   Suppose one of your friends usually doesn't wear his seatbelt and you want to encourage him to do so. Briefly explain how you can use dissonance to help him change his behavior.

6. **Fear Appeals**
   Describe a situation in which a fear appeal would be most persuasive to its audience.

When You Have Finished . . .

Applications of Attitudes to Your Life

1. We form attitudes about virtually every possible topic that has some degree of relevance to our lives. As such, we should be interested in how attitudes develop and influence behavior.

2. Since we often try to persuade others and vice-versa, an understanding of how persuasion works may make our efforts more viable while helping us to realize when others are trying to cause us to change our attitudes.

3. We can use dissonance in such a way to help promote healthy behaviors and lifestyles when it is related to a person's hypocrisy.

4. We often wonder whether a person's attitude will influence and predict their behaviors. By

understanding the attitude-behavior link, we are more apt to make accurate predictions.

5. If you've ever wondered from where your own attitudes have originated, then consider looking at the attitudes of parents and other relatives, given the importance of social learning.

Let's revisit point #2. Watch an hour or two of prime time television (e.g., between 8-10 p.m.) and pay particular attention to the *television commercials*. For each commercial you see, decide the method of persuasion that's being used and rate this method on a 1 to 5 scale (where "5" is the *most* persuasive) consider how persuasive the commercial is to you.

Internet Sites

http://realmagick.com/articles/49/549.html: Explains different kinds of priming in the context of asking "does subliminal influence work?"

http://www.rickross.com/reference/scientology/scien258.html: Contains an article from Skeptical Inquirer, "Brought into the fold: Scientology as a case study on influence and persuasion in religion, which applies social psychological theories to Scientology's practices." In particular, the Elaboration Likelihood Model is discussed, and Cialdini's principles of influence are discussed as illustrations of influence through the peripheral route.

http://www-unix.oit.umass.edu/~aizen/tpb.html: Ajzen's site on the theory of planned behavior. Includes guidelines for designing a theory of planned behavior questionnaire and conducting an intervention guided by the theory.

http://members.aol.com/psychneuro/subliminal/WhatisSubl.html: Another good article on cognitive psychology's approach to subliminal perception.

http://www.poleshift.org/sublim/: Illustrations of different subliminal advertising techniques.

This site guides you to other sites that have collections of ads you can view or hear online. (In particular, check *http://www.adflip.com/:* for print ads and *http://www.televisioncommercials.com* for television commercials).

Crossword Puzzle

ATTITUDES

Across

1. efforts to change others attitudes
3. basic form of learning
5. process of comparing ourselves to other
6. advance knowledge
7. resistance to persuasion
11. systematic attitude change
17. behavior and attitude inconsistent
18. evaluations of the social world
19. a technique for reducing dissonance
20. say one thing do another
21. learning from others
22. overestimate media impact underestimate self's impact

Down

2. stimuli that are below conscious awareness
4. processing information using mental shortcuts
8. extension of the theory of reasoned action
9. careful consideration of ideas
10. positive and negative evaluations of the same attitude object
12. induced to say something inconsistent with true attitudes
13. expectations about how people will behave
14. learning from observation
15. change in attitude due to peripheral cues
16. learning from reinforcement

Created by Puzzlemaker at DiscoverySchool.com
http://school.discovery.com/

5 THE SELF: HOW WE ANSWER THE QUESTION "WHO AM I?"

Before You Read . . .

This chapter considers the important aspect of our self-identity. You'll learn about the many unique components of your own identity by reviewing what is known as your self-concept. The general attitudes that you have about yourself in terms of your own worth or self-esteem will also be explored and gender differences in self-esteem will be discussed as well. You'll also be presented with an overview of other key dimensions of self-functioning, such as self-focusing, self-monitoring, and self-efficacy. You will then discover that looking inward is not always the best route to self-insight. You'll also have a good understanding, through a personal example offered by one of the authors (Nyla Branscombe), about the emotional consequences of stereotypes on our identities and what the implications of these beliefs are for our lives.

Chapter Objectives

After reading this chapter, you should be able to:

- Understand the components and dimensions of a person's social identity.
- State and define the three types of self-awareness.
- Consider how the self-concept functions and provide at least two examples of a specific type of self-concept.
- Describe how external factors can shape one's self-concept.
- Explain how we evaluate our self-esteem and how social comparison processes function in this respect.
- Offer a definition of a downward social comparison and an upward social comparison and an example of when we would use each.
- Contrast the consequences of low versus high self-esteem.
- Be able to discuss gender differences with regard to the topic of self-esteem.
- Offer a definition of self-focusing and why this is important in our lives.

- Contrast the differences between low and high self-monitors.
- Explain when individuals use the concept of ingratiation.
- Discuss how self-efficacy affects our lives and offer some examples of specific types of self-efficacy.
- Understand what a stereotype threat is and give an example of one.
- Explain the emotional reaction that a stereotype threat produces from the targeted individual.

As You Read . . .

Important Terms to Remember! Below are a list of some of the key terms and concepts from this chapter. Make flashcards in order to enhance your recall ability of these terms. Refer to the definitions that are either in boldface or in the margins of this chapter for help. You may also want to include additional terms from this chapter as you deem necessary.

Social identity	Self-concept	Subjective, objective, and symbolic self-awareness
Self-reference effect	Self-serving biases	Social self
Possible selves	Above average effect	Black sheep effect
Self-esteem	Self-assessment	Self-insight
Downward vs. upward social comparison	Existential terror	Self-focusing
Care ethic	Self-monitoring	Self-efficacy
Ingratiation	Independent self-concept	Identity interference
Interdependent self-concept	Intergroup comparison	Intragroup comparison
Justice ethic	Personal-social identity continuum	Objective self-awareness
Self-complexity	Self-evaluation maintenance model	Social-identity theory
Stereotype threat	Terror management theory	Collective self-efficacy
Performance deficits		

Thinking About the Self: Personal versus Social Identity

1. Explain the difference between your **social self-identity** and your **personal self-identity**

2. List two future **possible selves** that are inspiring to you.

3. It is well-known that ______________________culture emphasizes an independent self-concept,

whereas _______cultures emphasize an independent self-concept.

4. A **justice ethic** involves_________________________while a **care ethic**

is______________________.

5. Explain the difference between **objective self-awareness** and **symbolic self-awareness**.

6. List three activities that you have high self-efficacy in.

Self-Esteem: Attitudes Toward One's Self

1. In your own words, define "self-esteem."

2. State and describe the three possible motives for self-evaluation.

3. List the negative traits that are associated with very high self-esteem.

   a.______________________

   b. ______________________

   c.______________________

4. Do women and men differ in their level of self-esteem? Discuss the current research results with regard to gender differences in self-esteem between men and women.

Beyond the Headlines: As Social Psychologists See It: "Fugitive Blames Police for Not Capturing Him Fast Enough"

1. List two risks that are involved when an individual complains to others about unfair treatment.

➢ Social Comparison: Knowing The Self

1. What's going on? For each of the following two scenarios, discuss what you're doing exactly, the impact of what you're doing is for your self-esteem, and why is this impact happening.

   a.) You're making a downward social comparison with a stranger…

   b.) You're making an upward social comparison with a member of your in-group…

2. The self-evaluation maintenance model and the social identity theory both build on

   ______________________.

3. The black sheep effect is when ____.

➢ Self-Presentation and Self-Regulation

1. Name that aspect of self-functioning! I'll provide the key characteristics/effects and *you* name the aspect of self-functioning that's being described.

Aspect of Self-Functioning	Key Characteristics/Effects
	Engage in role playing in order to obtain positive evaluations from others
	Comparing ourselves to someone of lesser ability
	Presenting ourselves as admiring others
	Being true to yourself

➢ Making Sense of Common Sense--Is Looking Inwardly the Best Route to "Self-Insight?"

1. Explain the harmful effects of intense introspection.

2. List two positive effects of introspection.

➢ The Self as Target of Prejudice

1. Explain how a target of prejudice maintains his or her level of self-esteem.

2. The cognitive effects of being a target of prejudice include____________________________.

3. The behavioral effects of being a target of prejudice include____________________________.

4. Give an example of when you were the victim of a stereotype threat.

After You Read...

Practice Test 1

1. One's self-definition when compared with other members of a group, using an intragroup comparison, is likely to reflect
   a. perceived differences between yourself and other group members.
   b. perceived similarities between yourself and other members of your group.
   c. perceived personal inferiority.
   d. perceived personal anxiety.

2. With respect to our self-concept, we tend to do all of the following, *except*
   a. find excuses for any inconsistencies.
   b. maintain a level of self-consistency.
   c. question the efficacy of our motives.
   d. protect our self-image from threatening information.

3. Only humans appear to have ____ self-awareness.
   a. accurate
   b. symbolic
   c. subjective
   d. objective

4. The basic reason for the self-reference effect is that
   a. humans tend to be overly self-focused.
   b. self-relevant material is processed more efficiently.
   c. we typically are not able to process information that is irrelevant to the self.
   d. humans don't care about social information unless it directly pertains to them.

5. When we try to make others like us by conveying that we like them this is an example of
   a. care ethic.
   b. image presentation.
   c. self-monitoring.
   d. ingratiation.

6. The social self consists of ____ key components.
   a. two
   b. three
   c. four
   d. five

7. Culture influences social self-concepts
   a. in very rare instances.
   b. such that the welfare of the group, rather than the individual, is emphasized in Western cultures.
   c. such that the welfare of the group, rather than the individual, is emphasized in Eastern cultures.
   d. only if an individual is living in a harsh environment of some sort.

8. ____ are mental representations of what we might become.
   a. Working self-concepts
   b. Unrealized selves
   c. Potential selves
   d. Possible selves

9. Suppose Peter, who just completed his Ph.D. in psychology, is now a professor. As such, he'll probably experience
   a. a change in his self-concept.
   b. decreased self-esteem.
   c. the lack of a need for other possible selves.
   d. a stable self-image.

10. All of the following are motives for self-evaluation, *except*
    a. self-assessment.
    b. self-criticism.
    c. self-enhancement.
    d. self-verification.

Practice Test 2

1. Downward social comparisons tend to have ____ effect(s) on self-esteem and upward social comparisons tend to have ____ effect(s) on self-esteem when made with a stranger.
   a. positive; negative
   b. no; positive
   c. negative; no
   d. positive; no

2. Which of the following statements about self-esteem is *true*?
   a. Paradoxical self-esteem only refers to unrealistically high self-esteem.
   b. Low self-esteem has more negative consequences than variable self-esteem.
   c. Aggressive people typically have high self-esteem.
   d. Low self-esteem does not affect the body's immune system.

3. ______ allows organisms to differentiate themselves from the physical environment.
   a. Objective self-awareness
   b. Subjective self-awareness
   c. Existential self-awareness
   d. Social self-awareness

4. ____ is the act of directing attention toward oneself.
   a. Self-focusing
   b. Self-esteem
   c. Self-monitoring
   d. Self-efficacy

5. The observation that people show a preference for objects owned by and reflective of the self is termed the _____.
   a. objective self-awareness effect
   b. self-reference effect
   c. interdependent self effect
   d. social comparison effect

6. When a member of our ingroup behaves in way that threatens the value of our group identity and is intensely derogated as a means of protecting one's group identity. This is an example of
   a. identity interference.
   b. discrimination.
   c. black sheep effect.
   d. stereotype threat.

7. High self-monitors tend to possess all of the following characteristics, *except*
   a. fewer and longer lasting romantic relationships.
   b. engaging in role playing in order to obtain positive evaluations from others.
   c. the use of third person when talking about themselves.
   d. more positive self-esteem.

8. A shared belief by members of a group that together they can produce desired effects is known as ____ self-efficacy.
   a. social
   b. collective
   c. general
   d. self-regulatory

9. Dreaded possible selves can cause us to _____certain behaviors.
   a. give up
   b. increase
   c. maximize
   d. attain

10. High self-esteem is correlated with an increased likelihood of
    a. agreeableness.
    b. conscientiousness.
    c. openness.
    d. interpersonal aggression.

Practice Test 3

1. Upward social comparisons at the personal level can be_______.
   a. comforting.
   b. gratifying.
   c. painful..
   d. satisfying

2. Downward social comparisons at the personal level can be
   a. dissatisfying.
   b. comforting.
   c. painful.
   d. depressing.

3. Stereotype threat involves the undermining of performance in ___ people.
   a. incapable.
   b. capable.
   c. threatening.
   d. friendly

4. ___________plays a crucial role in stereotype threat effects.
   a. Positive affect
   b. Negative affect
   c. Anxiety
   d. Aggressiveness

5. Women do on average have __________self-esteem than men.
   a. greater
   b. the same
   c. higher
   d. lower

6. People often present themselves in an ingratiating manner to be
   a. liked.
   b. protected.
   c. Respected.
   d. thought of as intelligent.

7. People cope with stereotype threat by ____________ the performance domain.
   a. forgetting
   b. eliminating
   c. moving themselves closer to
   d. distancing themselves from

8. The social comparison theory was developed by
   a. Branscombe.
   b. Kelley.
   c. Bem.
   d. Festinger.

9. Low self-monitoring involves focusing on _____cues.
   a. internal
   b. external
   c. positive
   d. negative

10. High self-monitoring involves focusing on _____cues.
   a. internal
   b. external
   c. positive
   d. negative

Comprehensive Test

(NOTE: Items 1-15 are multiple-choice questions and items 16-23 are true-false questions.)

1. The ____ effect refers to the finding that information about the self is more readily processed and remembered than other information.
   a. self-efficacy
   b. self-focusing
   c. self-monitoring
   d. self-reference

2. Those who are most vulnerable to feedback indicating that they lack the necessary skills to enter their chosen profession are those who have
   a. a complex view of their possible selves.
   b. a limited number of possible future selves.
   c. possible selves that are unrealistically grounded.
   d. cultural taboos about thinking too much about the future.

3. One's ____ is measured in terms of a self-evaluation made along a positive-negative dimension.
   a. self-esteem
   b. self-concept
   c. self-schema
   d. self-monitoring

4. A downward comparison with someone who is very close to oneself
   a. raises self-esteem.
   b. doesn't influence self-esteem.
   c. produces a contrast effect.
   d. has a negative effect on self-esteem.

5. A very competent person with unrealistically negative self-esteem would exhibit
   a. evaluative-integrated self-organization.
   b. compartmentalized self-esteem.
   c. variable self-esteem.
   d. paradoxical self-esteem.

6. Persons who tailor their behavior to specific situations and audiences are said to be
   a. low in self-efficacy.
   b. high in self-efficacy.
   c. low in self-monitoring.
   d. high in self-monitoring.

7. High self-monitors tend to use _____when they speak.
   a. third person pronouns
   b. first person pronouns
   c. no pronouns
   d. few pronouns

8. Low self-monitors tend to use ______when they speak.
   a. third person pronouns
   b. first person pronouns
   c. no pronouns
   d. few pronouns

9. Descriptions of the self at the social identity level are ____________in nature.
   a. independent
   b. interdependent
   c. intragoup
   d. intergroup

10. Introspection is to __________ "who we are."
   a. publicly think about
   b. privately think about
   c. not acknowledge
   d. accept

11. Personal identity self-descriptions can be thought of as _____in nature.
   a. independent
   b. interdependent
   c. intragroup
   d. intergroup

12. ______________of us show the above average effect.
   a. Most
   b. Very few
   c. Some
   d. None

13. People with high self-esteem are _______vulnerable to threat following a failure experience.
   a. more
   b. less
   c. increasingly
   d. none of the above

14. Chinese students attribute their success in school to their __, and American students attribute their success in school to their ________.
   a. skill; skill
   b. teachers; teachers
   c. teachers; skill
   d. skill; teachers

15. Only humans show _____ self-awareness.
   a. meaningful
   b. symbolic
   c. objective
   d. subjective

Questions 16-23 are True/False Questions

16. There does *not* appear to be a difference between Americans and Japanese individuals in terms of how frequently they show self-enhancement and self-criticism.

17. The self-reference effect helps to explain why you likely would pay particular attention to a person who has the same last name as yours.

18. An athlete who identifies strongly and exclusively with the role of an athlete will probably be more upset by an athletic injury than an athlete with a variety of future selves.

19. A high self-monitor tends to regulate his or her behavior on the basis of internal factors, such as values, beliefs, and attitudes.

20. Chinese students are more likely to explain their failures as stemming from their own flaws.

21. Americans tend to explain their failures as being due to "someone else's fault."

22. High self-esteem has been found to be the root of many ills including drug abuse.

23. High self-esteem is associated with bullying and interpersonal aggression.

Short Answer/Essay Questions

1. **Self-Concept**
   Compare and contrast the similarities and differences between men and women in terms of their self-concepts.

2. **Social Comparisons**
   Suppose you make an upward social comparison with a stranger, a member of your in-group, and a close friend. Explain what the consequences of each of these comparisons will likely be—and why.

3. **Aspects of Self-Functioning**
   Janet tends to act and say things that are consistent with the actions and attitudes of those around her. Given this information, what characteristic is Janet displaying?

4. **Stereotype Threat**
   Give an example of when a stereotype threat has affected your life.

When You Have Finished . . .

Applications of the "Self" to Your Life

1. As trite as it may sound, the person who knows you the best is *yourself.* As such, we should all be aware and reflective of the components of our unique identities.

2. We live in a world where strong stereotypes about gender abound. By being more aware of these stereotypes, perhaps we may someday be able to live in a world where men and women are truly recognized and valued as a function to their abilities—and not by their sex.

3. Since very low and even very high levels of self-esteem can be harmful to our mental health and well-being, we should take an interest in having a fairly positive evaluation of our own worth.

4. We should also be aware of the type of social comparisons that we make on a daily basis either upward or downward and realize that a mix of these comparison is most optimal for good mental health.

Let's revisit point #2. Pick a day to focus on any gender stereotypes that you observe, whether these are from media sources (e.g., television, magazine ads, roadside billboards), personal interactions or observations involving yourself or others, or from other sources. Try to note the occurrence and prevalence of such stereotypes and also note instances where you found examples of behavior that was inconsistent or contrary to such stereotypes.

Internet Sites:

http://www.self-esteem-nase.org/links.shtml: The website of the National Association for Self-Esteem. This site provides many useful links to building self-esteem and self-esteem surveys.

http://pubpages.unh.edu/~ckb/SELFMON2.html or *http://www.css.edu/users/dswenson/web/OB/self-monitoring%20test.htm*: Two links to Mark Snyder's Self-Monitoring Scale posted online.

http://www.earthcam.com/: Click on "society and people cams." People's lives, live on the Internet. See question #14 below. People's diaries on the Internet. Finally, look at *http://www.sosig.ac.uk/iriss/papers/paper21.htm* for an article, "The Presentation of Self in WWW Home Pages" by Hugh Miller and Russell Mather. What kinds of self-presentation are going on, and what is the implication of this technological revolution for how people will come to understand themselves?

http://www.queendom.com/tests/personality/self_esteem_r_access.html: This site provides an online self-esteem test and feedback about your score.

http://www.prenhall.com/divisions/hss/app/social/chap5_3.html. An online test that measures and calculates your level of private self-consciousness.

Crossword Puzzle

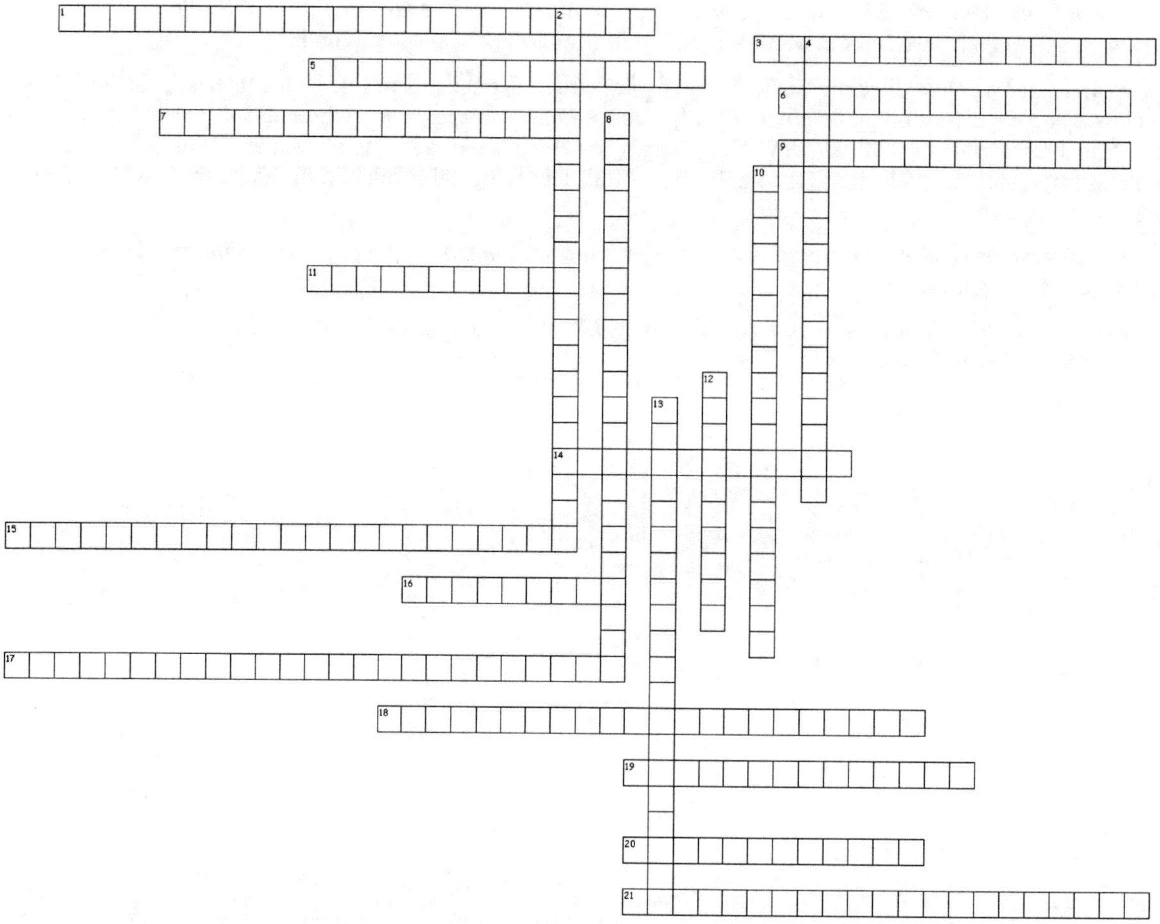

Across

1. comparing to someone less than self
3. being derogated
5. judged in light of a negative stereotype about your group
6. images of future self
7. anxiety about dying
9. monitoring behavior
11. application of universal rules
14. belief one can achieve a goal
15. self is separate from environment

16. justice and ethics orientation
17. collectivistic cultures self-concept
18. Festinger's theory
19. how self-concept is organized
20. making others like us
21. confronting own death

Down

2. comparisons between groups
4. rate your self above average
8. concept in individualistic cultures
10. orientation toward self
12. attitude toward self
13. social identities in conflict

Created by Puzzlemaker at DiscoverySchool.com
http://school.discovery.com/

6 PREJUDICE: ITS CAUSES, EFFECTS, AND CURES

Before You Read . . .

This chapter addresses the very serious and important issue of prejudice in terms of why it happens, its effects, and how to prevent it. First, your text considers the general nature of prejudice and explains how it differs from discrimination. Afterward, a thorough overview regarding the origins of prejudice is presented. As you might expect, prejudice is derived from a variety of sources, such as social learning, intergroup conflict, social categorizations, stereotypes, illusory correlations, and out-group homogeneity. In this chapter, you'll have a good understanding as to why each of these sources may contribute to prejudice. A discussion of how targets of prejudice cope and react to bigotry is also discussed. Your text also offers an encouraging perspective as to why prejudice is *not* inevitable. You'll consider the many ways to reduce prejudice, such as learning techniques, direct intergroup contact, recategorization, cognitive interventions, and social influence.

Chapter Objectives

After reading this chapter, you should be able to:

- Explain how schemas and negative emotions provide the basic foundations for prejudice.
- State the two basic reasons for why prejudice persists.
- Contrast the key difference between prejudice and discrimination.
- Understand how modern racism operates in contrast to "old-fashioned" racism.
- Describe how racial attitudes have been measured as a function of the "bogus pipeline" and the "bona fide pipeline."
- Consider why tokenism exists and its implications.
- Explain how realistic conflict theory helps to understand the origins of prejudice.

PREJUDICE

- Discuss the general methods and findings of the famous "Robber's Cave" study and why it is relevant to the study of prejudice.

- Contrast historical and contemporary social psychological views of whether poor economic conditions foster prejudice.

- Discuss how the social learning view of prejudice affects how a person develops attitudes about other racial or ethnic groups.

- Understand the nature and effects of social categorization and, in doing so, highlight the relevance of the ultimate attribution error and social identity theory.

- Offer a basic overview of what stereotypes are and how they operate.

- Compare and contrast how illusory correlations, in-group differentiation, and the illusion of out-group homogeneity all relate to the development of prejudice.

- Explain how the contact hypothesis and the extended contact hypothesis differ in terms of their predictions for how we can reduce prejudice.

- Consider how recategorizations, cognitive interventions, and social influence can all be used to reduce prejudice.

- Understand how individuals cope with prejudice.

- Explain how hostile and benevolent sexism function.

- Discuss how gender stereotypes and differential respect often provide the foundation for the cognitive bases of sexism.

- Understand why subtle forms of discrimination—particularly in the workplace—may still exist and, in doing so, explain what is meant by a "glass ceiling."

As You Read . . .

Important Terms to Know! Below are a list of some of the key terms and concepts from this chapter. Make flashcards in order to enhance your recall ability of these terms. Refer to the definitions that are either in boldface or in the margins of this chapter for help. You may also want to include additional terms from this chapter as you deem necessary.

Prejudice	Discrimination	Schemas
Stereotypes	Hate crimes	Modern racism
Subtype	Bogus vs. bona fide pipeline	Tokenism
Realistic conflict theory	Superordinate goals	Social learning view
Social categorization	In- vs. out-group	Ultimate attribution error
Social identity theory	Illusory correlations	In-group differentiation
Illusion of out-group homogeneity	Threat	Contact vs. extended contact hypotheses
Recategorization	Common in-group identity model	Category-driven processing
Stereotype threat	Sexism	Hostile vs. benevolent sexism
Subjective scales	Differential respect	Glass ceiling
Ambivalent racial attitudes	Benevolent sexism	Collective guilt
Gender Stereotypes	Glass ceiling	Hostile Sexism
Implicit associations	Incidental feelings	Minimal groups
Priming	Schemata	Social creativity responses

The Nature and Origins of Stereotyping, Prejudice and Discrimination

➢ Stereotyping: Beliefs About Social Groups

1. In your own words describe a stereotype. Give an example of a stereotype type.

2. A stereotype is______________________________.

   Prejudice is ______________________________.

   Discrimination is______________________________.

3. Discuss some of the origins of stereotypes, prejudice and discrimination

4. Explain what the term "glass ceiling" means.

5. Benevolent sexism views suggest that __________are superior to ___________in various ways.

6. Discuss the question "Are gender stereotypes accurate?" More specifically, which gender stereotypes are accurate?

7. Give two examples of gender-typed illusory correlations that we commonly see on TV.

8. For each of the following descriptions, place an "X" to the left of the item if it tends to be associated with attitudes and behaviors expressed by most women.

    ____ holding lower expectations about one's career

    ____ feeling outraged over lower salaries for women than men

    ____ comparing themselves with men and women

    ____ expressing lower self-confidence than men in achievement-related situations

    ____ using self-promoting strategies

9. How do people tend to react to women in positions of authority? Do they hold them in equally high regard as men?

The Science of Social Psychology: Making Sense of Common Sense

➢ Shifting Standards: Does no difference in evaluations indicate no difference in meaning?

1. Based on information from this insert, explain why "same" does not necessarily mean "equal" with regard to the absence of stereotyping.

2. In your opinion has stereotype-based discrimination been eliminated in the United States? Why or why not?

➢ Prejudice and Discrimination: Feelings and Action Toward Social Groups

1. Identify the two main reasons why prejudice persists.

2. Provide three recent examples of well-known hate crimes in the United States.

3. How does "modern racism" differ from "old-fashioned racism?"

4. Compare and contrast the research methodology associated with the "bogus pipeline" versus the "bona fide pipeline." What, precisely, are these measuring?

5. What is "tokenism?" Explain the consequences and impact of tokenism.

6. Why does prejudice occur according to realistic conflict theory?

7. Summarize the methods employed by Sherif and colleagues (1961) in the famous "Robber's Cave" study. What did this study reveal about why prejudice occurs—and how we can reduce it? Also, what were some of the limitations of this classic study?

8. In your own words, what is a "stereotype?" What do we do with information that's inconsistent with our stereotypes? Also, why might implicit stereotypes be a better predictor of subtle expressions of bias than explicit measures obtained through attitude questionnaires?

9. Evaluate the veracity of each of the following statements. If you believe the statement is *false*, then modify the *italicized* word in order to make the statement *true*.

   a.) According to the *social learning view*, prejudice is the end result of acquired negative attitudes from parents or friends that are rewarded in some way.

   b.) For white college students, concern with acting in a prejudiced manner tends to be positively related to pleasant interactions with blacks in *high school*.

   c.) Historically, minorities were cast in *low-status or comic roles* in the television and movies.

10. White Americans tend to overestimate crime rates among African-American males. How is this an example of an illusory correlation?

11. Why would the statement, "You know what they're like; they're all the same," be an example of prejudice?

PREJUDICE

12. The tendency to divide the social world into two separate categories is known as ________________ ________________; these two categories are the ____________________ and the ____________ ________________. Sometimes, this reality often leads to the ultimate attribution error which is ____ ____ __________. This type of social categorization can lead to prejudice through social identity theory, which is ____.
However, this tactic can succeed only to the extent that ________________________________ ____. Because all individuals are subject to the same tendencies, the final result is inevitable: ________________ ____.

13. Why do people tend to perceive members of other groups as more homogeneous than members of our own group?

> **<u>Beyond the Headlines: As Social Psychologists See It—"Reactions to the Harmful Actions of Members of Our Own National Group"</u>**

1. Explain the concept of "collective guilt."

2. What defensive strategies did the soldiers at Abu Ghraib employ after feeling collective guilt about torturing the prisoners of war?

Why Prejudice is Not Inevitable: Techniques for Countering Its Effects

1. Evaluate and summarize the evidence that bigots are made, not born.

2. Define the contact hypothesis and state the three reasons why it truly can be effective in reducing prejudice. Also, note the conditions that must be met for it to work effectively.

3. What is the extended contact hypothesis and how does it differ from the contact hypothesis? State the four ways that it works to reduce prejudice.

4. Define the terms "recategorization" and "common in-group identity model."

5. How can we induce people belonging to different groups to perceive each other as members of a single group?

6. How can we reduce the impact of stereotypes as a means of reducing prejudice and discrimination?

After You Read…

Practice Test 1

1. Prejudice is a phenomenon that affects
   a. minorities only.
   b. either those who hold racist views and the targets of racism.
   c. virtually everyone at some time or another.
   d. American society only.

2. Attitude is to behavior as
   a. discrimination is to prejudice.
   b. prejudice is to discrimination.
   c. prejudice is to schema.
   d. discrimination is to schema.

3. The two key reasons why prejudice persists are that it
   a. allows prejudiced persons to bolster their own self-image and it saves cognitive effort.
   b. saves cognitive effort and it enhances one's social status.
   c. provides an emotional outlet for aggressive tendencies and it is associated with reproductive success.
   d. minimizes one's life problems and it causes us to be more respected in the eyes of the prejudice target.

4. Dramatic instances of hate crimes
   a. rarely occur nowadays in the United States.
   b. are exploited and overemphasized by the media.
   c. continue to occur with disturbing frequency.
   d. appear to increase during harsh economic conditions.

5. Even though Chuck rarely discusses his views on race, he confesses to his friend that "people of color are given too many benefits in society." Chuck's views illustrate
   a. old-fashioned racism.
   b. modern racism.
   c. the bogus pipeline.
   d. the bona fide pipeline.

6. The bogus pipeline is to the bona fide pipeline as
   a. old-fashioned racism is to modern racism.
   b. modern racism is to old-fashioned racism.
   c. implicit is to explicit.
   d. explicit is to implicit.

7. Suppose Juanita discovers that she primarily was hired by a company because she is a Hispanic female. Upon learning this news, she will likely
   a. feel a bit troubled, but simply grateful for her job.
   b. realize that such hiring practices are the norm for most organizations.
   c. exhibit lowered self-esteem and confidence.
   d. feel greater motivation to showcase her talents.

8. According to realistic conflict theory, the main source of prejudice stems from
   a. a lack of communication.
   b. competition over valued resources.
   c. a need to enhance one's self-esteem.
   d. learned experiences.

9. Sherif's famous "Robber's Cave" study shows that competition can
   a. lead to violent conflict.
   b. promote healthy social interactions.
   c. decrease prejudice.
   d. be destructive only if it is not direct.

10. All of the following are shortcomings or limitations of the "Robber's Cave" study, *except*
   a. the study took place over a limited amount of time.
   b. all of the participants were boys.
   c. the study failed to yield concrete solutions as how to reduce prejudice.
   d. the participants had a fairly homogeneous background.

Practice Test 2

1. _______ refers to hiring based on group membership or to situations in which individuals perform trivial positive actions for out-group members, then use this as an excuse for not taking more meaningful positive actions at a later time.
   a. Prejudice
   b. Modern Racism
   c. Tokenism
   d. The glass ceiling

2. Implicit racial attitudes appear to be related to positive interactions with blacks during
   a. preschool.
   b. elementary school.
   c. high school.
   d. college.

3. Nowadays, media portrayals of minorities are
   a. fairly infrequent.
   b. consistent with low-status or comic roles.
   c. overwhelmingly positive.
   d. shown in a somewhat more favorable manner than in the past.

4. Social categorization refers to the notion that people typically form two distinct groups known as
   a. in-groups and out-groups.
   b. we-groups and other-groups.
   c. us-groups and them-groups.
   d. friendly-groups and hostile groups.

5. Suppose Jason, an Italian-American, says "Italian-Americans tend to be hard working—but I just don't see that work ethic in other ethnic groups." His statement would be consistent with
   a. social identity theory.
   b. an illusory correlation.
   c. the fundamental attribution error.
   d. the ultimate attribution error.

6. Consistent with social identity theory, the key reason individuals identify with specific social groups is to
   a. denigrate members of other groups.
   b. enhance the self-esteem of the individual in question.
   c. highlight one's pride with respect to his or her social group.
   d. enhance one's self-understanding.

7. Which of the following statements about stereotypes is *false*?
   a. When we become aware about inconsistent information regarding our stereotypes, we tend to no longer have that stereotype.
   b. Stereotypes are cognitive frameworks that strongly influence the processing of incoming social information.
   c. Stereotypes have been conceptualized as inferential prisons.
   d. A stereotype does not necessarily have an obvious negative connotation.

8. Suppose an individual is told that there are one thousand members of Group A and one hundred members of Group B; moreover, one hundred members of Group A were arrested by the police last year and that ten members from Group B were arrested during the same time period. For which group will this individual *most* likely have a less favorable opinion?
   a. Group A
   b. Group B
   c. Both groups will probably be evaluated in a similar fashion.
   d. Most individuals will be reluctant to rate the groups until they have further information about them.

9. The mirror image of the illusion of out-group homogeneity effect is called
   a. an illusory correlation.
   b. the illusion of in-group heterogeneity.
   c. in-group differentiation.
   d. the ultimate attribution error.

10. Prejudice against persons who aren't considered attractive in their society is known as ____ prejudice.
   a. fat
   b. weight-related
   c. appearance
   d. physical beauty-based

Practice Test 3

1. Currently, the vast majority of social psychologists tend to believe that prejudice is
   a. linked to genetic factors.
   b. learned from parents only.
   c. learned from a variety of social influences.
   d. caused by an interaction of genetic and environmental factors.

2. The key difference between the extended contact hypothesis and the contact hypothesis is that
   a. the extended contact hypothesis states that individuals must have far more contact with members of different groups in order to reduce prejudice than the contact hypothesis initially stated.
   b. the contact hypothesis is most effective in promoting acquaintances, whereas the extended contact hypothesis suggests how to build close friendships.
   c. the extended contact hypothesis lays out a variety of conditions that must be present for prejudice to be reduced, whereas the contact hypothesis does not do so.
   d. unlike the contact hypothesis, the extended contact hypothesis suggests that simply knowing that members of one's own group have formed close friendships with members of an out-group can reduce prejudice.

3. The common in-group identity model suggests that when individuals belonging to different social groups come to view themselves as members of ____, their attitudes toward each other become more positive.
   a. two separate but equal groups
   b. a single social entity
   c. two distinct groups
   d. as members of a variety of sub-groups within the two groups

4. Suppose Jim is trying to change Xavier's prejudiced views by convincing him that his views are out of line with most persons. Will such a technique decrease Xavier's prejudice?
   a. Yes. This technique has been shown to universally alter prejudicial thinking.
   b. Possibly. This technique has been shown to decrease prejudice—particularly if the bigoted person is convincing that someone he or she admires or respects doesn't approve of such views.
   c. No. This technique typically backfires and causes prejudiced persons to solidify their prejudiced views.
   d. At the current time, there is not enough research evidence to answer this question.

5. Stereotype threat refers to
   a. a concern that minorities will be evaluated in terms of stereotypes relating to their minority status.
   b. the notion that individuals are more likely to use stereotypes under threatening conditions.
   c. a belief that stereotypes are caused, in part, when an individual's self-esteem is threatened.
   d. how individuals process information that is inconsistent with their stereotypes.

6. In terms of sexist views, women
   a. rarely, if ever, hold such sentiments.
   b. can hold such sentiments, but these are much milder than men's sexist views.
   c. sometimes hold such views—even more strongly than men.
   d. almost always hold such sentiments to some degree.

7. Janet strongly believes that women are truly necessary for men's happiness. Her views are consistent with
   a. old-fashioned sexism.
   b. hostile sexism.
   c. benevolent sexism.
   d. no form of sexism whatsoever.

8. Suppose Sally and Tim work at the same company where there is a female and male co-president. Given this information, which of the following statements is *most* accurate?
   a. Sally and Tim will probably show equal levels of respect for their co-presidents.
   b. Sally will show more respect for the female co-president, whereas Tim will show more respect for the male co-president.
   c. Sally will show more respect for the male co-president, whereas Tim will show more respect for the female co-president.
   d. Sally and Tim will probably show more respect for their male co-president.

9. A final barrier that prevents women, as a group, from reaching the top positions in many companies is known as a(n)
   a. artificial barrier.
   b. glass ceiling.
   c. brick wall.
   d. cement floor.

10. Women tend to have ____ salary expectations since they usually compare themselves with ____.
    a. high; other women
    b. low; other women
    c. high; men
    d. low; men

Comprehensive Test

(NOTE: Items 1-15 are multiple-choice questions and items 16-23 are true-false questions.)

1. Prejudice refers to
   a. any kind of bias or inclination toward anything or anyone that may be considered inherently irrational.
   b. positive attitudes of a special kind.
   c. an usually negative attitude toward the members of some social group.
   d. attitudes of the majority toward the minority.

2. In the famous "Robber's Cave" study by Sherif and colleagues
   a. interactions between groups were hostile even before the study began.
   b. antagonism between the groups was caused because of boxing matches forced on the boys by the experimenters.
   c. the boys began to identify with their groups early.
   d. the boys had trouble developing group identities.

3. When we conceptualize "us" versus "them,"
   a. the "us" component is viewed in highly favorable terms.
   b. the "them" component is viewed in neutral terms.
   c. the "us" and "them" components are seen as complementary in nature.
   d. the "us" and "them" components are seen as merely dissimilar in nature and not antagonistic.

4. Recategorization refers to a(n)
   a. technique for collapsing the boundaries between antagonistic groups by having them pursue common goals.
   b. way for groups to switch their identities.
   c. ineffective technique designed to reduce prejudice.
   d. process by which children acquire prejudiced views.

5. According to the social learning view of prejudice, which of the following factors is *least* likely to cause the development of prejudiced views?
   a. sex role training
   b. inborn social tendencies
   c. parents and friends
   d. sociopolitical factors

6. Relative to men, women tend to be
   a. more ambitious.
   b. more concerned about money.
   c. less creative.
   d. less confident.

7. Tokenism refers to
   a. refusing to accept even a token gesture of friendship from an object of prejudice.
   b. being occasionally unfriendly to objects of prejudice.
   c. passing out to "tokens," such as small rewards or praise, to others who take a stand against discrimination.
   d. hiring a person solely on the basis of his or her racial or ethnic group membership and not his or her qualifications.

8. The bona fide pipeline makes use of ____ in order to study implicit racial attitudes.
   a. deception
   b. priming
   c. attributional biases
   d. one's self-concept

9. Social psychologists believe that prejudice is
   a. inevitable
   b. not inevitable
   c. a cycle that cannot be broken
   d. is irreducible

10. Superordinate goals are ones that are
   a. desired by two separate groups.
   b. unpleasant for two separate goals.
   c. desired by one group and undesired by the other.
   d. tend to promote further disagreements between groups.

11. Recent research on the effects of gender stereotypes in the workplace (Jackson, Esses, and Burris, 2001) has demonstrated that men are given _____ than women, which results in _____.
   a. less respect, higher hiring recommendations for men
   b. More respect, lower hiring recommendations for men
   c. more respect; higher hiring recommendations for men
   d. less respect; lower hiring recommendations for men

12. Illusory correlations operate on the premise that
   a. individuals typically do not understand statistics.
   b. infrequent events are distinctive.
   c. people tend to perceive members of out-groups to be fairly similar to one another.
   d. our views are greatly influenced by our parents and peers.

13. Information that is inconsistent with one's stereotype tends to
   a. change the individual's stereotype.
   b. make one's stereotype stronger.
   c. be changed in ways that allow it to be consistent with the stereotype.
   d. simply be forgotten.

14. Prejudiced people are
    a. fortunately rare.
    b. made, not born.
    c. more blatant in their expressions than they used to be.
    d. an inevitable consequence of a diverse society.

15. Gender stereotypes typically occur for ____ and tend to be ____ in nature.
    a. women only; negative
    b. men or women; negative
    c. women only; positive or negative
    d. men or women; positive or negative

Questions 16-23 are True/False Questions

16. According to Biernat when the same evaluation ratings are given to targets who are members of different groups, the ratings are still unequal regardless.

17. The soldiers at Abu Ghraib used a variety of mental strategies to reduce their feelings of collective guilt.

18. The boys in the famous Robber's Cave study came together once they received group therapy.

19. The social learning view of prejudice suggests that children can learn negative attitudes toward various groups from their parents.

20. Suppose George harbors racist views against African-Americans. When he hears a news report about an African-American who committed a crime, he feels that this provides further "proof" of his prejudiced views. This example illustrates an illusory correlation.

21. Schemas involve the use of one group as the comparison standard for in-group members but the use of a different comparison group for out-group members.
22. Superordinate goals are those goals that can be achieved only by cooperation between groups and can be useful in reducing prejudice.

23. Women leaders tend to be rated highly by other women.

Short Answer/Essay Questions

1. **Prejudice and Discrimination**
   Explain why the terms, "prejudice" and "discrimination," are NOT interchangeable.

2. **Realistic Conflict Theory**
   Briefly outline the main points of realistic conflict theory and note how it explains the hatred expressed by Osama bin Laden and his followers.

3. **Cognitive Mechanisms in Prejudice**
   Why do people tend to perceive members of other groups as more homogenous than members of their own groups?

4. **Coping with Prejudice**
   Define the stereotype threat and provide empirical evidence for its adverse effects.

5. **Strategies to Reduce Collective Guilt**
   Define the term collective guilt and list three strategies that individuals use to reduce the feelings of collective guilt.

When You Have Finished . . .

Applications of "Prejudice" to Your Life

1. Since we know the damaging effects of prejudice, we should all be encouraged to prevent it as best as possible.

2. Since all of us at some time may be victims of prejudice, we need to be mindful of why this occurs and how we can cope with it.

3. We need to be aware of how sexism operates—particularly in the workplace—so that men *and* women will be evaluated as a function of their abilities.

4. Tragically, we all saw how extreme prejudice can affect all of our lives on September 11, 2001.

5. We need to be aware that prejudice does *not* have to exist merely as a function of race or gender. Your text highlights that prejudice can take many forms—such as prejudice against obese persons.

Let's reconsider point #2. Think back to when you may have been a victim of prejudice. What were the circumstances and how did you deal with it? Looking back at the situation, do you feel that you would have handled it differently now? If so, how?

Internet Sites:

http://coe.sdsu.edu/eet/Articles/dissonance/index.htm: Website on how television promotes stereotyping.

http://www.theatlantic.com/issues/99aug/9908stereotype.htm: An article by Claude Steele on stereotype threat.

http://www.unt.edu/cpe/module1/resfile/res3-10.htm/: Provides a detailed description of Sherif's Robber's Cave study.

http://www.nytimes.com/library/world/europe/091399greece-turkey.html: An example of how a major earthquake and the need for cooperative interdependence helped reduce tensions between Greece and Turkey.

http://mentalhelp.net/psyhelp/chap7/chap7l.htm: Mental health net article reviews several social psychological theories of prejudice, including Allport's work, work on self-fulfilling prophecies, the role of conformity, and authoritarian personalities. The next page link discusses prejudice reduction, and the page after that discusses aggression reduction.

http://bostonworks.boston.com/globe/working_out/archives/022501_professor_wins.html: Article discusses a recent discrimination case in Boston and describes work on aversive racism.

*http://psychology.ucdavis.edu/rainbow/:*This site features work by Dr. Gregory Herek — a noted authority on sexual prejudice (or homophobia), hate crimes, and AIDS stigma — and his Northern California Community Research Group at the University of California, Davis. See especially *http://psychology.ucdavis.edu/rainbow/html/phobdefn.html* on definitions of terms, and *http://psychology.ucdavis.edu/rainbow/html/comeout1.html*, which reports on research by Herek showing that homosexuals who come out of the closet to their heterosexual friends and family members help to create more positive attitudes toward homosexuality. Relevant to the contact hypothesis.

http://cain.ulst.ac.uk/csc/reports/connolly99g.htm: Sectarianism, Children, and Community Relations in Northern Ireland. Discusses applications of the contact hypothesis.

http://splcenter.org: Southern Poverty Law Center. An organization devoted to fighting hate crimes. Information about hate crimes and the fight against it, information on the bulletin *Teaching Tolerance* published by the SPLC.

http://www.adl.org/: The Anti-Defamation League. Information on hate crimes. On their education page, you can order their publication, *No place for hate: 101 ways to fight prejudice.*

Crossword Puzzle

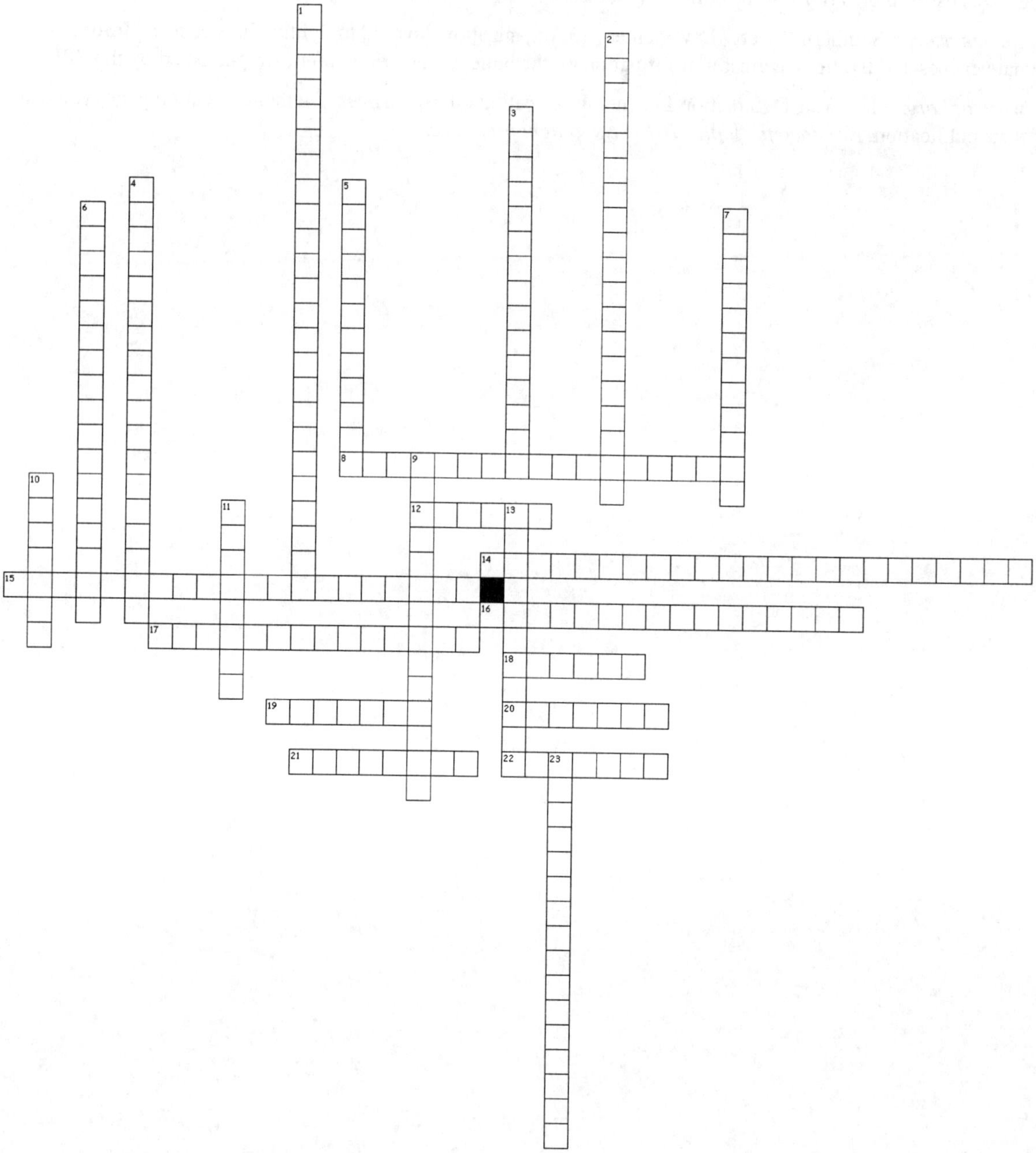

Across

8. stereotypes about females or males

12. prejudice based on gender
14. theory that direct competition creates prejudice
15. dividing into categories
16. shifts inboundaries between groups
17. prejudice acquired through experience
18. makes ones self-esteem in jeopardy
19. being seen as having worth
20. stimulus makes accessible information
21. the group that you do not belong to
22. a subset of the group not consistent

Down

1. self serving attributional bias the group level
2. perception of association between two variables
3. group guilt
4. goals achieved by group cooperation
5. prevents females from getting to the top
6. contact reduces prejudice
7. subtle belief of superiority
9. negative behavior toward members
10. the group you belong to
11. hiring based on group membership
13. beliefs about individuals
23. priming measures racial attitudes

Created by Puzzlemaker at DiscoverySchool.com

7 INTERPERSONAL ATTRACTION: MEETING, LIKING, BECOMING ACQUAINTED

Before You Read . . .

This chapter outlines interpersonal attraction by focusing on the early stages of how we become acquainted with someone and may grow to like him or her. Did you know that some of the earliest phases of attraction may be related to such seemingly mundane things as how physically close you are located to a person? Your general emotions or affect can also greatly influence how you feel about a person (e.g., a positive evaluation of the person if you are laughing with him or her). This chapter also makes the interesting point that there are individual differences and situational cues that are linked to our need to affiliate—and this also greatly influences how we become acquainted with others. The chapter will also discuss people's perceptions of physical attractiveness and their perceptions of what a president of the United States should look like. Have you ever wondered which of these two famous sayings, "birds of a feather flock together" or "opposites attract," is accurate with respect to interpersonal attraction? Well, social psychologists believe that the former saying is, for the most part, quite correct. A very thorough consideration of how and why similarity affects attraction is discussed. This chapter also helps to serve as an introduction of the next chapter, which focuses on the study of close relationships.

Chapter Objectives

After reading this chapter, you should be able to:

- Provide an overview of the four key factors that need to be operating before individuals progress to the final stage of interpersonal attraction.
- State the two most important characteristics of affect and note how emotions can influence attraction.
- Describe how laughing is a "social lubricant" and leads to liking and attraction.
- Understand how proximity and repeated exposure can influence attraction (for better and sometimes worse).
- Describe the need for affiliation, including its key characteristics and modes of expression.
- Consider how and why people evaluate others on the basis of physical attractiveness—particularly from an evolutionary perspective. Offer an overview of the key sex differences in terms of how men and women evaluate attractiveness

INTERPERSONAL ATTRACTION

- Note the key features associated with physical attractiveness (regardless of one's sex).
- Consider the degree to which certain stereotypes about physical attractiveness are accurate.
- Discuss people's perceptions of what a president of the United States should look like or their stereotype for this image.
- Understand the role that similarity plays in attraction.
- Highlight the key predictions of balance theory.
- Explain the repulsion hypothesis and how it is viewed by most contemporary social psychologists.
- Conceptualize the overall themes of interpersonal attraction with particular emphasis on the role of the affect-centered model of attraction.

As You Read . . .

Important Term to Know... Below are a list of some of the key terms and concepts from this chapter. Make flashcards in order to enhance your recall ability of these terms. Refer to the definitions that are either in boldface or in the margins of this chapter for help. You may also want to include additional terms from this chapter as you deem necessary.

Interpersonal attraction	Proximity	Repeated exposure
Affect and its characteristics	(In)direct effects of emotion	Need for affiliation
Explicit vs. implicit motives	Needs for positive stimulation, social support, attention, and social comparison	Physical attractiveness
Appearance anxiety	"Average" attractiveness	Contrast effect
The "similarity hypothesis"	Attitude similarity	Proportion of similar attitudes
Balance theory and its three main states	The repulsion hypothesis	Stereotypes of the president
Adaptive response	Mere exposure effect	The affect-centered model of attraction
Humor as a social lubricant	Unplanned contact	Complementarity
Similarity-dissimilarity effect	Consensual validation	

Interpersonal Attraction: Meeting, Liking, Becoming Acquainted

INTERPERSONAL ATTRACTION

1. In your own words, define "interpersonal attraction."

2. Provide an overview of the four factors that can eventually lead to liking.

Internal Determinants of Attraction: The Need to Affiliate and the Basic Role of Affect

➢ The Importance of Affiliation for Human Existence

1. Explain what is meant by the "need for affiliation." Also, how can this be expressed as a trait *and* a state?

2. What is the basic difference between an explicit versus an implicit motive to affiliate?

3. State and define the four other dispositional expressions of the need for affiliation.

4. Why should real-life events and laboratory manipulations of anxiety arouse the need for affiliation? Is it beneficial for us to do so?

➤ Affect as a Basic Response System

1. What's wrong here? Each of the following statements is *false*. Your task is to modify each statement in some fashion in order to make it accurate.

a.) The two most important characteristics of affect are feelings and moods.

b.) All emotions fall along a single dimension—positive at one end and negative at the other.

c.) People typically don't experience a mixture of positive and negative affective states at the same time.

d.) An associated effect occurs when another person says or does something that makes you feel good or bad.

e.) The general idea behind indirect effects of emotion are based on instrumental conditioning.

f.) When an individual has continued contact with a stigmatized person, he or she shows an increased perception of threat.

g.) Most voters are too savvy to believe that a political candidate's affective expressions reveal basic personality characteristics of that individual.

h.) A single negative aspect about a political candidate usually doesn't influence voters' perceptions of that candidate.

➢ Additional Implications of the Affect-Attraction Relationship

1. Explain what the phrase "humor is a social lubricant," means.

External Determinants of Attraction: Proximity and Observable Characteristics

1. Define "proximity" and explain why it is an important factor that allows strangers to become acquaintances.

2. Provide at least one example of repeated exposure effects shown in an experimental study.

3. Identify the most important exception to the repeated exposure effect.

4. Describe evidence that suggests that proximity can lead to attraction in natural settings. What evidence is there that this relationship is *causal* in nature?

5. If you want to become friends with someone in one of your classes, you should try to ______________ ____ and avoid selecting a seat that is ______ ____.

➢ Observable Characteristics: Instant Evaluations

1. In your own words, define "physical attractiveness" and "appearance anxiety."

2. Which of the following characteristics is *not* universally associated with attractiveness?

   Intelligence Sexual warmth Integrity Adjustment Social competence

3. Identify which stereotypes based on appearance are *correct.*

4. Complete the chart below by listing facial features or characteristics that are generally viewed as attractive for men only, women only, and both men and women.

Men only	Women only	Both men and women

5. For each of the following pairs, circle the characteristic that most people will typically like:

    a.) A person who is underweight vs. a person who is overweight.

    b.) Rapid eye blinking vs. slow eye blinking.

    c.) A firm handshake vs. a loose handshake.

    d.) An expression of anger vs. an expression of sadness.

    e.) A dominant male vs. a noncompetitive male.

    f.) The name "Joshua" vs. the name "Roscoe."

Beyond the Headlines: As Social Psychologists See It

➤ Voting for the Candidate Who Looks Like a President

1. Explain how the concept of "height" affects voters' perceptions of presidential candidates.

2. Is the stereotype with regard to "height" a correct predictor of future political performance, why or why not?

Interactive Determinants of Attraction: Similarity and Mutual Liking

➢ Similarity: Birds of a Feather Actually Do Flock Together

1. Most laypersons are familiar with the contradictory sayings, "birds of a feather flock together" and "opposites attract." Which saying is correct? Why? Be sure to provide research evidence to support your claims.

The Science of Social Psychology: Making Sense of Common Sense

➢ Complementarity: Do Opposites Attract?

1. Describe two specific situations in which complementarity of traits would work.

2. List some advantages and disadvantages to being attracted to an individual who has opposite personality traits.

➢ Explaining the Effect of Similarity-Dissimilarity on Attraction

1. Identify and define the three possible states as predicted by balance theory. What are the consequences of being in these states?

2. Are there evolutionary reasons for why genocide and war occurs? Evaluate the evidence.

➢ Mutual Evaluations: Reciprocal Liking or Disliking

1. Once two people discover that they're sufficiently similar to be able to move toward establishing a friendship, one additional step is crucial. That step is ______________________________ ______________________________.

2. When Person A and Person B interact, list all of the processes that are occurring according to the affect-centered model of attraction.

After You Read.. . Practice Tests

Practice Test 1

1. ____ signifies the final step or stage of interpersonal attraction.
   a. The need to affiliate
   b. Positive emotions
   c. Physical proximity
   d. Mutual liking

2. You would expect to have a ____ level of attraction for a superficial acquaintance.
   a. mild liking
   b. neutral
   c. mild disliking
   d. strong disliking

3. Another term for physical proximity is
   a. closeness.
   b. affiliation.
   c. similarity.
   d. physical attraction.

4. The underlying factor as to why proximity tends to promote liking is due to
   a. perceived similarity.
   b. repeated exposure.
   c. positive affect.
   d. personality differences.

5. Suppose Billy hears a song on the radio that he initially dislikes and continues to hear it played on the radio many additional times. The additional exposures to this song will likely cause him to
   a. increase his liking for the song.
   b. increase his dislike for the song.
   c. not change his attitudes about the song.
   d. reconsider his feelings about the song.

6. Suppose Sarah and Jon are two college students who live in a college dormitory designed for students who are Jewish or have interests in Jewish culture. They live right across the hall from each other and soon start dating each other. Given this information, which of the following statements is *most* accurate?
   a. Their proximity is causing attraction.
   b. Their attraction has caused their proximity.
   c. Their ethnicity has lead to their attraction and proximity.
   d. Their attraction is unrelated to their proximity or ethnicity.

7. The two key characteristics of affect are
   a. emotions and feelings.
   b. positive and negative.
   c. intensity and direction.
   d. degree and quality.

8. Positive and negative emotions are usually conceptualized as
   a. two separate and independent dimensions.
   b. opposite ends of the same dimension.
   c. being unable to experience positive and negative states at the same time.
   d. having an inverse relationship with each other.

9. Suppose Jill reacts harshly to a stranger while shopping at a store simply because she had a major fight with her boyfriend. This is an example of a(n) ____ effect of emotion on attraction, which is based on ____ conditioning.
   a. direct; classical
   b. indirect; classical
   c. direct; instrumental
   d. indirect; instrumental

10. When an individual interacts with a stigmatized person for the first time, he or she will likely experience all of the following, *except*
   a. increased blood pressure.
   b. a feeling of threat.
   c. diminished performance.

d. information overload

Practice Test 2

1. Affective influences on voters tend to be strongest when voters are
   a. politically uninformed.
   b. politically informed.
   c. not consciously motivated to evaluate the candidates.
   d. moderate in their political orientation.

2. Which of the following individuals illustrates the need for affiliation as a trait?
   a. Zeke, who is trying to comfort his neighbors after they experienced a major tornado.
   b. Sue, who tends to work in a very cooperative manner with her co-workers.
   c. Jeff, who after being diagnosed with cancer, decides to seek out support from other cancer patients.
   d. Mindy, who along with her fellow concert-goers, is dancing at a rock concert.

3. Our need for ____ pertains to the desire to obtain knowledge and reduce uncertainty.
   a. social support
   b. social comparison
   c. attention
   d. positive stimulation

4. Being independent and successful are two characteristics that are associated with attractiveness in
   a. men only.
   b. women only.
   c. men and women.
   d. neither men nor women.

5. An undue concern with one's looks is called
   a. appearance anxiety.
   b. physical attractiveness concerns.
   c. social anxiety.
   d. physical appearance phobia.

6. All of the following characteristics appear to be associated with attractiveness across most cultures, *except*
   a. adjustment.
   b. sexual warmth.
   c. intelligence.
   d. integrity.

7. An example of a stereotype based on appearance that is largely accurate is
   a. only physically unattractive individuals commit heinous deeds or crimes.
   b. kind and intelligent people tend to be physically unattractive.
   c. those who are most attractive are (correctly) believed to more popular and have greater interpersonal skills.
   d. non-existent—all of the stereotypes based on appearance are false.

8. From an evolutionary perspective, the point that men tend to place a greater premium on physical attractiveness and youth is due to
   a. a variety of societal and environmental influences.
   b. the point that most women realize that is superficial to make definitive judgments about a mate solely on the basis of their looks.
   c. women's common knowledge that relationships with extremely attractive men tend to end in failure.
   d. the fact that women have a limited period of their lives where they are fertile in contrast to men.

9. A possible limitation of the evolutionary perspective in terms of mate selection is that
   a. it overly emphasizes the importance of environmental factors.
   b. gay men often show an analogous preference for male partners in the same that heterosexual men have for female partners.
   c. even though this theory predicts that women should value a man's social status, research on this topic has confirmed otherwise.
   d. it fails to explain why certain characteristics of "attractiveness" should be associated with reproductive success.

10. Women with ____ are generally considered to be attractive.
   a. childlike, but not mature features
   b. mature but not childlike features
   c. either childlike or mature features
   d. neither childlike nor mature features

Practice Test 3

1. Suppose Dr. Smith has collected pictures of ten women and intends to create composite images of them on her computer. Most individuals will likely find the *most* attractive face to be
   a. any single picture.
   b. a composite of half (or five) of the faces.
   c. a composite of all ten faces.

d. debatable—based on this information, there likely will not be a general consensus.

2. Facial symmetry is associated with
   a. sexual promiscuity.
   b. general health.
   c. extremely masculine or feminine characteristics.
   d. physical unattractiveness.

3. Suppose Ryan has a thin, angular body shape. Consequently, people will likely judge him as being
   a. sad and sloppy.
   b. in good health, yet having few intellectual interests.
   c. intelligent and fearful.
   d. dynamic and rigid.

4. If a political candidate has a specific ethnic last name, then this is considered to be an
   a. overall net negative.
   b. overall net positive.
   c. overall net positive if it is popular within a given geographic area.
   d. overall net positive if the candidate is a male.

5. Physically attractive women have ____ weight and diet concerns with respect to less attractive women since ____.
   a. greater; physically attractive women tend to be more concerned with being thin.
   b. less; physically attractive women tend to be more concerned with being thin.
   c. the same; all women have an equal concern with being thin.
   d. less; less attractive women are trying harder to lose weight and diet.

6. Suppose you find out that your sister is having a baby and you are trying to offer her some advice about baby names. On the basis of research in this area, what advice should you offer?
   a. Be sure to select a name that is considered to be "trendy" at the time of the baby's birth.
   b. Just go with a name that sounds "right"—one's name really makes very little difference in terms of interpersonal perceptions.
   c. If she has a girl and wants to name her "Hillary," assure her that very few people would associate her in any way with Senator Hillary Rodham Clinton.
   d. Be aware that various male and female names are associated with specific positive and negative stereotypes.

7. The general idea that similarity fosters interpersonal attraction was first noted by scholars
   a. within the past few decades.
   b. during the 1920s.
   c. well over a century ago.
   d. well over two thousand years.

8. Suppose Phil and Jake discuss six issues and are in agreement on two of them. Their proportion of similar attitudes would be ____.

a. 2
b. .33
c. .67
d. 4

9. Suppose Carla and Heather dislike each other. As such, they are in a state of____.
   a. balance
   b. imbalance
   c. unbalance
   d. nonbalance

10. The evolutionary perspective would likely predict that genocide and human animosity is ____ with this perspective since ____.
    a. consistent; we often have harsh reactions to dissimilarity.
    b. consistent; we realize that this behavior is a way to showcase our strengths.
    c. inconsistent; we understand that this is destructive to the human race.
    d. inconsistent; we perceive such behaviors to be incompatible with reproductive success.

Comprehensive Test

(NOTE: Items 1-15 are multiple-choice questions and items 16-23 are true-false questions.)

1. Subliminal repeated exposure has been shown to
   a. produce no change in liking for the exposed stimulus.
   b. cause subjects to dislike the exposed stimulus.
   c. increase liking for the exposed stimulus.
   d. produce recognition of the exposed stimulus, but no change in liking.

2. Moreland and Beach (1992) had female assistants attend a college class not at all, a few times, or several times. When members of the class rated the assistant for likeability, it was found that
   a. how often assistants attended class didn't affect likeability.
   b. assistants who attended a few times were rated more likeable.
   c. assistants who attended several times were rated more likeable.
   d. frequency of attendance wasn't important; the one significant factor was the assistants' attractiveness.

3. Consistent with research on proximity in the classroom, you would expect that
   a. people seated at the end of a row make more friends than those in the middle.
   b. when seating is alphabetical, friendships seldom form with people whose names begin with the same or a nearby letter.
   c. someone seated to your right or left is not likely to become your friend.
   d. changing seat assignments once or twice a semester results in each student having more acquaintances.

4. All of the following are considered attractive, *except*
   a. “childlike” features in women.
   b. “mature” features in women.
   c. an “average” face created by digitizing.
   d. an asymmetrical face.

5. Rosenbaum’s repulsion hypothesis states that
   a. opposite views lead to attraction.
   b. we respond to physically unattractive individuals with rejection.
   c. we are most likely to terminate a romantic relationship when we are repulsed by our partner’s behavior.
   d. we dislike a stranger who holds dissimilar attitudes than our own.

6. When two people like each other and agree there is____; however, when two people like each other and disagree, there is ____.
   a. balance; imbalance
   b. balance; nonbalance
   c. nonbalance; imbalance
   d. imbalance; balance

7. Jim truly believes that “almost everyone agrees with me.” Such a sentiment is consistent with the
   a. false consensus effect.
   b. need for affiliation.
   c. repulsion hypothesis.
   d. asymmetric reasoning effect.

8. The affect-centered model of attraction contains all of the following elements, *except*
   a. it is a conceptual framework pertaining to attraction.
   b. it assumes that negative emotions are more important than positive emotions.
   c. emotion can be aroused from a variety of sources.
   d. when two individuals interact, they are simultaneously reacting to and processing information about each other.

9. ____ refers to an attitude about another person.
   a. Interpersonal influence
   b. Interpersonal attraction
   c. Social cognition
   d. Person perception

10. Continued contact with a stigmatized person tends to ____ the threatening element of the interaction for an individual.
   a. increase
   b. decrease
   c. stabilize
   d. highlight

11. __________________ is an undue concern with how one looks.

a. Appearance anxiety
b. Appearance nervosa
c. Naricissism
d. Appearance neuroticism

12. The ____ of attractiveness stereotypes depends on which characteristics are valued by a particular culture.
    a. objective validity
    b. general nature
    c. specific content
    d. overall use

13. Height has been found to be a ________________predictor of behavior.
    a. good
    b. poor
    c. inconsistent
    d. the studies have yielded inconclusive results

14. Suppose Jerry, after viewing pictures of extremely attractive women, finds his own girlfriend to be less attractive. Given this information, this could be explained by
    a. Jerry's dispositional tendencies.
    b. the fact that their relationship is troubled.
    c. the false consensus effect.
    d. the contrast effect.

15. The basic premise behind the "similarity hypothesis" is that
    a. similarity is merely correlation with attraction.
    b. similarity causes attraction.
    c. attraction causes similarity.
    d. either similarity or dissimilarity can promote attraction.

Questions 16-23 are True/False Questions

16. Tall people are found to earn more than short people throughout their careers.

17. There is no evidence based on multiple experiments that opposites attract.

18. People tend to *not* show much agreement over the specific characteristics that are associated with attractiveness.
19. The repulsion hypothesis stipulates that attitude similarity causes decreased attraction.

20. Marcia and Fran are good friends, but they are in disagreement over a certain issue. As such, there is an imbalance with respect to their friendship.

21. Consistent with evolutionary theory, men and women place an equal value on a potential mate's physical appearance.

22. Charlie likes to spend time with others as much as possible. As such, he appears to have a need for acceptance.

23. Consistent with the affect-centered model of attraction, if you were in a bad mood while interacting with a particular person, then there is a strong likelihood that you will form a negative view of this person.

Short Answer/Essay Questions

1. **Proximity and Repeated Exposure**
   Summarize how proximity and repeated exposure usually function in natural settings and discuss whether there is a causal relationship between these variables.

2. **The Need to Affiliate**
   Define what is meant by a person's need for affiliation and briefly outline the difference between how this need is shown as a function of traits and states.

3. **Physical Attractiveness**
   Briefly outline why physical attractiveness should matter from an evolutionary perspective.

4. **Balance Theory**
   John and Steve are good friends, but they find themselves in some disagreement over a political issue that they are discussing. Consistent with balance theory, how would you describe the state of their relationship and how will John and Steve likely contend with this state?

5. **Similarity versus Dissimilarity: The Repulsion Hypothesis**
State the repulsion hypothesis and evaluate its veracity.

When You Have Finished . . .

Applications of Interpersonal Attraction to Your Life

1. We are always meeting a new person on a regular basis and evaluating them: This is what interpersonal attraction is all about!

2. Given the overwhelmingly importance of similarity in fostering interpersonal attraction, this information should help to give you a better understanding on the likelihood that you will become good friends with someone.

3. We can use some basic findings with respect to proximity and repeated exposure to either encourage or decrease the likelihood that we will make new friends.

4. By understanding the importance of affect in interpersonal attraction, we are better equipped to realize its effects when we are becoming acquainted with someone.

5. We should be mindful that—whether we like it or not—physical appearance and one's general style can often have a great impact on whether we like someone. By simply being aware of this information, we also can realize that interpersonal attraction may be greatly influenced by seemingly trivial or superficial factors.

Internet Sites:

http://www.mhhe.com/hper/health/personalhealth/labs/love/activ6-2.html: Sternberg's Triangular Love Scale online. Also see *http://www.spods.net/personality/tests/tests.php3* and *http://www.freshy.com/personality/index.php3.*

http://www.photo-seminars.com/Seminars/MereImage/Mere%20Image.htm: A photographer uses the principles of mere exposure theory and people's familiarity with their own mirror images to suggest how photographers can improve their sales of portraits.

http://www-psych.nmsu.edu/~vic/faceprints:. Participate in an experiment on perceptions of facial beauty.

http://salmon.psy.plym.ac.uk/year3/PSY339EvolutionaryPsychology/EvolutionaryPsychology.ht: Excellent site on evolutionary psychology, courtesy of the University of Plymouth Department of Psychology. Includes background information about evolutionary theory and discussions of how it applies to relationships, altruism, and why men rape.

http://cornell-magazine.cornell.edu/Archive/Nov1999/NovRoommates.htm: An article that students will find interesting on how different colleges assign freshman roommates; applies social psychology theories in understanding how such pairings will work out.

Crossword Puzzle

INTERPERSONAL ATTRACTION

Across

4. formulations of Heider and Newcomb
6. emotional state

12. Rosenbaum's proposal

Down

1. repeated exposure effect
2. individuals who share same attitudes
3. beautiful
5. worry about one's physical characteristics
7. a person's attitude about another
8. characteristics increasing reproductive success
9. closeness of two individuals
10. mere exposure effect
11. motive to seek interpersonal relationships

Created by Puzzlemaker at DiscoverySchool.com
http://school.discovery.com/

8 CLOSE RELATIONSHIPS: FAMILY, FRIENDS, LOVERS, AND SPOUSES

Before You Read . . .

In the last chapter, we considered the initial stages of attraction. This chapter considers the nature of our well-established, ongoing close relationships. In particular, you'll quickly discover the important and defining role of interdependence in close relationships. Then this chapter discusses our earliest types of close relationships—those with our parents and siblings. In doing so, the increasing importance of attachment styles is fully considered. A consideration of how close friendships operate will also be featured. You'll also consider what life is like for lonely people who do *not* have any close, intimate relationships. The possible roots of loneliness will then be discussed. Have you ever wondered just "what is this crazy little thing called *love*?" Well, we'll consider the nature of love and sexuality in romantic relationships. The topic of people's perceptions of gay marriages will also be touched upon. Then we consider the realities of married life. Have you ever wondered what is the "secret" of a happy marriage? Many of these so-called secrets will be revealed in the latter part of this chapter. You'll also consider why marriages sometimes fail and how people cope with a failing marriage or intimate romantic relationship.

Chapter Objectives

After reading this chapter, you should be able to:

- Understand the concept of interdependence and its relevance to close relationships.
- Outline some of the major characteristics of parent-child and sibling relationships.
- Consider the nature of close friendships and highlight how same-sex and opposite-sex friendships tend to function.
- Detail and contrast the three initial types of attachment outlined (in the study of parent/mother-infant interactions) with the four types offered by Bartholomew and colleagues.
- Consider why loneliness develops, its consequences, and ways to overcome it.

CLOSE RELATIONSHIPS

- Explain why and how a romantic relationship differs from a close friendship.
- Discuss the disadvantages and advantages to meeting a romantic partner through the internet.
- Clarify how passionate love differs from unrequited and companionate love.
- Contrast the elements of Hendrick and Hendrick's (1986) love styles with that of Sternberg's (1986) triangular model of love.
- Outline how sexuality and sexual practices have differed over the course of the past several decades and discuss the implications of these changes.
- Understand the varying opinions with respect to gay marriages.
- Discuss the importance and role of similarity, assumed similarity, individual differences, and sexual interactions in a marriage.
- Consider the benefits and challenges of marriage.
- Discuss how parenthood affects marriage and note how the prototype of the American family has been changing over the past few decades.
- Outline some of the common problems faced by married couples and helpful ways to deal with these issues.
- Discuss the behavioral options for those in a troubled marriage or intimate relationship.

As You Read . . .

Important Terms to Know... Below are a list of some of the key terms and concepts from this chapter. Make flashcards in order to enhance your recall ability of these terms. Refer to the definitions that are either in boldface or in the margins of this chapter for help. You may also want to include additional terms from this chapter as you deem necessary.

Close relationships	Interdependence	Characteristics of parent-child and sibling relationships
Close friendships	Attachment style	Working models
Bilateral Symmetry	Interpersonal trust	Secure, fearful-avoidant, preoccupied, and dismissing attachment styles
Loneliness	Personal negativity and hopelessness	Cognitive therapy
Social skills training	Close friendships vs. romances	Belief in romantic destiny
Love	Passionate love	Unrequited love
Companionate love	Hendrick and Hendrick's six love styles	Sternberg's triangular model of love
Consummate love	Intimacy	Passion
Decision/commitment	Exit, voice, neglect, and loyalty	(Un)Restricted sociosexual orientation
Unwanted pregnancies/teenage pregnancy epidemic	Sexually transmitted diseases/HIV and AIDS	Assumed similarity
Narcissism	Cohabiting	Qualities of marital love and parenthood
Communal behavior	Causes of and solutions for marital problems	

Interdependent Relationships with Family and Friends versus Loneliness

➢ Family: Where Relationships and Attachment Styles Begin

1. Identify and discuss the common factor included in all close relationships.

2. What's wrong here? Each of the following statements is *false*. Modify some aspect of each statement in order to make it *true*.

   a.) Infants are ready to interact with others at around two months of age.

   b.) The nature of parent-child interactions depends solely on the personality of the child.

   c.) Adolescents routinely report that they dislike their parents.

   d.) Mothers never report that they were closer to one of their grown children than to the others.

   e.) Siblings tend to be very close in early childhood, but then grow and stay apart.

➢ Beyond the Family: Friendships

1. Note the characteristics of a close friendship.

2. Discuss the role of gender in friendships.

➢ Loneliness: Life without Close Relationships

1. In your own words, define "loneliness." Why does it occur and what are its consequences?

2. Discuss the role genetics and environmental factors play in loneliness.

3. Is there any hope for lonely people to overcome their loneliness? If so, identify the ways by which they can overcome loneliness.

Romantic Relationships and Falling in Love

➢ Romance: Moving Beyond Friendship

1. *She loves me, she loves me not*...Place a star next to each of the following statements *if* it is consistent with behavior that you'd expect to find in a romantic relationship.

   Expecting that one's partner be honest and loyal in a homosexual relationship.

   A preference for someone who will provide accurate feedback relevant to his or her self-concept.

   A relationship built on fantasy.

   A tendency for there to be a happy relationship when an individual matches his or her partner's ideals.

   A keen ability to predict how long their relationship will last.

2. Define the term "bilateral symmetry" and its effect on romantic relationships.

The Science of Social Psychology: Making Sense of Common Sense

1. Describe the advantages and disadvantages to meeting a romantic partner on the Internet.

2. Compare this method to speed dating discussed in Chapter 3, which method is most effective?

➢ Love: Who Can Explain It? Who Can Tell You Why?

1. *Crazy little thing called love*...There have been countless songs and poems about love—so, let's consider what social psychologists have said about this topic. Actually, let's evaluate the statements being said in the following hearts and denote the type of love being illustrated.

"I would rather suffer myself than let my lover suffer."

____

"When I told her how much I loved her, she said the feeling wasn't mutual."

____

"Even though we're not as intense as we once were, our lives are deeply intertwined."

____

"I love him so much, I can't stop thinking about him!"

____

"It wasn't easy to get, but our love has passion, commitment, and intimacy."

____

"I prefer to love someone who's like me."

____

Marriage: Happily Ever After--and Otherwise

➤ Marital Success and Satisfaction: Similarity, Personality, and Sexuality

1. Complete the sentences below by filling in the blanks.

   a.) Couples who've been married for many years show ________________________ in their degree of similarity over time.

   b.) ____________________ refers to the point that spouses tend to assume greater similarity than is the case.

   c.) Marital success is _________________________ by whether a women uses her own surname or not.

   d.) A ________________________ feels superior to most people or lacks empathy for others.

   e.) The most sexually active couples are ____.

➤ Love and Marriage, Careers, Parenthood, and Family Composition

1. Is being married better than being single?

2. What type of love is essential for success in a marriage?

3. How do husbands and wives distribute work inside and outside the home?

4. How do husbands and wives respond to parenthood?

5. Is "married with children" the norm in the United States?

➢ When Relationships Fail: Causes, Preventives, and Consequences

1. Describe the possible problems that spouses may face. In doing so, discuss the role of communal behavior.

2. Outline helpful and hurtful ways to react to marital problems.

3. Outline the four possible ways to respond to a troubled relationship.

4. State the three factors that can enable a couple to reconcile a deteriorating relationship.

Beyond the Headlines: As Social Psychologists See It

1. Discuss the attitudes held by various ages of voters about the legality of gay marriages.

After You Read . . . Practice Tests

Practice Test 1

1. The common element to all close relationships is
   a. intimacy.
   b. sexual warmth.
   c. equity.
   d. interdependence.

2. Human infants are ready to interact with others
   a. from birth.
   b. at around their second week of life.
   c. at around their first month of life.
   d. between ages two to three months.

3. Adolescents typically respond to their parents
   a. with general contempt.
   b. with overwhelmingly positive feelings.
   c. by being less close and dependent on them than they were in childhood.
   d. with great fluctuations in emotion so that one moment they love them and the next they do not.

4. Boys appear to be at greatest risk for behavior problems if they
   a. have an aloof father.
   b. are an only child.
   c. only have a sister.
   d. have a high level of contact with their siblings and a rejecting, punitive mother.

5. Two key characteristics of close friendships is that the individuals tend to avoid
   a. self-disclosure and mutual support.
   b. bragging and lying.
   c. modesty and lying.
   d. doing varied activities and sensitivity.

6. In the earliest work on attachment, it was argued that there were ____ styles of attachment.
   a. two
   b. three
   c. four
   d. five

7. The two central cognitions that an infant and his or her caregiver develop pertain to
   a. self-esteem and interpersonal trust.
   b. empathy and sympathy.
   c. self-esteem and self-awareness.
   d. interpersonal warmth and interpersonal trust.

8. A significant negative effect associated with a secure attachment style is
   a. overly inflated self-esteem.
   b. a tendency to dominate others in relationships.
   c. putting others ill at ease.
   d. apparently nonexistent—at this time, there appears to be no negative effects associated with this attachment style.

9. Joyce has low self-esteem and generally holds negative views about others. As such, she'd likely be classified as having a ____ attachment style.
   a. fearful-avoidant
   b. dismissing
   c. secure
   d. preoccupied

10. If Jack, an infant, has a secure attachment with his parents, will he necessarily have a secure attachment with close others when he is an adult?
    a. Yes, he will definitely have a secure attachment as an adult.
    b. Not necessarily, there are many other factors that could affect his attachment style.
    c. No, there is evidence that individuals tend to develop an adult attachment style that is markedly different from that with their parents.
    d. Since researchers have not considered this issue at all, there is no way to evaluate this question.

Practice Test 2

1. Loneliness develops as a result of
   a. individual experiences only.
   b. cultural influences and individual experiences only.
   c. genetics and individual experiences.
   d. genetics, individual experiences, and cultural influences.

2. Extreme loneliness may culminate in
   a. feelings of personal negativity.
   b. sense of complete hopelessness.
   c. a yearning to have friends.
   d. suicide

3. A need for acceptance is particularly important and accurate feedback is *not* usually desired in a
   a. friendship.
   b. marriage.
   c. romantic relationship (at least at the beginning).
   d. parent-child relationship.

4. The Internet offers all of the following advantages pertaining to relationship development, *EXCEPT*
   a. increased anonymity.
   b. reduced importance of physical appearance.
   c. greater control over the time and place of interactions.
   d. increased pressure to make the first move in a relationship.

5. Experiences of unrequited love are particularly likely to occur for
   a. women.
   b. elderly individuals.
   c. those with an anxious-ambivalent attachment style.
   d. those with an avoidant attachment style.

6. ____ love is characteristic of those who are concerned with themselves and their own independence.
   a. Companionate
   b. Consummate
   c. Game-playing
   d. Logical

7. In Sternberg's triangular model of love, intimacy plus passion equals
   a. romantic love.
   b. infatuation.
   c. fatuous love.
   d. empty love.

8. Nowadays, ____ report having sexual intercourse for the first time on their wedding night ____.
   a. women; more frequently than they used to
   b. men and women; more frequently than they used to
   c. women; rarely
   d. men and women; rarely

9. Sam believes that a sexual relationship is acceptable only when accompanied by affection and tenderness. This view is consistent with a(n) ____.
   a. unrestricted sociosexual orientation
   b. restricted sociosexual orientation
   c. unrestricted psychosexual orientation.
   d. unrestricted psychosexual orientation.

10. A general, heightened awareness of the dangers of sexually transmitted diseases and unwanted pregnancies began during the
    a. 1960s.
    b. 1970s.
    c. 1980s.
    d. 1990s.

Practice Test 3

1. The incidence of HIV infections in the United States is considerably higher among all of the following groups (compared with the national average), *except*
   a. women who are in their thirties.
   b. gay men.
   c. the poor.
   d. minority groups.

2. Similarity is to assumed similarity as
   a. correct is to incorrect.
   b. objective is to subjective.
   c. subjective is to objective.
   d. incorrect is to correct.

3. Joe feels superior to most other individuals, lacks empathy for others, and is sensitive to criticism. As such, he would be considered to be
   a. psychotic.
   b. a narcissist.
   c. high in neuroticism.
   d. suffering from social phobia.

4. ____ couples tend to share household chores in an equitable manner.
   a. African-American
   b. Latino
   c. Lesbian
   d. Cohabiting

5. As the number of children increases in a marriage, ____ report decreased satisfaction with the marriage.
   a. only men
   b. only women
   c. men and women
   d. neither men nor women

6. In the United States, the "married with children" household
   a. is the norm.
   b. was the norm until the 1990s.
   c. is quickly becoming the norm again.
   d. hasn't been the norm for several decades.

7. All of the following are possible sources of trouble in a long-term marriage, *except*
   a. growing costs of the relationship.
   b. changing in different directions as a couple.
   c. discovering that the actual similarity for the couple is different than their assumed similarity.
   d. expressing relationship problems in an agreeable way.

8. Suppose a couple decides to take a cross-country trip across America in the hope of making their relationship "less boring." This decision will likely
   a. have no effect on the quality of their relationship.
   b. enhance their relationship.
   c. worsen their relationship.
   d. promote negative affect.

9. Successful marriages tend to have all of the following characteristics, *except*
   a. lustful attraction.
   b. friendship.
   c. a consistent determination to create positive affect.
   d. social support.

10. About ____ of American children have divorced parents.
    a. one-quarter
    b. one-third
    c. one-half
    d. two-thirds

Comprehensive Test

(NOTE: Items 1-15 are multiple-choice questions and items 16-23 are true-false questions.)

1. Loneliness is
   a. feeling alone under any circumstance.
   b. any perception of solitary that is (in fact) valid.
   c. the unmet desire to engage in high quality close interpersonal relationships.
   d. the desire to not have too many people around oneself regardless of circumstances.

2. The sexual revolution involved all of the following, *except*
   a. fear of sexual disease.
   b. acceptance of premarital sexual intercourse.
   c. a greater tolerance of sexual practices in general.
   d. a disappearance of sex differences in sexual experience.

3. Cohabiting of unmarried couples is
   a. a strong predictor of marital discord.
   b. on the decline.
   c. against the law in many states.
   d. unrelated to (eventual) marital satisfaction.

4. Passionate love is characterized by
   a. falling head over heels.
   b. thoughtfulness.
   c. a certain comfortable feeling.
   d. initially very little sexual interest.

5. Married people tend to be
   a. universally unhappy.
   b. fairly unhappy, even though historically they used to be extremely happy.
   c. happy, even though they used to be fairly unhappy until recently.
   d. happier than those who aren't married.

6. Women tend to have ____ close friendships compared to men.
   a. ambivalent
   b. superficial
   c. fewer
   d. more

7. Suppose Ken, a toddler, is separated from his mother for about a half hour. When they are reunited, he rejects his mother and shows emotional restraint towards her. Consistent with initial conceptualization of attachment, Ken would have a(n) ____ attachment.
   a. secure
   b. generic insecure
   c. avoidant
   d. ambivalent

8. Jordan has a very favorable view of himself, yet most others don't describe him in favorable terms. As such, he'd likely be classified as having a ____ attachment style.
   a. fearful-avoidant
   b. dismissing
   c. secure
   d. preoccupied

9. Sally is receiving intervention and treatment for her feelings of loneliness, whereby a therapist encourages her to think differently about herself and her life. This type of intervention is chiefly known as
   a. client-centered therapy.
   b. desensitization.
   c. social skills training.
   d. cognitive therapy.

10. Of the following, ____ is considered to be one of the Hendrick's love styles.
    a. agog
    b. thanatos
    c. pragma
    d. alpha

11. Greg and Carol have been married for over twenty years and their shared passion has begun to fade a bit. Consistent with Sternberg's triangular model of love, their relationship would likely be characterized as
    a. companionate love.
    b. empty love.
    c. consummate love.
    d. liking.

12. An index of whether a marriage is going well is whether
    a. there is frequent contact with the in-laws.
    b. the couple has children.
    c. the couple speaks harshly to each other.
    d. the couple ever has any disagreements.

13. Overall, ____ percent of married persons claim that they never disagree.
    a. 1.2
    b. 13.8
    c. 33.3
    d. 45.7

14. ____ behavior occurs when one performs an act at some cost to the individual that is beneficial to one's partner and relationship.
    a. Communal
    b. Empathic
    c. Companionate
    d. Risk-taking

15. Voice represents a(n) ____ response to a troubled relationship.
    a. active negative
    b. active positive
    c. passive negative
    d. passive positiv

Questions 16-23 are True/False Questions

16. Older voters, ages 65 and up, overwhelmingly support gay marriages.

17. Women indicate that they have closer friendships than men do.

18. Men are more attracted to females who have bilateral symmetry to their faces.

19. Two common techniques used in order to primarily alter one's attachment style are social skills and cognitive therapy.

20. In general, if a sibling relationship is close during childhood, it tends to remain close over the siblings' lifespan.

21. About half of all marriages are second marriages for at least one of the individuals.

22. Whether a woman changes her name is unrelated to the success of her marriage.

23. Wendy and Bill have been married for thirty years. As such, we should expect that they show a higher degree of interpersonal similarity now than when they initially wed.

When You Have Finished . . .

Top Ten Reasons Why the Study of Close Relationships Has Great Relevance For *Your* Life

1. Most people believe that their close relationships are one of—if not *the*—most important and meaningful aspects of their life. Given this reality, we should all be interested in the study of close relationships!

2. Those who are married—or hope to be married someday—can all benefit from the research on what makes for a happy relationship.

3. For those who feel lonely (or for those who are concerned about a lonely individual), we should be aware that there are some very effective therapeutic techniques to overcome this condition.

4. In order to improve the nature of one's family relationships, it is helpful to be cognizant of some of the trends of this field.

5. In an age where sexually transmitted diseases and unwanted pregnancies still are very serious health and societal concerns, we should all seek to avoid these conditions for our own and others' health and well-being.

Consistent with many of the points described above, review the different styles of attachment outlined in your text. Now, try and figure out in which category you and some of your close others would belong. Also, if you are currently involved in a romantic relationship, try and determine the appropriate love category (or categories) that best describes your relationship.

Short Answer/Essay Questions

1. **Attachment Styles**
   Chris describes himself in unrealistically positive terms, yet he tends to view others less positively and limited in social ability. What type of attachment style does he likely have?

2. **Loneliness**
   Discuss two environmental factors that can contribute to loneliness. Next, provide a brief overview of the two primary interventions that are often used for individuals to combat their feelings of loneliness.

3. **Love**
   Bret constantly thinks of his new girlfriend, Holly. He often feels that he has an overwhelming, all-consuming love for her. As such, what type of love does this illustrate?

4. **Sexuality**
   Contrast the characteristics of an unrestricted sociosexual orientation with a restricted sociosexual orientation.

5. **Marriage**
   Discuss the importance of love in a marriage. In particular, what type of love appears to be *most* important in a happy marriage?

Crossword Puzzle

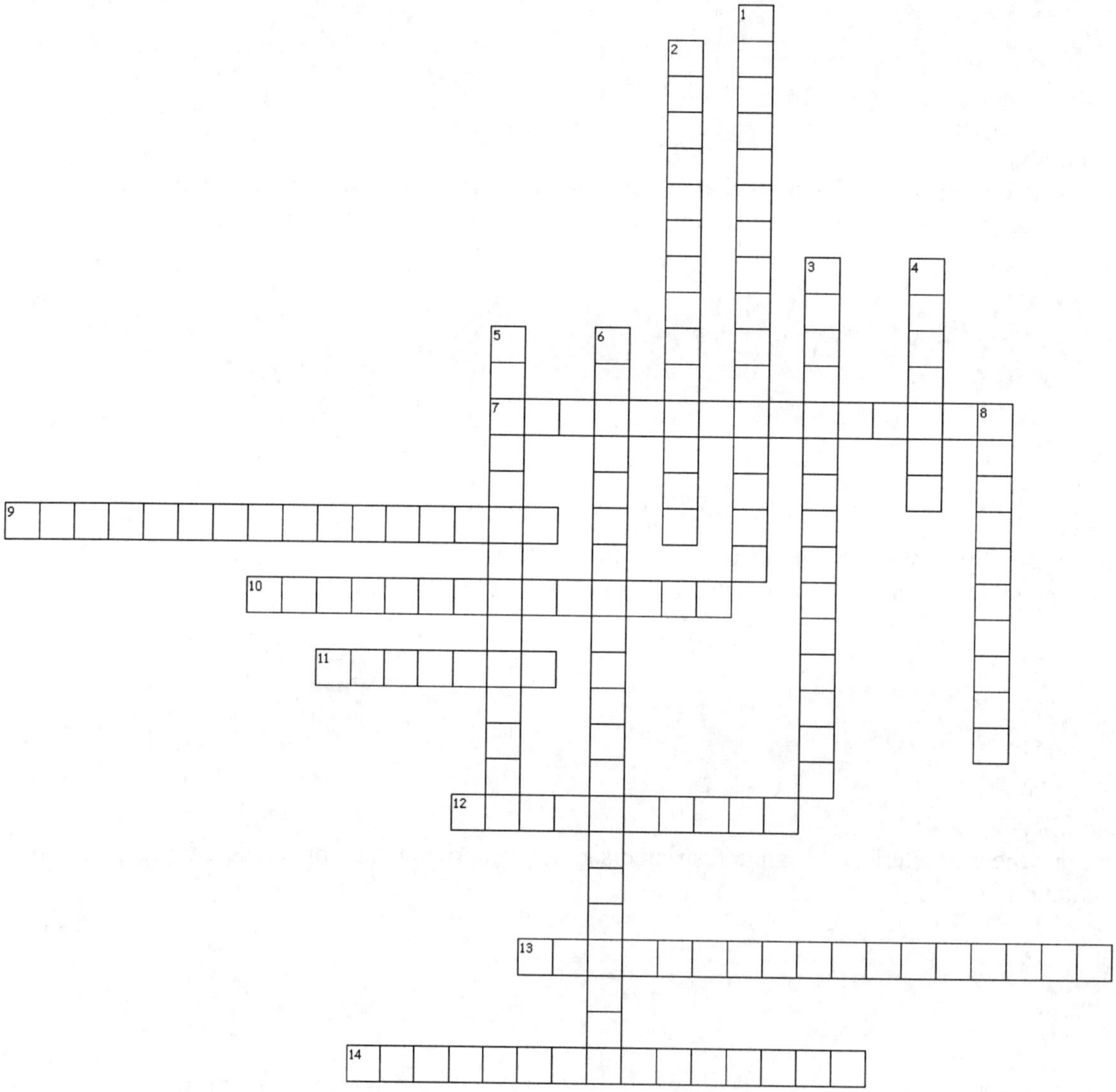

Across

7. socially rejecting another
9. benevelent acts in a relationship
10. unreciprocated love
11. ________similarity
12. one's attitude about oneself
13. face is symmetrical
14. different styles of attachment

Down

1. love based on friendship
2. complete ideal love
3. two people spend a lot of time together
4. sexual excitement
5. unrealistic response to another person
6. Sternberg's theory
8. self love

Created by Puzzlemaker at DiscoverySchool.com
http://school.discovery.com/

9 SOCIAL INFLUENCE:
CHANGING OTHERS' BEHAVIOR

Before You Read...

In this chapter you will develop a good understanding of "social influence," which is how others try to get us to change our attitudes or behaviors. At the beginning of this chapter one of the authors shares a personal and touching story with us about social influence (resisting the pressure to drive with a drunk driver). The author uses this example throughout the chapter to illustrate the concept of conformity, one of three prominent forms of social influence that will be introduced to you. You will realize how powerful the pressure to "change our behavior to match that of others" is and that sometimes we put our own lives on the line just to "fit in" with others. The chapter will then discuss one of the hallmark studies on conformity conducted by Solomon Asch. You will learn that there are various factors that play a role in whether or not we will conform, such as how many people are surrounding us and whether or not we are close to them.

The second form of social influence that you will be introduced to is compliance. You will learn first-hand the strategies salespersons and politicians use to get us to agree to their requests. Finally, the chapter saves the strongest form of social influence for last, obedience. You will be riveted to learn about the famous Milgram study in which individuals were willing to harm an innocent stranger simply by being obedient to the commands of an authority figure. Afterward, you will learn that obedience is great, but can be resisted and countered as so many instances in history exemplify.

Learning Objectives

After reading this chapter, you should be able to:

- Distinguish between the three prominent forms of social influence: conformity, compliance and obedience.
- Describe what a "social norm" is and give an example of an injunctive norm.
- Discuss the main findings and applications of the Asch conformity study as well as outline the various components that affect whether or not conformity will occur.
- Define the *normative focus theory* and then describe the difference between an injunctive norm and a descriptive norm.

- Explain the difference between normative and informational social influence with respect to why we choose to "go along" and conform in certain situations.
- Provide two factors that help us in resisting the pressure to "go along" and conform.
- Describe how an individual's gender can affect the degree to which he or she conforms.
- Provide an example of how the minority can influence the majority.
- Describe Cialdini's six principles of compliance and the seven principles for gaining compliance.
- Define symbolic social influence and give an example of this principle.
- Give highlights from the Milgram obedience study, such as ethical issues, findings and applications to other events in history.
- Define the concept of destructive obedience, while providing a few strategies as to how an individual can resist the effects of it.
- Discuss the most effective compliance tactics that can be used in the workplace.

As You Read...

IMPORTANT CONCEPTS TO KNOW- The table below provides some of the key concepts from this chapter. By making flashcards of these terms and concepts you will increase your ability to recall these terms for future use. Be aware that there may be additional terms in the chapter that you might want to add to this existing list.

Forms of social influence	Normative social influence	Deadline technique
Conformity	Informational social Influence	Social validation
Compliance	Individuation	Relational schemas
Obedience	Conformity and gender effects	Milgram obedience study
A social norm	Minority effects	The velvet glove
An injunctive norm	Six compliance principles	Destructive obedience
A descriptive norm	Foot-in-the-door technique	Gradual escalation
Cohesiveness and group size	Door-in-the-face technique	Transfer of responsibility
Solomon Asch	Lowball procedure	Visible signs of authority
Normative focus theory	That's not-all technique	
Situational norms	Playing hard to get	

Conformity: Group Influence in Action

➢ Asch's Research on Conformity: Social Pressure—The Irresistible Force?

Match the Concepts

1. **Instructions:** Match each phrase, word, or sentence on the left side of the page with an identifying concept on the right side of the page. Each item on the right should be used only once.

_____1. A strategy used to get others to say "yes" to a request A. destructive obedience

_____2. Commanding others to do specific behaviors B. compliance

_____3. Thinking or behaving in a way so to "fit in" with a group C. obedience

_____4. Obeying orders from a relatively powerless authority D. conformity

2. *Norms Norms Norms!*

Instructions: Underline those norms that are explicit and circle those norms that are implicit.

"Face forward in an elevator."

"Come to a complete stop at a stop sign."

"Wait your turn in the ATM line."

"Arrive at parties fashionably late."

"No speeding in a construction zone-- fine doubled in this zone."

"Tip your waitperson."

3. *"Asch's Asch's"*

Instructions: In Solomon Asch's line-judgment study, there were many relevant numbers. For each number listed below, explain its relevance in terms of Asch's study.

a.) Twelve out of eighteen problems

b.) Almost 25 percent

c.) 37 percent of the time

d.) 76 percent

e.) usually six to eight

➢ **The Bases of Conformity: Why We Often Choose to "Go Along"**

Match the concepts

1. **Instructions:** Match each phrase, word, or sentence on the left side of the page with an identifying concept on the right side of the page. Each item on the right should be used only once.

__1. The degree that we like and admire some group of persons A. descriptive norms

__2. What most people do in a certain situation — B. cohesiveness

__3. What ought to be done — C. normative focus theory

__4. Increasing the group size — D. injunctive norms

__5. Norms influence behavior if they're relevant for the person — E. increases conformity

- **Beyond the Headlines: As Social Psychologists See It--The Rocky Road to Social Acceptance? Why On Earth Do Many People Collect Big Rocks?**

1. Discuss your thoughts as to what is influencing people like Ms. Williams to spend her hard-earned money on purchasing large boulders? What could you say or do to prevent people from buying these large objects?

- **We've Come a Long Way**

1. Instructions: Consider how social norms were studied during the era of Solomon Asch's line-judgment study (1930s) and how social norms and the topic of conformity are studied today. Compare and contrast the research techniques of these two times as well as the views of the times.

	Then	**Now**
Research Methodology:		
Views about Norms:		

- **The Bases of Conformity: Why We Often Choose to "Go Along"**

1. Define **informational social influence** and **normative social influence**.
   a. Give an example from your life of when you conformed due to an information influence.

   b. Give an example from your life of when you conformed due to a normative influence.

2. Define the concept **"situational norm."**
   a. Give an example from your life of when a situational norm influenced your behavior.

➢ **Resisting Pressure to Conform: Why, Sometimes, We Choose Not to Go Along**

1. **Instructions:** Fill in the table below by noting why the following factors may not allow or cause a person to NOT conform.

Factor	Why conformity does not occur
The desire to be in control of our lives	
The desire to retain our individuality	
Having a prosthetic limb	
Being homosexual	

➢ **The Science of Social Psychology: Making Sense of Common Sense--Do Women and Men Differ in the Tendency to Conform?**

1. Discuss the past and current findings with regard to gender and conformity.

2. Describe two situations that you think that women would be more likely to conform in than men and two situations where men might be more likely to conform than women. Discuss your rationale for each situation.

➢ **Minority Influence: Does the Majority Always Rule?**

1. Give two examples from history when an individual with a minority view was able to influence the majority.

2. Under what conditions do minorities succeed in influencing majorities?

3. Explain how the minority view produces *positive effects* even if the view does not influence the majority.

Compliance: To Ask—Sometimes—Is To Receive

➢ Compliance: The Underlying Principles

1. **Instructions:** Examine each of the following statements and then decide which compliance principle it exemplifies:

a.) "I helped her with her homework because she gave me a ride last week when my car broke down."___________________

b.) " The advertisement said that time was running out to buy the tickets so I bought them immediately." ______________________________

c.) "Maria is my dear friend, so of course I helped her move her boxes into her new apartment." _______________________

d.). "I told everyone that I was going to start being punctual, so I must be on time for the event."

____

e.) "Yes I bought a natural gas powered car. All of the celebrities these days own one."

____

f.) "My doctor just discussed with me the positive aspects of eating organic food. I am going to purchase organic produce from now on."_____________________

➢ Tactics Based on Friendship or Liking: Ingratiation

1. Consider the concept of impression management (discussed in Chapter 2). One particular aspect of impression management is ingratiation. Explain when a person would use this particular impression management technique? What ingratiation technique works best?

- **Tactics Based on Commitment or Consistency: The Foot-in-the-Door and the Lowball**

1. Compare and contrast the foot-in-door technique with the lowball technique by explaining how each operates.

2. Give an example from your life in which you were the victim of the foot-in-the-door technique and an example with regard to the lowball tactic.

- **Tactics Based on Reciprocity: The Door-in-the Face and the "That's Not All" Approach**

1. Compare and contrast the door-in-the-face technique with the "that's-not-all" technique by explaining how each operates.

2. Give an example from your life in which you were the victim of the door-in-the-face technique and an example with regard to the "that's not all" approach.

- **Tactics Based on Scarcity: Playing Hard to Get and the Fast-Approaching Deadline Technique**

1. Compare and contrast the playing hard to get technique with the deadline technique by explaining how each operates.

2. *Applying your knowledge*: Give an example of how a car salesperson might use both the "playing hard to get" technique and the "fast approaching deadline" technique to sell a car to a customer.

> **Symbolic Social Influence: How We Are Influenced By Others Even When They Are Not There**

1. Define a relational schema. Give an example from your life of symbolic social influence on your behavior.

Social Influence: Obedience to Authority

> **Obedience to Authority: Would You Harm An Innocent Stranger if Ordered to Do So?**

1. Persons who possess authority and could use it tend to prefer to exert influence through the "velvet glove" meaning that____________________

2. Stanley Milgram's interest in studying destructive obedience came apart, in part, from a desire to understand the horrors of________________________________

3. Outline step by step, what each of Milgram's subjects ("teachers") did as they participated in Milgram's initial study of obedience.

4. ____________percent of Milgram's participants showed total obedience in his initial obedience study.

5. Describe the two variations of the Milgram obedience study and summarize the results from these follow-up studies.

6. What were the ethical issues associated with Milgram's study? Could Milgram's study be conducted today in the United States? Why?

7. Why does destructive obedience occur in natural settings?

8. List four ways to resist the effects of destructive obedience.

➢ **Social Influence Goes to Work: Influence Tactics in Work Settings**

1. Identify the nine most common influence tactics used in work settings.

2. Give an example of how a politician would use each of the three most popular influence techniques to get your vote.

3. Describe two influence tactics that are the least popular in the workplace. Describe a situation where these tactics might be well-received.

After You Read...

Practice Test 1

1. The author's personal story of a drunk driving incident at the beginning of the chapter exemplified the concept of
   a. compliance
   b. conformity
   c. obedience
   d. intense indoctrination

2. ____is when an individual orders another person to behave in a certain way, while ___is an effort to get others to say yes to various requests.
   a. Compliance, conformity
   b. Obedience, conformity
   c. Conformity, obedience
   d. Obedience, compliance

3. "Don't stare at strangers." This is an example of a ____ norm
   a. implicit
   b. explicit
   c. social
   d. both a and c

4. In Asch's famous conformity studies, roughly ____percent of his subjects never yielded to the group pressure.
   a. 5
   b. 15
   c. 25
   d. 75

5. Which of the following exemplifies a cohesive group of individuals?
   a. strangers standing together on an elevator
   b. patrons shopping at a supermarket
   c. students taking an examination in class
   d. friends getting together for a group study session

6. When cohesiveness is ____, people tend to conform.
   a. absent
   b. low
   c. moderate
   d. high

7. The behavior of picking up an empty soda can and putting it into a trash can after another individual inadvertently dropped it, can be best understood according to ______
   a. injunctive norm salience
   b. normative focus theory
   c. descriptive norms
   d. explicit social norms

8. Research has found that individuals in an unfamiliar context with the strong desire to be accurate or correct are ____ to conform.
   a. more likely
   b. less likely
   c. unaffected in their desire
   d. dissuaded

9. All of the following factors increase the possibility that a minority will alter the majority view, except
   a. consistency.
   b. flexibility.
   c. operating within the current social context.
   d. angrily expressing views.

10. Recent research indicates that because they feel greater concern over being right, minorities tend to _________the number of persons who share their views.
    a. underestimate
    b. overestimate
    c. not realize
    d. neglect

Practice Test 2

1. All of the following are considered compliance principles EXCEPT
   a. reciprocity.
   b. scarcity.
   c. social responsibility.
   d. authority.

2. Ingratiation is considered to be a compliance tactic based on
   a. scarcity.
   b. commitment.
   c. authority.
   d. liking.

3. The foot-in-the-door tactic rests on the principle of
   a. commitment.
   b. scarcity.
   c. reciprocity.
   d. liking.

4. If you've agreed to purchase something after a salesperson has decided to sweeten the deal, you've likely shown compliance as a result of the
   a. lowball technique.
   b. "that's-not-all technique.
   c. pique technique.
   d. playing hard to get technique.

5. The door-in-the-face technique rests on the principle of
   a. commitment.
   b. scarcity.
   c. reciprocity.
   d. social validation.

6. Suppose Iris decides to buy a certain shirt because she claims "it's what everyone who's like me is wearing." This example depicts the importance of compliance tactics based on
   a. scarcity.
   b. liking.
   c. authority
   d. social validation.

7. The extent to which other persons are present in our thoughts may trigger _______ schemas.
   a. explicit
   b. relational
   c. functional
   d. factional

8. When individuals use the ____technique in the area of romance by suggesting that it is difficult to win their affections, this tends to _____their desirability.
   a. playing hard to get; increase
   b. playing hard to get; decrease
   c. foot-in-the-door technique; increase

d. foot-in-the-door technique, decrease

9. Fitzsimmons and Bargh (2003) found that when participants in their study were asked if they would be willing to help the researcher by answering a long set of questions, those who thought about a friend were ________ to help.
   a. more willing
   b. less willing
   c. unaffected in their willingness
   d. the results were inconclusive

10. All of the following careers are often synonymous with "compliance professionals," EXCEPT
    a. advertisers.
    b. politicians.
    c. salespeople.
    d. medical doctors.

Practice Test 3

1. Obedience is less frequent than conformity or compliance because even persons who possess authority and could use if often prefer to exert influence through the velvet glove, through _____ rather than ____.
   a. requests; direct orders
   b. direct orders; requests
   c. subtle hints; explicit threats
   d. explicit threats; subtle hints

2. Milgram began his interest in obedience with an attempt to better understand the events surrounding
   a. the Civil War.
   b. World War I.
   c. the Great Depression.
   d. the Holocaust.

3. ______ percent of the participants in Milgram's study showed total obedience
   a. 100
   b. 85
   c. 75
   d. 25

4. In Milgram's experiments the transfer of authority and responsibility for the learner was
   a. implicit.
   b. explicit.
   c. not mentioned.
   d. gradual.

5. The Milgram study relied on what compliance tactic?
   a. The door-in-the-face technique
   b. The foot-in-the-door technique
   c. The lowball technique
   d. The that's not all technique

6. A practical consequence of the Milgram study is that it led to.
   a. a worldwide understanding of the harmful effects of destructive obedience.
   b. a thorough condemnation of Milgram's work by the psychological community.
   c. stricter ethical guidelines in research.
   d. strong criticism from Holocaust survivors.

7. The presence of disobedient models has been found to _____unquestioning obedience in others.
   a. increase
   b. reduce
   c. motivate
   d. have no effect on

8. A prominent example of where the power of authority was resisted in order to produce positive outcomes was
   a. The overthrow of many Eastern European governments in the 1980s and 1990s.
   b. The oil embargo of the 1970s.
   c. When the U.S. Supreme Court ruled in George W. Bush's favor in the *Bush v. Gore* case.
   d. The Vietnam War.

9. Destructive obedience stems from use of the _____technique.
   a. door-in-the-face
   b. scarcity
   c. foot-in-the-door
   d. lowball

10. All of the following are influence tactics used in the workplace setting EXCEPT
    a. consultation
    b. rational persuasion
    c. ingratiation
    d. all of the following are used

Comprehensive Test

(NOTE: Items 1-15 are multiple-choice questions and items 16-23 are true-false questions.)

1. An example of an implicit norm would be
   a. "We should speak softly in the library."
   b. "Posted speed limit is 65."
   c. "Students not registered by August 28 will be charged a late fee."
   d. "Those above the age of seventy are granted a lower tax rate by order of the city council."

2. All of the following are popular influence tactics used in the workplace EXCEPT
   a. pressure.
   b. inspirational appeal.
   c. rational persuasion.
   d. consultation.

3. Social influence is
   a. simply being influenced by others.

b. the influence of society on us.
c. influencing how society operates in the present and future.
d. the efforts on the part of an individual to alter the behavior or attitudes of others.

4. Compliance occurs when individuals
   a. respond favorably to a person's direct request
   b. mimic each other
   c. question the conventions of society
   d. change their behavior in order to fit that of other persons in their group

5. Social influence is an effort by one or more individuals to change all of the following EXCEPT
   a. attitudes.
   b. behaviors.
   c. perceptions.
   d. all of the following can be changed by social influence.

6. In Asch's line-judgment study almost _____percent of the participants never yielded to the group pressure
   a. 75
   b. 55
   c. 45
   d. 25

7. Current research has found that conformity tends to _____as group size ____.
   a. decrease, decreases
   b. decrease, increases
   c. increase, decreases
   d. increase, increases

8. One reason we tend to conform is so that we can win the approval and acceptance of others. This is referred to as
   a. informational social influence
   b. normative social influence
   c. implicit social influence
   d. explicit social influence

9. A compliance tactic based on reciprocity is the
   a. lowball technique.
   b. foot-in-the-door technique.
   c. door-in-the-face technique.
   d. playing hard to get technique.

10. The compliance tactic based on consistency is the
    a. lowball technique.
    b. foot-in-the-door technique.
    c. door-in-the-face technique.
    d. playing hard to get technique.

11. Suppose a minority fails to influence the majority on some issue. A possible consequence of this action is that
    a. it will serve as an impetus for the minority to become radical.

b. it will serve as an impetus for the majority to become radical.
c. it may cause the majority to engage in systematic processing.
d. the minority view will likely be forgotten.

12. __________is seen to play a role in why people are spending tremendous sums of money to buy collections of large boulders.
a. Informational social influence
b. Normative social influence
c. Implicit social influence
d. Explicit social influence

13. ______and ______ serve to reduce conformity.
a. Our desire to retain our individuality; the desire to retain control over our lives
b. Our desire to decrease our individuality; the desire to decrease control over our lives
c. Our desire to decrease our individuality; the desire increase control over our lives
d. Our desire to increase our individuality; the desire to decrease control over our lives

14. In sum, current gender research on conformity has found that women are ______ accepting of social influence than men.
a. extremely more
b. less
c. not much more
d. the results are still unclear

15. The lowball procedure rests on the principle of
a. consistency.
b. scarcity.
c. commitment.
d. friendship.

(Questions 16-23 are True/False items.)

16. The desire to be liked and correct are two powerful reasons why we conform.

17. Special uniforms, badges, and titles do little to increase the power of authority.

18. Pressuring others to comply with your requests is an effective compliance tactic in the workplace.

19. Gradual escalation of shock levels in the Milgram study served to lower obedience.

20. The velvet glove technique makes requests of others instead of giving direct orders.

21. In Asch's famous conformity studies, about a quarter of the subjects went along with the false judgment at least once.

22. Public conformity tends to routinely predict private acceptance.

23. The desire to be accurate coupled with an unfamiliar context, decreases our desire to conform.

Short Answer/Essay Questions

1. **Social Influence Factors**
   Jorge is taking his first college history course. Jorge's history professor has assigned him to complete a group project with three of his close friends. Once the project is complete all four members of the group will receive a group grade based on the accuracy of their assignment. All three of Jorge's friends agree on the main answer to their assignment, but despite Jorge's feeling that the answer is not quite right, he goes along and agrees with the group. What conformity factors are occurring that push Jorge to go along with the group's answer?

2. **Minority Influence**
   State the three key factors that need to be in place in order for the minority to have a viable chance to influence the majority.

3. **Compliance Tactics**
   Judy has found the car of her dreams for $2,000 less than at any other car dealership. She immediately signs the contract and then calls her friends to tell them about her purchase. Five minutes later the salesperson reappears with disappointing news that his boss is forcing him to sell the car for $2,000 more than the original asking price. Reluctantly Judy agrees to purchase it at this price. What type of compliance tactic does this illustrate?

When You Have Finished……

The Applications of Social Influence to Your Life

1. We frequently experience direct or indirect pressure to change our views or behaviors in some way. This is what social influence is all about!

2. By being aware of the various compliance tactics, we are less likely to be hoodwinked into accepting a deal of some sort that really isn't much of a bargain.

3. Despite the fact that authority figures can exert a tremendous amount of pressure for us to obey their commands, we should also be aware that there are ways to combat destructive obedience.

4. If you ever find yourself in a minority role, then you will want to note the most effective ways to influence a majority.

5. By understanding the nature of conformity, you will have a better appreciation for why we often "go along" and why this isn't always a "bad thing."

Let's reflect on point #3 and, more specifically, on Milgram's classic study of obedience. How do YOU think you would have acted if you were a research participant in Milgram's initial study of obedience? If you say that you would not go along with the experimenter's orders, how can you be so sure that you wouldn't simply obey?

Here are some web links to provide you with additional information about the topics covered in this chapter:

Internet Resources

http://www.influenceatwork.com. This site, developed by Kelton Rhoads, is based on Cialdini's principles of influence. Go to the "academic" side for an excellent tutorial on principles of persuasion, and on the "corporate" side, take an online test of knowledge of influence principles.

http://www.stanleymilgram.com/main.html. This site, developed by Thomas Blass, focuses on the work of social psychologist Stanley Milgram.

http://remus.rutgers.edu/~rhoads/PerilsofObedience.html. A 1974 *Harper's Magazine* article, "The Perils of Obedience," written by Milgram.

http://www.outofservice.com/freak/. A need for uniqueness scale on the Web. How strong is your need *not* to conform?

http://www.stophazing.org/ "Educating to Eliminate Hazing." Site covering many aspects of hazing including fraternity, sorority, athletic, high school, and military hazing. Includes news on hazing, discussion of what can be done to prevent or decrease it, and some pro-hazing views as well.

Crossword Puzzle

Across

5. unpopular compliance tactic
7. basis of foot-in-the-door
10. alter behavior or attitude
15. changing the deal at the last minute
16. key to milgram study
18. conformity researcher
19. obedience researcher
20. harming the innocent
21. time is running out
23. tactic based on friendship

Down
1. degree of attraction
2. five-hundred dollar fine
3. percent of obedient people in milgram study
4. what is commonly done
6. basis of that's not all
8. ordering behavior
9. large then small request
11. small then large request
12. influence researcher
13. compliance professionals
14. tactic to sweeten the deal
17. normative behavior
22. saying yes to requests

Created by *<u>Puzzlemaker</u>* *at DiscoverySchool.com*
http://school.discovery.com/

10 PROSOCIAL BEHAVIOR: HELPING OTHERS

Before You Read . . .

This chapter reviews research regarding prosocial or helping behavior. You'll learn very quickly that there are many important factors to consider when trying to determine whether an individual will help someone in an emergency. It truly is amazing how many factors can determine whether one helps—everything from whether others are around to individual difference or personality factors and motivational or emotional states. It's also interesting to note that who you are (or appear to be) can influence whether you receive help; this chapter will consider these factors. You should also be aware that social psychologists have long considered why people decide to help others in the first place. You will be reviewing the major the hypotheses regarding this issue.

Chapter Objectives

After reading this chapter, you should be able to:

- Explain the key differences between "prosocial behavior" and "altruism."
- Understand the concept of "heroism."
- Be familiar with the term "bystander effect" and how it functions.
- Outline Latane and Darley's (1971) five essential steps to a prosocial response in an emergency and note at what point help may be given.
- Discuss three important situational factors that can either enhance or inhibit helping.
- Contrast the following terms: egoism, self-interest, moral integrity, and moral hypocrisy.
- Explain how a bystander's emotional state may influence his or her decision to help.
- Discuss the nature of empathy, how it develops, and why people may differ as a function of it.
- Understand the concept of "reciprocal altruism" and why people would be willing to put their lives on the line for a stranger in a dangerous situation.

- Outline other personality factors (other than empathy) associated with prosocial behavior and pay particular attention to the qualities of the altruistic personality.
- Explain the various motives for volunteering.
- Consider the role that gender plays in helping behavior.
- Note the general reactions of those who receive help in terms of how it feels to receive such assistance.
- State, define, and contrast the key models or hypotheses of why we engage in prosocial behavior.

As You Read . . .

Important Terms to Know... Below are a list of some of the key terms and concepts from this chapter. Make flashcards in order to enhance your recall ability of these terms. Refer to the definitions that are either in boldface or in the margins of this chapter for help. You may also want to include additional terms from this chapter as you deem necessary.

Prosocial behavior	Altruism	Diffusion of responsibility
Bystander effect	Latane and Darley's five step model	Pluralistic ignorance
Prosocial models	Egoism	Self-interest
Moral integrity	Moral hypocrisy	Empathy and its components
The major types of perspective taking	Inclusive fitness	Kin selection
Implicit bystander effect	Altruistic personality and its components	Volunteering and its functions
Generativity	Empathy-altruism hypothesis	Negative-state relief model
Personality disposition	Pluralistic ignorance	Reciprocal Altruism
Empathic joy hypothesis	Genetic determinism model	Mimicry
Selective altruism	Heroism	

Responding to an Emergency: Will Bystanders Help?

1. What's the key difference between "prosocial behavior" and "altruism?"

➢ When a Stranger is Distressed: Heroism or Apathy?

1. In your own words describe the concept of "heroism." Give an example of this concept.

The Science of Social Psychology: Making Sense of Common Sense

➢ Do More Witnesses to an Emergency Mean that More Help is Given?

1. In your own words, what's the difference between "diffusion of responsibility" and the "bystander effect?"

3. Describe how Darley and Latane (1968) demonstrated the bystander effect in the laboratory.

4. To what degree do *you* believe that diffusion of responsibility and the bystander effect accounts for why people often don't offer help in an emergency?

➢ Five Crucial Steps Determine Helping versus Not Helping

1. Complete the following flowchart that outlines Latane and Darley's five essential steps to a prosocial response in an emergency. (You may want to pay particular attention to the chart in your text.)

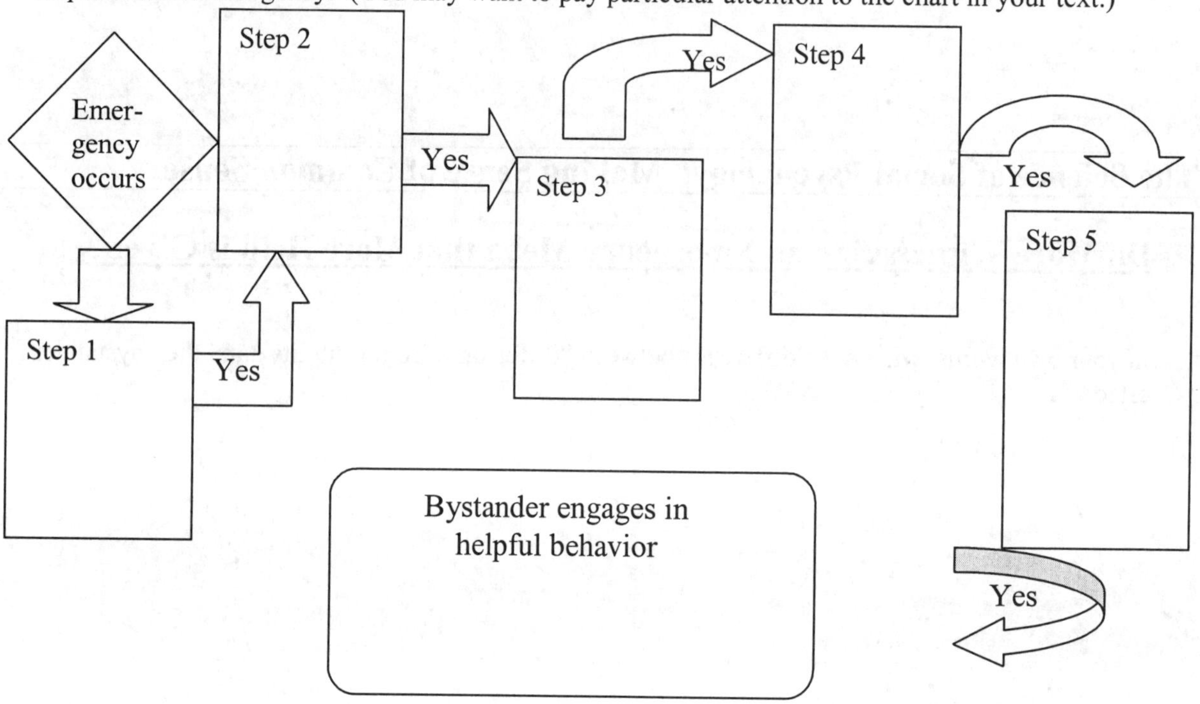

If the answer is "no" to any of these questions then ______________________________

____.

External and Internal Influences on Helping Behavior

1. *To help or not to help, that is the question.* For each of the following situations, indicate whether help will be offered.

a.) Helping a stranger who appears similar to you in some way: ______________

b.) Helping a stranger with a stigma: ______________

c.) Helping someone whose problems are perceived as controllable: ______________

d.) Helping someone who appears too much like yourself: ______________

e.) Helping someone after watching the TV show, *Lassie*: ______________

f.) Helping someone after watching the TV show, *South Park*: ______________

2. A ________________ is the automatic tendency to imitate the behavior of those with whom we interact.

➢ Empathy and Other Personality Dispositions Associated with Helping

1. Empathy consists of ______________ and __________ responses to another person's emotional state and includes sympathy.

2. Discuss briefly the evidence that suggests that the personality trait of empathy is inherited.

3. Altruistic individuals tend to have the following five traits …

   a. ________________________________

   b. ________________________________

   c. ________________________________

   d. ________________________________

   e. ________________________________

Long-Term Commitment to Prosocial Action and the Effects of Being Helped

1. Differentiate the following terms: egoism, self-interest, moral integrity, and moral hypocrisy.

2. Identify some of the key reasons why a person might volunteer. In doing so, emphasize the rationale for AIDS volunteerism, as well as the role of generativity in volunteering.

➢ How Does It Feel to Be Helped?

1. Complete the following sentences by underlining the term or phrase that makes the statement correct.

   a.) Men are (likely, unlikely) to help women in distress.

   b.) A possible reason why men may help women in distress may be related to the (third, fourth) step of Darley and Latane's model of helping behavior.

   c.) Men who are driving (alone, with other male friends) are likely to help a female who's experiencing car trouble.

   d.) (Elderly, young) adults don't readily ask for help that often.

   e.) After you receive help, it is fairly common to experience (overwhelming happiness, discomfort).

The Basic Motivation for Engaging in Prosocial Acts

➢ Empathy-Altruism: It Simply Feels Good to Help Others

1. As your text notes, there is a common belief that being in a good mood makes it more likely that you'll help someone, whereas being in a negative mood has the opposite effect. Describe the evidence that *supports* these claims as well as instances that does *not support* these claims.

2. What's wrong here? Each of the following statements is *false*. Modify the statement in some way in order to make it correct.

   a.) Empathy simply involves an affective component.

   b.) When someone feels empathy for a fictional character, they're taking the "imagine other" perspective.

   c.) Empathy does *not* have a genetic component whatsoever.

d.) Robert Coles believes that children can learn empathy by remembering a variety of social rules and regulations.

e.) Women are just as likely as men to show prosocial behavior.

f.) People tend to help the victims of a disaster no matter what.

3. Match it! Match each phrase, word, or sentence on the left side of the page with an identifying concept on the right side of the page. Note that each item on the right should be used *only once*.

___1. Helping that has evolutionary benefits	A. empathic joy hypothesis
___2. Helping that makes the helper feel good	B. genetic determinism model
___3. Empathy directed at a single group member	C. empathy-altruism hypothesis
___4. Helping done in order to make the helper have less negative affect	D. empathy avoidance
___5. Helping simply done for the sake of helping	E. selective altruism
___6. A motivation to not engage in high-cost helping	F. negative-state relief model

4. Consistent with the negative-state relief model, it doesn't matter whether the bystander's negative emotions were ____ ____.

5 The emotion that is elicited by performing a prosocial act is sometimes called ____________, which refers to ____.

6 Consistent with the genetic determinism model, we tend to help our ______________, particularly those who are ____

➢ Beyond The Headlines: As Social Psychologists See It--Is Helping as Joyful as Eating Ice Cream?

1. Briefly discuss why a stranger would pull another stranger out of a burning car with so much at stake. How was reciprocal altruism a focus in this incident?

After You Read . . . Practice Tests

Practice Test 1

1. ____ is an unselfish concern for the welfare of others.
   a. Empathy
   b. Sympathy
   c. Altruism
   d. Prosocial behavior

2. An important lesson from the infamous Kitty Genovese murder is that people tend to
   a. feel indifferent about crime and crime victims.
   b. be apathetic, unless a matter directly concerns them.
   c. people are much less likely to help when others are around.
   d. offer help to others, only if they live in a rural area.

3. A key reason why the bystander effect occurs is that people tend to
   a. gawk and stare when an accident or emergency occurs.
   b. only focus on their own well-being during an emergency.
   c. feel less responsible for offering aid to a victim.
   d. denigrate the victim and wonder whether he or she caused their lot.

4. According to Latane and Darley (1970), there are ____ essential steps to responding to an emergency.
   a. three
   b. four
   c. five
   d. six

5. A bystander will offer help, according to Latane and Darley's (1970) model if an affirmative response is given to ____ of the stages.
   a. all
   b. a majority
   c. none
   d. any

6. Interpreting an emergency as such is considered the ____ stage of the Latane and Darley (1970) model.
   a. first
   b. second
   c. third
   d. fourth

7. Of the following, an individual would be *most* likely to help a stranger who
   a. appeared to be involved in some domestic dispute.
   b. had a stigma of some sort.
   c. appears to be similar to the individual in some way.
   d. appears to have caused his or her dilemma in some way.

8. Non-prosocial models that aren't necessarily violent, such as the characters on *South Park*, appear to
   a. surprisingly enhance prosocial behavior in others.
   b. adversely affect prosocial behavior in others.
   c. have no effect whatsoever on prosocial behavior.
   d. impact individuals in ways that have not yet been fully examined by researchers.

9. ____ is an exclusive concern with one's own personal needs.
   a. Egoism
   b. Self-interest
   c. Moral integrity
   d. Moral hypocrisy

10. When faced with a certain moral dilemma, Marilyn decides to perform a behavior that satisfies her own needs and desires. In this example, it appears that Marilyn's ____ was stronger than her ____.
    a. moral hypocrisy; moral integrity
    b. self-interest; moral integrity
    c. moral integrity; moral hypocrisy
    d. self-interest; moral hypocrisy

Practice Test 2

1. If a person is in a good mood and is faced with a situation that might require him or her to help,
   a. assistance is uniformly given.
   b. he or she will likely do so provided that his or her prosocial act doesn't spoil his or her good mood.
   c. such an individual tends to shy away from offering help.
   d. he or she will only offer help if his or her positive mood is due to situational causes.

2. Empathy has a(n)
   a. affective component only.
   b. cognitive component only.
   c. affective and a cognitive component.
   d. biological component only.

3. The Native American expression, "walking a mile in my moccasins," pertains to the ____ aspect of empathy.
   a. feeling sympathetic
   b. perspective taking
   c. altruistic
   d. personality

4. Apparently, genetics is ____ involved in affective empathy and is ____ involved in cognitive empathy.
   a. partially; partially
   b. not; not
   c. not; partially
   d. partially; not

5. Some psychologists suggest that the key to fostering prosocial behavior in children is to
   a. keep them away from television.
   b. teach them to be kind.
   c. instruct them about the benefits of helping.
   d. simply attend church on a regular basis.

6. During the Nazi Holocaust, the gender breakdown of non-Jewish Germans who helped rescue Jews tended to be
   a. women by a ratio of two to one.
   b. men by a ratio of two to one.
   c. women by a ratio of four to one.
   d. an equal ratio of men and women.

7. Suppose Bill, a conservative, and Tom, a liberal, learn that a major flood has hit a town bordering the Ohio River in the United States. Who is *most* likely to help?
   a. Bill
   b. Tom
   c. They are equally likely to help.
   d. Since political ideology doesn't predict helping in the wake of a disaster, more information is needed in order to answer this question.

8. Among the many lessons of the September 11, 2001 catastrophe is that
   a. people tend to help as a means of expressing relief that they haven't been personally affected by a disaster.
   b. in order for people to help in a major catastrophe, they must feel some sort of similarity to the victims.
   c. people usually don't offer help to victims unless they have personally experienced such a disaster.
   d. a helper often jeopardizes his or her life when offering assistance.

9. Empathy tends to be ____ related to achievement motivation and ____ related to aggression.
   a. positively; negatively
   b. negatively; not
   c. not; negatively
   d. not; not

10. All of the following are components of the altruistic personality, *except*
   a. the belief in a just world.
   b. low egocentrism.
   c. an external locus of control.
   d. social responsibility.

Practice Test 3

1. AIDS volunteerism
   a. has greatly increased in recent years since most people don't fear AIDS anymore.
   b. is just as likely to occur for a homosexual or drug user than for someone who got AIDS through a blood transfusion.
   c. is often viewed by potential volunteers as having too many costs associated with it.
   d. usually is not viewed as personally rewarding by those who partake in it.

2. The protective function of volunteerism allows a person to
   a. potentially address personal problems.
   b. act on important values.
   c. grow and develop psychologically.
   d. gain career-related experience.

3. ____ are particularly likely to help a female motorist with car trouble.
   a. Young men driving alone
   b. Young men driving with other men
   c. Middle-aged men
   d. Women

4. A fairly common reaction from individuals who receive help is
   a. relief.
   b. profound gratitude.
   c. feeling overjoyed.
   d. discomfort.

5. Of the following groups, ____ are the *most* likely to ask for help.
   a. elderly adults
   b. those with an ambivalent attachment style
   c. those with low socioeconomic status
   d. young adults

6. The ____ states that prosocial behavior is motivated solely by the desire to help someone in need.
   a. genetic determinism model
   b. empathy-altruism hypothesis
   c. empathic joy hypothesis
   d. negative-state relief model

7. Even though Jean was interested in working at a battered women's shelter, once she realized that the cost of helping was high, her interest in helping dramatically decreased. This example illustrates
   a. empathy avoidance.
   b. selective altruism.
   c. empathic joy.
   d. a helper's high.

8. Since Jon was in a foul mood, he decided to offer assistance to a man who just fell in the hope of making himself feel better. The ____ is probably provides the *best* explanation for why Jon offered help.
   a. genetic determinism model
   b. empathy-altruism hypothesis
   c. empathic joy hypothesis
   d. negative-state relief model

9. Of the four major explanations for prosocial behavior, the one that does *not* emphasize the role of emotion is the
   a. genetic determinism model.
   b. empathy-altruism hypothesis.
   c. empathic joy hypothesis.
   d. negative-state relief model.

10. There is some empirical evidence that shows that you are *most* likely to help
    a. any person with whom you have a close relationship.
    b. a fairly close relative regardless of their age or gender.
    c. a fairly young, close relative.
    d. any biological relative.

Comprehensive Test

(NOTE: Items 1-15 are multiple-choice questions and items 16-23 are true-false questions.)

1. The bystander effect refers to the
    a. inhibition of helping when there are several witnesses present during an emergency.
    b. indifference to the plight of someone in distress.
    c. apathy shown by the victim of a calamity.
    d. tendency for people to "kick someone when he or she is down."

2. Diffusion of responsibility involves
    a. spreading the responsibility for helping from oneself to others present in an emergency.
    b. absorbing the responsibility to help from others present in an emergency.
    c. whether and why someone helps when there is only a single witness to an emergency.
    d. the techniques needed in order to help someone in a responsible and thoughtful manner.

3. According to Robert Coles, children learn moral intelligence
    a. by watching and listening to their parents.
    b. from television.
    c. from their peers.
    d. by learning a set of rules and regulations.

4. Of the following, a(n) ____ is *most* likely to help.
    a. middle-aged person
    b. person with an internal locus of control
    c. individual with a history of having their need for approval punished after helping
    d. male

5. The negative state relief model postulates that
    a. people help in order to reduce a victim's negative affect.
    b. emergency situations cause negative moods.
    c. individuals help in order to relieve his or her own negative emotions.
    d. victims in negative moods are helped less often than those in positive moods.

6. Of the following, the *most* important factor in helping behavior is
    a. a history of being in need of help.
    b. the ability to take the perspective of another person.
    c. one's physical fitness.
    d. having some kind of disability or other affliction.

7. ____ is part of a "helper's high."
   a. Warmth
   b. Relaxation
   c. Contemplation
   d. A peak experience

8. ____ is involved in the empathic joy hypothesis.
   a. Warmth
   b. A peak experience
   c. Feeling good about accomplishing something
   d. Getting rid of a bad mood and putting someone else in a good mood

9. Suppose you are at a movie theater and notice smoke coming from one of the vents in the theater. Even though you and many other people in the audience notice the smoke, no one decides to do anything about it. This illustrates
   a. the bystander effect.
   b. the diffusion of responsibility.
   c. pluralistic ignorance.
   d. moral hypocrisy.

10. Even though Caleb stresses the importance of exercise to others, he rarely exercises himself. This is an example of
    a. moral integrity.
    b. self-interest.
    c. egoism.
    d. moral hypocrisy.

11. The positive effect of negative emotions in helping behavior is *most* likely to be observed if the
    a. negative feelings are very intense.
    b. emergency is not ambiguous.
    c. act of helping will be difficult.
    d. individual usually experiences negative emotions.

12. After watching a very sad movie, Julia feels very sorry for the lead character when he died. Julia's perspective involved
    a. imagining the self.
    b. imagining the other.
    c. fantasy.
    d. theoretical understanding.

13. All of the following personality characteristics contribute to helping behavior, *except*
    a. the need for approval.
    b. sociability.
    c. interpersonal trust.
    d. Machiavellianism.

14. A possible reason why men readily help women may be related to the nature of the ____ stage of Latane and Darley's (1970) model of responding to an emergency.
    a. second
    b. third
    c. fourth
    d. fifth

15. Receiving help often ____ the recipient's self-esteem, particularly if the helper is a ____.
    a. reverses the current state of; stranger
    b. decreases; stranger
    c. increases; friend
    d. decreases; friend

Questions 16-23 are True/False Questions

16. Reciprocal altruism also benefits the larger group to which the helper and victim belong.

17. Being mimicked decreases one's prosocial tendencies.

18. Leon has just retired and is very concerned about the well-being of future generations. As such, his concerns are related to the concept of generativity.

19. Those with an altruistic personality were particularly likely to rescue and help Jews from Nazi persecution.

20. The empathic-joy hypothesis states that individuals are motivated to help in order to reduce one's negative emotional state.

21. Men tend to help because they are more empathic than women.

22. Heroism involves courageous actions to obtain a socially valued goal.

23. There is a definite gene for prosocial behavior.

When You Have Finished . . .

Applications of Prosocial Behavior to Your Life

1. Most of us would like to think that if we needed help, it would be offered to us *and* if we could, we'd offer help to others. The study of prosocial behavior helps to pinpoint the conditions when this is most likely to occur.

2. By understanding the five essential steps to helping in an emergency, governmental agencies and laypersons alike can understand why and how individuals may help under these conditions.

3. Parents can certainly benefit from an understanding of the importance of how to foster empathy in their children.

4. Even though it may not represent altruism in the "purest" sense, people may be more likely to help others if they realize that they're more likely to feel good after helping someone.

5. In the aftermath of the September 11, 2001 disaster, we all dramatically witnessed how prosocial behavior from helpers can truly save lives—even though it may potentially take the life of the helper.

Let's try to reflect a bit more on point #4 by thinking about a time when you offered help to someone. Did you truly feel better after doing so? If yes, how? Also, do you think that people can truly show altruism without really expecting *anything* in return? Justify your answer. You may also want to ask this question to your friends and see what they have to say.

Short Answer/Essay Questions

1. **Prosocial Responses in an Emergency**
   Outline Latane and Darley's (1971) model of the five essential steps to a prosocial response in an emergency.

2. **Prosocial Models**
   Briefly describe the three types of models shown on television and other media that may influence a child's prosocial behavior (for better or worse).

3. **Moods and Helping Behavior**
   Briefly discuss when a person who is in a good mood may *not* be likely to help a stranger.

4. **Volunteering**
   Explain why someone might volunteer as a function of generativity.

5. **Theoretical Explanations for Prosocial Behavior**
   Consistent with the genetic determinism model, what type of individual should you be *most* likely to help?

Internet Sites:

http://www.apa.org/pubinfo/altruism.html: contains a readable article from the APA public information website on how to make children more caring.

http://www.giraffe.org/heroes.html: is the website for the Giraffe Project, which brings attention to people who "stick out their necks for the common good." This section of the site has brief biographies of altruists from a variety of communities.

http://www.volunteermatch.com: provides an easy way to find opportunities for volunteering, from one-day to long-term. Indexed by location and by type of organization.

http://www.thehungersite.com: allows the site-user to help contribute to help the hungry. The viewer clicks on the site, and corporations pay to provide the help. There are also links to other sites where one can help for "free" (the breast cancer site, rainforest site, etc.).

http://www.myhero.com/hero.asp?hero=binti: has the story of Binti Jua, the gorilla described in the text who saved a 3-year-old boy who fell into her cage. This site also provides links to other animal heroes.

Crossword Puzzle

Across

1. courageous actions
4. one individual is helped when a large group is in need
6. concern with one's personal needs
7. unselfish behavior
9. cooperative behavior among strangers
10. motivation to appear moral
11. kin selection
12. imitation

13. inclusive fitness
14. help effected by the number of bystanders present
15. concern for future generations

Down
2. decrease in helping behavior by thinking about being in a group
3. responsibility of bystanders is shared
4. egoism
5. putting yourself in others shoes
8. motivation to be moral

Created by Puzzlemaker at DiscoverySchool.com
http://school.discovery.com/

11 AGGRESSION: ITS NATURE, CAUSES, AND CONTROL

Before You Read . . .

In many respects, this chapter reflects the exact opposite of the previous chapter on helping behavior—here we look at behavior that is designed to harm others in some way, or aggressive behavior. First, you will consider various theoretical perspectives on aggression: In other words, why should we show aggression anyway? Afterward, you will be presented with a variety of personality/individual difference, social/situational and cultural factors that can cause or produce aggression. Then you will consider a couple of examples of aggression that may occur in a long-term relationship—namely, bullying and workplace violence. Finally, you'll consider a variety of practical techniques that may reduce various forms of aggression. You actually might be quite surprised by some of the techniques that can help to reduce aggression—and by some of the popular techniques that do *not* appear to reduce aggression.

Chapter Objectives

After reading this chapter, you should be able to:

- Contrast the views of Freud, Lorenz, and evolutionary perspectives in terms of how aggression develops.
- State the purpose of drive theories of aggression and note the most well-known of these theories.
- Outline the variables involved in the general affective aggression model and briefly explain how this model operates.
- Identify the ways by which social psychologists study aggression in the laboratory.
- Discuss why the original frustration-aggression hypothesis is *not* considered to be accurate by most contemporary social psychologists.
- Understand what a "culture of honor" is and the role it plays in sexual jealousy.
- Outline the major points of excitation transfer theory.
- Identify individual difference or personal causes of aggression by discussing (among others) the Type A behavior pattern, hostile and instrumental aggression, and the hostile attributional bias.

- Identify the nature of gender differences in aggression.
- Define Munchausen's Syndrome and why mothers intentionally harm their children.
- Discuss how temperature and alcohol may influence aggression.
- Contrast the characteristics of bullies, victims, and bully/victims and note the ways by which bullying behavior can be reduced.
- Note the prevalence of workplace violence and summarize the three main categories of aggression in the workplace.
- Consider whether punishment can be an effective deterrent to violence.
- Evaluate the veracity of the catharsis hypothesis.
- Identify the various techniques (cognitive and non-cognitive interventions) that can be used in order to reduce aggression.

As You Read . . .

Important Terms to Know... Below are a list of some of the key terms and concepts from this chapter. Make flashcards in order to enhance your recall ability of these terms. Refer to the definitions that are either in boldface or in the margins of this chapter for help. You may also want to include additional terms from this chapter as you deem necessary.

Aggression	Death wish/thanatos	Fighting instinct
Drive theories	General affective aggression model and its related variables	Aggression machine and the point subtraction and aggression paradigm
Frustration-aggression hypothesis	Provocation	(Triggered) Displaced aggression
Culture of honor	Media violence	Desensitization
Excitation transfer theory	Type A/Type B behavior patterns	Hostile vs. instrumental aggression
Hostile attributional bias	Direct vs. indirect aggression	Sexual coercion
Negative-affect escape model	Bullying, bullies, victims, and bully/victims	Workplace violence vs. workplace aggression
Expressions of hostility	Obstructionism	Overt aggression
Punishment and its four conditions for success	The catharsis hypothesis	Forgiveness
Cognitive deficits and preattribution	The incompatible response technique	

Theoretical Perspectives on Aggression: In Search of the Roots of Violence

➢ The Role of Biological Factors: From Instincts To The Evolutionary Psychological Perspective

1. In your own words, define "aggression."

2. Compare and contrast how Sigmund Freud and Konrad Lorenz conceptualized aggression.

3. How would an evolutionary psychologist explain why aggression occurs?

➢ Drive Theories: The Motive to Harm Others

1. What is a drive theory of aggression? Identify the most famous of these theories.

➢ Modern Theories of Aggression: The Social Learning Perspective and the General Aggression Model

1. Identify and define the variables involved in the general affective aggression model. Be sure to label these in the order in which these occur.

Causes of Human Aggression: Social, Cultural, Personal and Situational

➢ Social Determinants of Aggression: Frustration, Provocation, Displaced Aggression, and Media Violence

1. In each of the following pairs, one of the factors is likely to produce aggression: Circle that factor.

   a.) frustration due to fact that a person is behind schedule vs. frustration that seems illegitimate

   b.) provocation from someone we believed meant to harm us vs. provocation from an authority figure

   c.) a mild provocation when we're having a bad day vs. a mild provocation when we're on vacation

   d.) exposure to a violent television show vs. exposure to a nonviolent film

2. When we watch scenes of violence, we often experience ________________, where we become hardened to the pain of others. Such viewing may also prime __________________ thoughts.

➢ Heightened arousal: Emotion, cognition, and aggression

1. Suppose you just found out that your sister was involved in a major car accident. In your attempt to rush to the hospital, you bump into someone who accidentally causes you to fall. On the basis of excitation transfer theory, describe the circumstances that may cause your aggression level to increase or not increase.

2. ________________ sexual arousal reduces aggression because ______________________________

____, while more explicit

sexual stimuli ____

____. In short, the

relationship between sexual arousal and aggression is _______________________________.

➢ Cultural Factors in Aggression: "Culture of Honor" and Sexual Jealousy

1. Cultures of honor are cultures in which there are ___________________________________.

2. Give an example of a modern day culture of honor.

3. Discuss briefly the general results of studies examining sexual jealousy in cultures of honor.

➢ Personal Causes of Aggression

1. Listed below are a variety of personal causes of aggression. Your job is to detail how and why these factors are associated with aggressive tendencies.

Personal cause of aggression	How and why it's associated with aggression
Type A behavior pattern	
Hostile aggression	
Instrumental aggression	
Hostile aggression bias	
Narcissism	

2. *Boys will be boys…or will they?* For each of the scenarios below, identify whether aggression is more likely to happen with respect to men, women, or equally in both.

a.) Situations where intense provocation is present: ____________________

b.) Direct aggression: ________________________

c.) Indirect aggression: ______________________

d.) Sexual coercion: _________________________

➢ Situational Determinants of Aggression: The Effects of High Temperature and Alcohol Consumption

1. In contrast to those who don't consume alcohol, those who consume substantial doses of alcohol have been found to ____ ____. Additionally, those individuals with relatively ________________ tendencies to aggress become more aggressive when intoxicated; those with relatively ______________________ tendencies to aggress become slightly less aggressive when intoxicated.

Aggression in Long-Term Relationships: Bullying and Workplace Violence

➢ Bullying: Singling out Others for Repeated Abuse

1. Compare and contrast the characteristics of bullies, bully/victims, and victims.

2. Identify some practical steps to reduce bullying, particularly in school settings.

➢ Workplace Violence: Aggression on the Job

1. What is the difference between workplace violence and workplace aggression?

2. For each of the following examples, identify the category of workplace aggression involved:

   a.) Patty simply throws out memos from Tina: ______________________________

   b.) Mark threw one of Tom's pictures off his desk in anger: __________________________

   c.) Polly is so disgusted by Anne's behavior that she talks behind her back whenever possible: _____________________________

3. When individuals feel that they've been treated unfairly by either others in their organization or the organization itself, they experience _________________________________ and often seek to ____. However, workplace aggression isn't a new or unique form of behavior; rather, it is ______________________ ____.

The Prevention and Control of Aggression: Some Useful Techniques

➢ Punishment: Just Desserts Versus Deterrence

1. In your own words, what is meant by "punishment?" Under what conditions will it succeed? Given these conditions, do you think the death penalty is a "good" punishment?

The Science of Social Psychology: Making Sense of Common Sense

➤ Catharsis: Does Getting It Out of Your System Really Help?

1. *Well, does it?* Explain what the catharsis hypothesis is and then consider whether getting it out of your system is helpful.

➤ Cognitive Interventions: Apologies and Overcoming Cognitive Deficits

1. Consider how and why apologies and other procedures that help us overcome cognitive deficits (such as preattribution) often prevent aggression.

➤ Other Techniques for Reducing Aggression: Training in Social Skills, and Incompatible Responses

1. Complete the chart below by noting how the following techniques may help to reduce or prevent aggression.

Technique	How it works
Exposure to nonaggressive models	

Social skills training	
The incompatible response technique	

After You Read . . .

Practice Test 1

1. The notion that aggression stemmed from a powerful death wish was proposed by
    a. Arnold Buss.
    b. Konrad Lorenz.
    c. Sigmund Freud.
    d. Stanley Milgram.

2. Evolutionary psychologists often conceptualize (male) aggression by highlighting the importance of
    a. eliminating potential rivals for certain mates.
    b. observational learning.
    c. showcasing one's physical strength in order to boost one's self-esteem.
    d. social norms.

3. One reason why the frustration-aggression hypothesis has turned out to be largely false is that
    a. frustration does not cause aggression.
    b. aggression stems from many causes other than frustration.
    c. inconsistent with this hypothesis, aggression causes frustration, but frustration doesn't cause aggression.
    d. the importance of frustration as a predictor of aggression was greatly underestimated.

4. In the general affective aggression model, there are ____ general types of variables that impact ____ basic processes.
    a. two; two
    b. three; three
    c. two; three
    d. three; two

5. The key difference between the methodology employed by Arnold Buss versus Stanley Milgram involved the purported use of shocks is that

a. Milgram's subjects actually administered "real" shocks to others whereas Buss' subjects did not.
b. Milgram incorporated the use of a "teacher" and a "learner" in his study whereas Buss did not.
c. Milgram did not give his subjects free choice about the shock level used whereas Buss did allow for free choice.
d. Milgram, not Buss, was primarily interested in studying aggression.

6. Bob says to his co-worker Mike, "I never liked you jerk!" This is an example of
   a. displaced aggression.
   b. instrumental aggression.
   c. hostile aggression.
   d. provocation.

7. After Mark was yelled at by his wife, he screamed at his daughter just as he left his house. This scenario illustrates
   a. displaced aggression.
   b. instrumental aggression.
   c. hostile aggression.
   d. provocation.

8. After viewing a news report featuring some disturbing images of violence in the Middle East, Mary says "That's too bad—but this is to be expected in the Middle East." Mary's statement depicts the effects of
   a. prejudice.
   b. desensitization.
   c. heightened arousal.
   d. priming.

9. A key aspect of excitation transfer theory is that
   a. we tend to act aggressively when we are in a bad mood.
   b. arousal produced in one situation can persist and intensify emotional reactions in later situations.
   c. when we are overly excited, we often exhibit aggression.
   d. attributions play an essential role in determining why we sometimes show aggression.

10. Priming with sexual stimuli tends to prime
   a. aggressive thoughts in men and women.
   b. aggressive thoughts in men only.
   c. aggressive behaviors in men only.
   d. aggressive thoughts and behaviors in men only

Practice Test 2

1. Type A individuals tend to be extremely
   a. hostile.
   b. conscientiousness.
   c. relaxed.
   d. anxious.

AGGRESSION

2. In contrast to Type B individuals, Type A individuals tend to show
   a. high levels of instrumental aggression.
   b. high levels of hostile aggression.
   c. high levels of instrumental and hostile aggression.
   d. high levels of hostile aggression and low levels of instrumental aggression.

3. Those with a hostile attributional bias are particularly apt to perceive hostile intentions in others' actions when these actions are ____.
   a. overtly aggressive
   b. ambiguous
   c. inconsequential
   d. repetitive

4. Gender differences in aggression appear to be fairly small when
   a. an individual reaches the age of fifty.
   b. an individual lives in a collectivistic society.
   c. direct aggression is involved.
   d. a provocation is present.

5. When a fight occurs in a bar, we should automatically assume that
   a. alcohol is the reason why the fight began.
   b. a factor other than alcohol caused the fight.
   c. alcohol is one of the many possible factors that contributed to the fight.
   d. the fight would not have occurred if these same individuals were in a restaurant that did not serve alcohol.

6. The hypothesis that heat increases aggression up to a point is known as the
   a. heat-aggression paradigm.
   b. temperature-anger hypothesis.
   c. negative-affect escape model.
   d. environmental-affect promotion model.

7. There tends to be a ____ relationship between heat and aggression in the ____.
   a. linear; daytime
   b. linear; night
   c. linear; day and night
   d. curvilinear; night

8. In discussing a case in which airplane passengers were trapped on the tarmac for several hours, your text authors make the point that
   a. it is inevitable that airplane travel will prime aggressive thoughts and behaviors.
   b. people can only be pushed so far before they aggress.
   c. functioning or living in extreme conditions inevitably produces aggression.
   d. individuals need to learn how to cope with difficult circumstances.

9. A defining characteristic of bullying behavior is that it only tends to occur with respect to

a. children.
b. individuals who know each other.
c. prison inmates.
d. adolescents.

10. It is fairly____ for a child to be a pure bully; also, bullying behavior tends to be found ____.
    a. uncommon; throughout the world
    b. common; throughout the world
    c. uncommon; in America only
    d. common; in America only

Practice Test 3

1. Suppose Mrs. Kerns, a fifth-grade teacher, notices two boys engaged in bullying behavior. Consequently, she should
   a. realize that bullying is a normal part of growing up.
   b. shrug off the behavior and simply conclude that "boys will be boys."
   c. quietly take the boys aside and ask them to cease their current behavior.
   d. bring in an outside expert to address the problem if she won't herself.

2. Workplace violence is relatively ____ and is often performed by ____.
   a. common; coworkers
   b. rare; coworkers
   c. common; outsiders
   d. rare; outsider
3. Since Leigh is so frustrated with her co-worker Susan, she decides to launch a "whisper campaign" against her. This is an example of
   a. overt aggression.
   b. obstructionism.
   c. an expression of hostility.
   d. bullying.

4. Workplace aggression is
   a. a new, unique form of behavior.
   b. simply aggression occurring in one type of setting.
   c. overly emphasized by the media.
   d. as frequent as workplace violence.

5. If a robber believes that he'll spend six months (at most) in jail for stealing money, then clearly the prospect of a punishment has failed to serve as a deterrent since it does *not* appear to be
   a. strong.
   b. certain.
   c. prompt.
   d. justified.

6. A layperson would tend to describe catharsis as
   a. turning inward.
   b. "holding it in."
   c. "doing your thing."
   d. "blowing off steam."

7. The catharsis hypothesis
   a. is largely correct.
   b. is partially correct.
   c. is inaccurate.
   d. remains to be tested by social psychologists.

8. Right before a faculty meeting, Iris tells one of her colleagues, "I just know that Myrna is going to explode at today's meeting—but that's just Myrna!" This example illustrates how ____ can prevent or reduce aggression.
   a. apologies
   b. preattribution
   c. repression
   d. distractions

9. Those who frequently show aggression often lack
   a. moral values.
   b. social skills.
   c. exposure to others who are aggressive.
   d. the intellectual capacity to understand why aggression is harmful.

10. In order to reduce Jake's anger, Jeff attempts to tell him a joke. Such an attempt illustrates the use of
   a. the incompatible response technique.
   b. cognitive dissonance.
   c. preattribution.
   d. anger-management training.

Comprehensive Test

(NOTE: Items 1-15 are multiple-choice questions and items 16-23 are true-false questions.)

1. Aggression is
   a. any physical harm-doing.
   b. intentional or unintentional harm-doing.
   c. inflicting harm upon others.
   d. an attitude favoring violence.

2. The instinct theory of aggression suggests that people are
   a. unlikely to engage in aggression.
   b. likely to fear aggression by instinct.
   c. biologically "programmed" for aggression.
   d. primed to learn aggression.

3. Freud believed that aggression
   a. results from the death instinct.
   b. is learned.
   c. is determined by external factors.
   d. tends to be overemphasized as a factor relating to human motivation.

4. The hypothesis that aggression increases with temperature up to a point and then drops often since it becomes uncomfortable is called the
   a. GAAM model.
   b. negative affect escape model.
   c. excitation transfer theory.
   d. drive theory of aggression.

5. Of the following, the condition that is *not* needed for punishment to deter aggression is for it to be
   a. following the aggressive act closely in time.
   b. viewed as justified by recipients.
   c. involving multiple punishments.
   d. strong.

6. Social psychologists have solved the problem of studying aggression in the laboratory by
   a. using an "aggression machine."
   b. accepting the necessity of hurting subjects.
   c. resigning themselves to study only verbal aggression.
   d. abandoning the laboratory study of aggression.

7. Suppose Henry is a Type A individual. As such, you would expect him to show all of the following characteristics, *except*
   a. hostile or irritable tendencies.
   b. always being in a hurry.
   c. being extremely competitive.
   d. insensitivity to social concerns.

8. An example of how the incompatible response technique might reduce aggression is
   a. hitting a punching bag.
   b. watching someone else be aggressive.
   c. thinking hostile thoughts.
   d. watching a funny movie.

9. The key problem with the frustration-aggression hypothesis is that frustration
   a. always leads to aggression.
   b. never leads to aggression.
   c. only intensifies aggression that is already present.
   d. can lead to other responses than aggression.

10. The main conclusion of how alcohol affects the aggressiveness of high versus low aggression individuals is that
    a. high and low aggressives increased their aggressiveness when they were intoxicated.

b. high aggressives increased their aggressiveness when they were intoxicated.
c. low aggressives increased their aggressiveness when they were intoxicated.
d. alcohol consumption has no effect on aggressiveness for either.

11. Watching violent scenes may
    a. lower aggressive tendencies.
    b. prime hostile thoughts.
    c. make one more sympathetic toward the victims of violent crime.
    d. raise or lower aggression, depending on the age of the viewer.

12. Feelings of low self-esteem and perceived control coupled with high levels of Machiavellianism are associated with
    a. bullies.
    b. victims.
    c. bully/victims.
    d. bystanders to bullying.

13. In order to prevent or minimize workplace violence, organizations should try to
    a. increase salaries as frequently as possible.
    b. subject all of their employees to rigorous criminal background checks at least twice a year.
    c. address any feelings of perceived unfairness that employees may have.
    d. encourage employees to regularly update managers about "troublesome" individuals.

14. The general theme of drive theories of aggression is that
    a. genetic factors primarily explain why aggression occurs.
    b. aggression stems from external conditions that arouse a strong motive to harm others.
    c. aggression occurs, since it has proven to be adaptive over the course of evolution.
    d. internal forces, free of any external influences, cause aggression.

15. An example of ____ factor that is a determinant of human aggression would be the words or deeds of others.
    a. social
    b. personal
    c. situational
    d. genetic

Questions 16-23 are True/False Questions

16. Munchausen's Syndrome is where people make themselves sick in order to get attention.

17. Forgiveness is an ineffective way for reducing aggression.

18. Research shows evidence that the "code of male honor" is especially strong in Latin America.

19. As a general rule, men always show more aggression than women.

20. A common apparatus used to measure aggression in experimental studies is the violence machine.

21. Chris has been hitting a punching bag at a gym in the hopes of "blowing off steam." As a result of this action, he should show a decrease in his overall level of aggression.

22 The frustration-aggression hypothesis is largely accepted as accurate by most contemporary social psychologists.

23. Even though a passerby in the supermarket didn't intend to knock into Ken's cart, Ken interprets this action as indicative of hostile intent. This scenario is *most* consistent with Type A behavior.

Short Answer/Essay Questions

1. **Theories of Aggression**
   State the two main categories of variables in the general affective aggression model and give a couple of examples of each.

2. **Personal Causes of Aggression**
   Define the three main characteristics of the Type A behavior pattern.

3. **Alcohol and Aggression**
   Discuss how alcohol affects aggression for those who are low or high aggressors.

4. **Aggression in the Workplace**
   Briefly describe the three major categories of aggression in the workplace.

5. **Preventing and Controlling Aggression**
   Pete's friend, Josh, is very angry over the fact that he got passed over for a promotion at his job. Pete is trying to reduce Josh's anger by telling him silly jokes about his boss. What type of technique is Pete using in order to lower Josh's level of anger? Will it be effective in reducing Josh's anger?

When You Have Finished . . .

Applications of the Concept of Aggression to Your Life

1. By understanding the nature of aggression and its causes, we are in a better position to try and prevent aggression as best as possible.

2. Inevitably though, it is often quite difficult to *not* get at least a bit upset over certain matters from time to time. By understanding some of the useful techniques to prevent and control aggression, we can try to prevent a little anger from becoming full-blown aggression.

3. We should mindful of the situational determinants of aggression and try to avoid these situational influences as much as possible.

4. We should be mindful of the personality-based determinants of aggression and, if we exhibit such characteristics (e.g., Type A behavior), then we should make a conscious effort to alter this aspect of our personality.

5. We should realize the particularly harmful effects of aggression in long-term relationships, particularly as it applies to bullying and workplace violence. In doing so, let us strive to make the workplace and the worlds of our children as pleasant as they possibly be.

Let's revisit point #5. Think back to your childhood and adolescence. Can you still identify which of your peers were bullies, bully/victims, or victims? In which category did *you* find yourself? Were the characteristics of these three types of individuals that you knew consistent with the characteristics of bullies, bully/victims, or victims as discussed in your text? Did anyone (e.g., a teacher or parent) help to end the bullying? Now, as a parent or a potential parent (in the years ahead), how do *you* think you would work to prevent bullying behavior with respect to your own children and their peers?

Internet Sites:

http://cagle.slate.msn.com/news/schoolshooting/: This site contains political cartoons about school shootings, along with discussion questions on the issue geared towards secondary school students.

http://www.drdriving.org: Excellent site on road rage by University of Hawaii psychologist Leon James, who has written extensively on this issue. Includes self-tests for road rage and a description of a program for decreasing it.

http://www.theatlantic.com/issues/98aug/roadrage.htm: See this for a site critical of whether there is actually an increase in road rage; argues that the increase is a media fabrication.

http://www.media-awareness.ca/eng/med/home/resource/famvlnc.htm: contains the text of an article, "The Effects of Media Violence on Children," written by Dr. Jane Ledingham for The National Clearinghouse on Family Violence. Of particular interest are the sections on what parents can do.

http://www.apa.org/pubinfo/violence.html: provides a similar article, on the APA's public information site.
http://exn.ca/Stories/1998/06/16/55.asp contains an article that discusses several instigators of riots at sporting events, including deindividuation.

Crossword Puzzle

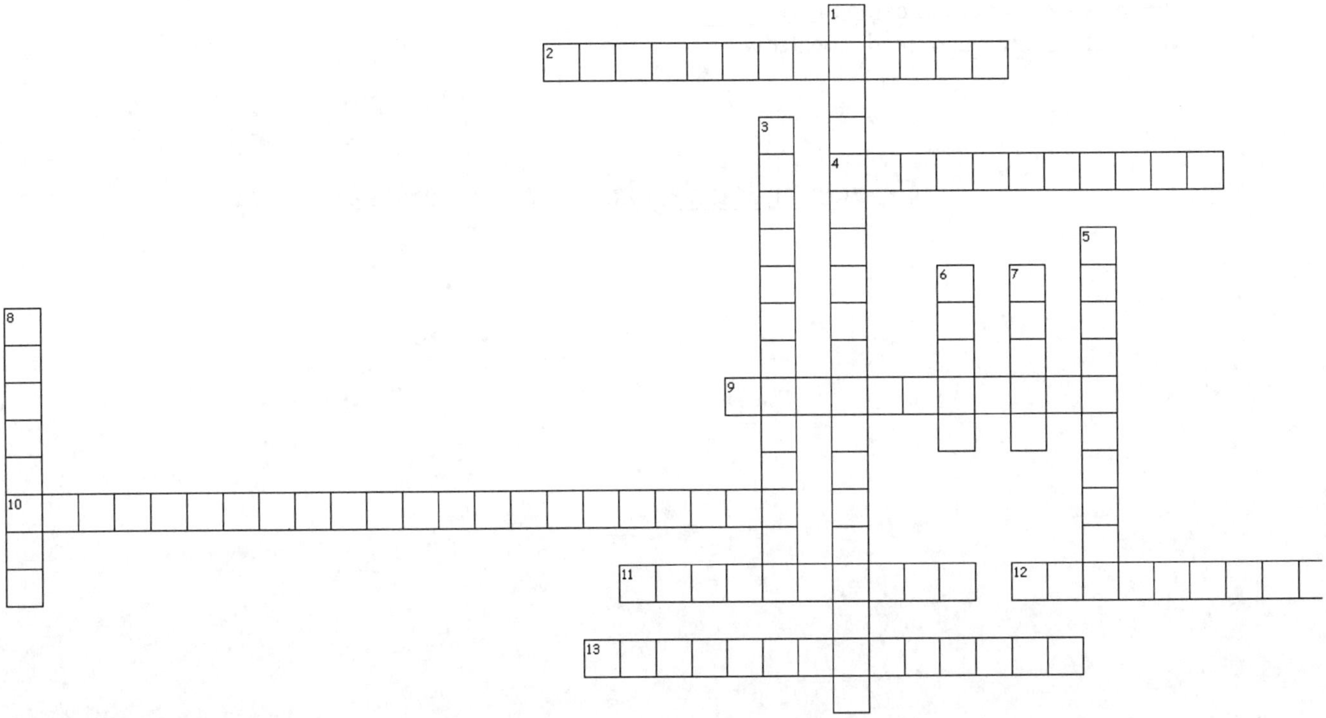

Across

2. theories suggesting that aggression stems from external conditions
4. actions that trigger aggression
9. reconciliation
10. goal to be aggressive to obtain something of value
11. behavior with goal of harming another

12. expressing angry impulses
13. culture where norms say aggression is ok to defend one's honor

Down

1. violence in the workplace
3. depictions of violent actions in the media
5. aversive consequences delivered
6. a behavior pattern of absence of Type A patterns
7. a behavior pattern of competitiveness
8. target person is assaulted repeatedly

Created by Puzzlemaker at DiscoverySchool.com

12 GROUPS AND INDIVIDUALS: THE CONSEQUENCES OF BELONGING

Before You Read . . .

In this chapter, you'll have a good understanding of various examples of groups and how they function through the use of roles, status, norms, and cohesiveness. You'll also note how groups can affect individual performance—for better or worse—as a function of social facilitation or social loafing. As you likely know from personal examples, groups can choose to cooperate or show conflict. This chapter will explore the consequences of both of these choices with a particular emphasis on conflict and how it can be resolved. You'll also have a better understanding of why perceived fairness is of the utmost importance in groups. This chapter concludes with a discussion of group decision-making processes. Interestingly enough, such processes can produce disastrous outcomes for those involved; the discussion of group polarization and groupthink makes this particular point very clear. The chapter will then end with various techniques to improve the decision making process.

Chapter Objectives

After reading this chapter, you should be able to:

- Define what is meant by a "group" and the role that entiativity plays in studying groups.
- Identify how roles, status, norms, and cohesiveness allow a group to function.
- Define what is meant by "social facilitation" and provide a detailed overview of how this topic has been studied throughout social psychology's history.
- Explain why social loafing occurs and ways to reduce it.
- Contrast the terms, "cooperation" and "conflict."
- Explain the dynamics of a social dilemma.
- Discuss how reciprocity, personal orientations, communication, and the discontinuity effect may influence the occurrence of cooperation.
- Identify the basic nature and causes of conflict, as well as ways to reduce it.

- Explain the importance of perceived fairness in groups and, in doing so, identify and describe the three main categories of justice. Also, consider how we react to feelings of perceived unfairness.
- Outline some of the social decision schemes that a group may decide to pursue.
- Discuss the nature and consequences of group polarization.
- Discuss the nature, underlying causes, and consequences of groupthink.
- Consider how and why the devil's advocate technique and authentic dissent may improve group decisions.

As You Read . . .

Important Terms to Know... Below are a list of some of the key terms and concepts from this chapter. Make flashcards in order to enhance your recall ability of these terms. Refer to the definitions that are either in boldface or in the margins of this chapter for help. You may also want to include additional terms from this chapter as you deem necessary.

Group	Entiativity	Four distinct categories of groups
Roles	Status	Norms
Cohesiveness	Depersonalized attraction	Social facilitation
Drive theory of social facilitation	Evaluation apprehension	Distraction-conflict theory
Additive tasks	Social loafing	The collective effort model
Expectancy-valence theory	Cooperation	Conflict
Social (Prisoner's) dilemma	Reciprocity	The discontinuity effect
Status quo bias	Bargaining	Integrative agreements and tactics to achieve these
Superordinate goals	Perceived unfairness	Distributive, procedural, and interactional justice
Social decision schemes and specific examples of them	Normative social vs. Informational social influence	Group polarization
Groupthink	Biased processing	The devil's advocate technique
Authentic dissent		

Groups: Why We Join....And Why We Leave

➢ Groups: Some Basic Aspects

1. Word find! Time for another really fun exercise...Use the clues below to find the words below. Look up, down, and diagonally. When you find the relevant word, write it next to the clue.

C	O	H	E	S	I	V	E	N	E	S	S
R	A	B	E	P	L	C	N	A	A	B	T
I	N	L	U	P	R	N	T	C	S	Z	A
R	O	O	A	N	G	A	I	I	U	O	T
R	R	L	S	T	U	I	A	P	G	Q	U
G	M	A	E	C	Y	P	T	P	O	S	S
S	S	N	V	S	J	I	I	J	W	Y	C
M	I	G	K	L	P	V	V	F	R	A	T
U	E	E	C	A	K	I	I	R	O	L	L
S	T	R	A	K	S	T	T	S	Y	C	H
I	N	T	I	M	A	C	Y	S	O	O	P

Clues:
1. A collection of persons believed to be bonded together in some way.
2. The extent to which a group is perceived as a coherent entity.
3. Family relationships often comprise this group.
4. Behaviors that individuals are expected to perform in a group.
5. Position or rank within a group.
6. Showing calm expressions of this emotion may enhance one's standing in a group.
7. Rules within a group about how to behave.
8. All forces that keep members in a group.

➢ The Benefits—and Costs—of Joining

1. List three benefits to joining a group

   a. ____________________

   b. ____________________

   c. ____________________

2. Discuss some reasons that groups splinter.

Beyond the Headlines: As Social Psychologists See It

➢ Groups to Die For?

1. Discuss how sorority hazing increases an individual's commitment to the group.

Effects of the Presence of Others: From Task Performance to Behavior in Crowds

1. Explain how social facilitation was studied by Allport over eighty years ago.

2. Explain the basis of the distraction-conflict theory.

➢ Social Loafing: Letting Others Do the Work

1. In your own words, define the terms, "additive tasks" and "social loafing."

2. How does the collective effort model explain why social loafing occurs?

3. Identify the five conditions when social loafing effects will be the weakest, as well as practical ways to reduce social loafing.

Coordination in Groups: Cooperation or Conflict?

➢ Cooperation: Working With Others To Achieve Shared Goals

1. Contrast the patterns of behavior shown with respect to cooperation and conflict.

2. Explain what is meant by a "social dilemma." Also, identify the possible steps that a person can take under such a condition.

3. State the three key factors that influence cooperation.

➢ Social Dilemmas: Situations in Which Cooperation Could Occur, But Often Doesn't

1. Explain the basis of the Prisoner's Dilemma.

➢ Factors Influencing Cooperation

1. List three factors that influence whether cooperation will occur in a situation.

➢ Conflict: Its Nature, Causes, and Effects

1. State the four key elements in conflict.

2. Complete the chart below by listing the four main causes and characteristics of conflict.

Factor	Characteristics

➢ Resolving Conflicts: Some Useful Techniques

1. Discuss the role of bargaining and superordinate goals in resolving conflicts.

Perceived Fairness in Groups: Its Nature and Effects

1. Match it! Match each phrase, word, or sentence on the left side of the page with an identifying concept on the right side of the page. Note that each item on the right should be used *only once*.

___1. Individual judgment as to whether they've received their fair share of rewards	A. procedural justice
___2. Fair procedures used to distribute available rewards	B. interactional justice
___3. Courtesy shown by those who distribute rewards	C. distributive justice

2. Suppose you received a "D" on a paper for which you were expecting at least a "B" and decide to speak with your professor about this matter. Under what conditions would you probably *not* feel a sense of interactional justice?

➢ Reactions to Perceived Unfairness: Tactics for Dealing with Injustice

1. Summarize how the issue of perceived unfairness factors into romantic relationships, particularly marriages.

Decision Making by Groups: How It Occurs and the Pitfalls It Faces

➢ The Decision-Making Process: How Groups Attain Consensus

1. In your own words, define "decision making."

2. Name that social decision scheme! Actually, first define a "social decision scheme:"

Now, consider the following hypothetical scenarios and identify the social decision scheme under use:

a.) After a group has been deadlocked as how to resolve the company's financial matter, a member simply says "Why don't we just cut back on our spending?" At that point, the group agrees to go with this suggestion.

b.) After spending many days arguing which job candidate should get the job position, a group member says "Listen, the majority of us felt that Jeff was the best candidate from the outset of our discussions, so I say we go with Jeff." After hearing this statement, the committee decides to offer the job to Jeff.

c.) After Anna suggests to her colleagues that it is important to reconsider her company's dress code, more and more members of her group agree with this position.

3. Explain how normative and informational social influence can cause individuals to go along with the group.

The Science of Social Psychology: Making Sense of Common Sense

➢ <u>Are Groups Really Less Likely Than Individuals To "Go Over the Edge"?</u>

1.a. Suppose a group of war veterans get together for their monthly meeting. They begin discussing their views on whether America is too involved in worldwide affairs. Their average view is represented by an "X" below. After they're done talking, place an "X" on the scale that will likely represent their average view on this issue once they're done talking.

1	5	X 10
America is too involved	Moderate	America isn't involved enough

b. Name and define the phenomenon that the above example illustrates. Why does it occur?

➢ Potential Dangers of Group Decision Making: Groupthink, Biased Processing, and Restricted Sharing of Information

1. What is "groupthink" and why does it occur? Identify at least two ways that faulty group decision making, such as groupthink, can be avoided and improved.

After You Read . . . Practice Tests

Practice Test 1

1. A collection of persons who are perceived to be bonded together in a coherent unit are called a(n)
   a. group.
   b. class.
   c. chunked unit.
   d. organization.

2. Of the following, ____ are considered to have the *least* amount of entiativity.
   a. people attending an athletic contest
   b. people in line at a bank
   c. members of a labor union
   d. women

3. Matthew is a Jewish-American who belongs to a certain synagogue. The type of group to which he belongs would be classified as a(n) ____.
   a. intimacy group
   b. weak social relationship
   c. task-oriented group
   d. social category

4. Harry belongs to an astronomy society where he is the co-president. As such, he appears to have much ____ within the group.
   a. status
   b. role conflict
   c. cohesiveness
   d. norm-related behavior

5. Adherence to norms within a group often leads to
   a. decreased cohesiveness.
   b. role conflict.
   c. increased status.
   d. profound difficulties for the group.

6. A key reason why cohesiveness develops in groups is due to
   a. genuine liking.
   b. destructive obedience.
   c. depersonalized attraction.
   d. the lack of external threats.

7. Early research by Allport (1920) found that when others were present, performance was
   a. enhanced.
   b. weakened.
   c. unchanged.
   d. enhanced only if the individual personally knew the other individuals who were present.

8. According to Zajonc's drive theory of social facilitation, the main reason why social facilitation occurs is due to
   a. social desirability concerns.
   b. self-efficacy.
   c. a desire to show off in front of others.
   d. arousal generated from the mere presence of others.

9. Zajonc and colleagues (1969) found that ____ were more able to complete a ____ maze when in the presence of other ____.
   a. roaches; simple; roaches
   b. roaches; complex; roaches
   c. college students; simple; college students
   d. college students; complex; college students

10. Distraction-conflict theory suggests that audiences produce social facilitation effects only when
    a. we believe that we are being critically judged by them.
    b. directing attention to them conflicts in some way with task demands.
    c. we feel unprepared to perform.
    d. it is in our own best interest to do so.

Practice Test 2

1. The end result of working with others on a project, rather than working individually, is that working with others tends to cause individuals to
   a. work harder.
   b. purposely create problems.
   c. make errors.
   d. reduce their effort.

2. Social loafing effects tend to *not* occur with respect to ____.
   a. men
   b. women
   c. individualistic cultures
   d. collectivistic cultures

3. ____ refers to a belief that better performance will be recognized and rewarded.
   a. Expectancy
   b. Instrumentality
   c. Valence
   d. Justice

4. Anthony owns a construction company and has noticed a great deal of social loafing. He can reduce this by
   a. making the output of each person readily identifiable.
   b. minimizing group members' commitment to successful task performance.
   c. downplaying the relative importance of a task.
   d. emphasizing that each workers' task is not unique.

5. All of the following terms are associated with the concept of conflict, *except*
   a. process.
   b. incompatible.
   c. negative results.
   d. shared.

6. In the prisoner's dilemma, the greatest risk for a given individual occurs when the individual ____ action and his or her counterpart ____ takes action.
   a. does not; does not
   b. does; does
   c. does not; does
   d. does; does not

7. Reciprocal altruism appears to have ____ evolutionary benefits.
   a. great
   b. minimal
   c. no
   d. negative

8. When available resources are increased so that both sides can obtain their major goals this is referred to as
   a. logrolling
   b. broadening the pie
   c. bridging
   d. cost cutting

9. Suppose Sally is facing a social dilemma of some sort and she focuses primarily on defeating others. Consequently, she appears to have a ____ orientation.
   a. competitive
   b. vindictive
   c. cooperative
   d. individualistic

10. The discontinuity effect refers to the
   a. greater tendency for groups instead of individuals to compete in mixed-motive situations.
   b. greater tendency for individuals instead of groups to compete in mixed-motive situations.
   c. general tendency for a consortium to show intergroup cooperation.
   d. finding that intragroup and intergroup cooperation is equally likely to occur.

Practice Test 3

1. The key elements of conflict include all of the following, *except*
   a. opposing interests between individuals or groups.
   b. recognition of opposition by relevant parties.
   c. the belief by each side that the other will act to interfere with these interests.
   d. the lack of specific actions that produce interferences for the parties.

2. Suppose Harriet dislikes Roz since she believes that Roz thwarted her efforts to get a raise at work. The major source of conflict in this case is likely
   a. a faulty attribution.
   b. faulty communication.
   c. the status quo bias.
   d. Harriet's Type A behavior.

3. The ____ tactic for reaching integrative agreements involves increasing available resources so that both sides can obtain their major goals.
   a. logrolling
   b. broadening the pie
   c. bridging
   d. cost cutting

4. Superordinate goals tend to
   a. create conflict.
   b. allow opposing groups to find a way to end their conflict by considering mutual interests.
   c. highlight differences between groups.
   d. hinder overt cooperation.

5. Heather decided to complain to her college dean about the manner in which her professor decided to handle grades in her class. As such, she appears to be *most* concerned with ____.
   a. distributive justice
   b. procedural justice
   c. interpersonal justice
   d. equitable justice

6. In marriages, perceived unfairness is
   a. the result of marital conflict (only).
   b. the cause of marital conflict (only).
   c. a potential result and cause of marital conflict.
   d. only of concern for women.

7. Suppose Joe is considered to be a "maverick" who won't follow the group's general views. In order to try to bring Joe into line, one of the group members presents data that supposedly contradicts Joe's beliefs. In this example, ____ is being used in order to attain consensus.
   a. informational social influence
   b. normative social influence
   c. the first-shift rule
   d. the truth-wins rule

8. ____ has (have) contributed to major historical blunders or disasters.
   a. Only group polarization
   b. Only groupthink
   c. Group polarization and groupthink
   d. Neither group polarization nor groupthink

9. If a jury was engaged in biased processing, then its members were likely
   a. attempting to ascertain whether any of the witnesses had a bias of some sort.
   b. refusing to comply with the judge's order.
   c. processing information in ways that allowed them to reach the decision they wanted.
   d. exhibiting groupthink.

10. Suppose Kathy says that she profoundly disagrees with the strategy that her co-workers appear to be in favor of adopting. Assuming that she wasn't instructed to make such a disagreement, her behavior illustrates ____.
    a. groupthink.
    b. the devil's advocate technique.
    c. authentic dissent.
    d. group polarization.

Comprehensive Test

(NOTE: Items 1-15 are multiple-choice questions and items 16-23 are true-false questions.)

1. Tom, Mary, and Sue are all part of a group where they are expected to accomplish different tasks for the group. This illustrates the importance of ____ in groups.
   a. status
   b. norms
   c. roles
   d. cohesiveness

2. If group members like each other and are united in pursuit of the group's goals, they are expressing a high amount of ____.
   a. cohesiveness
   b. groupthink
   c. interpersonal attraction
   d. cooperation

3. According to Zajonc's drive theory of social facilitation, the presence of others produces an increase in
   a. confidence.
   b. self-motivated interest.
   c. arousal.
   d. empathy.

4. Which of the following statements *best* describes social loafing?
   a. When people are doing a task, they work harder when getting paid for it.
   b. When people are doing a task, they work harder when it's their own project than one they've been assigned.
   c. When people work together on a joint task, each member exerts less effort than when they work alone.
   d. When people are doing a task, they work harder when being watched.

5. Judgments of distributive justice require that individuals perceive fairness in the
   a. procedures used to divide rewards among group members.
   b. considerateness and courtesy shown by those who divide available rewards.
   c. ratio of contributions to outcomes for themselves and for others in the group.
   d. outcomes they personally receive without regard to what others get.

6. ____ pertains to the considerateness and courtesy shown to group members by those responsible for distributing available awards.
   a. Distributive justice
   b. Procedural justice
   c. Interpersonal justice
   d. Equitable justice

7. The ____ rule suggests that the correct solution will ultimately be accepted by the group as its correctness is recognized by more and more members.
   a. social-comparison
   b. truth-wins
   c. majority-wins
   d. first-shift

8. Suppose a group composed of individuals who moderately approve of gambling get together to exchange their shared views. Group polarization would predict that after some discussion their views will likely be
   a. more extreme than the views they initially held.
   b. less extreme than the views they initially held.
   c. no different than the views they initially held.
   d. quite divided.

9. All of the following are determinants of groupthink, *except*
   a. leadership that is concerned with hearing all group members' views.
   b. a high level of cohesiveness among group members.
   c. pressure to maintain a high level of group consensus.
   d. group norms preventing a consideration of alternate courses of action.

10. Research on the pooling of information during group decision making suggests that group members are more likely to discuss ____ information and that this tendency ____ that groups will make the best decisions.
    a. shared; assures
    b. shared; jeopardizes
    c. unshared; assures
    d. unshared; jeopardizes

11. Situations where individuals can potentially enhance their own individual outcomes by acting in a particular way are referred to as ____.
    a. social dilemmas.
    b. negative frames.
    c. reciprocal conflicts.
    d. incompatible bargains.

12. ____ is a basic rule of social life suggesting that individuals tend to return the kind of treatment they have previously received from others.
    a. Cooperation
    b. Framing
    c. Distributive justice
    d. Reciprocity

13. When we believe that a group is ____ in entiativity, we tend to compare the group members with ____.
    a. low; each other
    b. high; each other
    c. low; other groups
    d. high; each other

14. It is often possible to acquire social status within a group by displaying
    a. indifference.
    b. sadness.
    c. overt rage.
    d. quiet anger.

15. All of the following are examples of ethically questionable ways to resolve conflict, *except*
    a. attacking an opponent's network.
    b. misrepresentation.
    c. making false promises.
    d. adopting superordinate goals.

Questions 16-23 are True/False Questions.

16. Logrolling is where each party makes concessions on low-priority issues in exchange for concessions on issues it values more highly.

17. Distributive justice pertains to whether a person believes that he or she has been treated fairly in a group and with courtesy and considerateness.

18. An additive task refers to group members' contributions combined into a single group output.

19. Social loafing is enhanced when a person works with others he or she doesn't respect.

20. The rules within a group telling members how they should behave are called roles.

21. Suppose a group of conservatives get together to talk about a host of issues. At the conclusion of their discussions, they find that their views have become even more conservative. This example illustrates groupthink.

22. The social decision scheme that serves to strengthen the initially most popular view is the truth-wins rule.

23. Groupthink has *not* been shown to have any negative consequences with respect to major, historical decisions.

Short Answer/Essay Questions

1. **How Groups Function**
   Briefly outline the four key factors that allow groups to function.

2. **Social Loafing**
   Provide an overview of the key predictions from expectancy-valence theory.

3. **Conflict**
   State and describe three major social factors that play an important role in terms of causing conflict.

4. **Judgments of Fairness**
   The Dean at a public university rewards faculty with pay bonuses as a function to each individual's contributions to the school. What type of justice does this example *best* illustrate?

5. **Decision-Making Processes**
   State and define three social decision schemes.

When You Have Finished . . .

Applications of the Study of Groups to Your Life

1. Virtually all of us at any given point in our lives is part of a group, whether it be at work, school, as part of a sports team, or a myriad of other possibilities. As such, we should all be interested in how to make these interactions as productive and pleasant as possible for all parties concerned.

2. Sometimes groups make devastating inaccurate decisions, often as a result of groupthink or group polarization. By being aware of these pitfalls, *you* may be in a position to help steer your particular group away from such faulty decisions.

3. Unfortunately, conflict often arises in groups—but it doesn't have to be a reality. The next time you face a conflict within or between groups, consider using some of the techniques outlined in your text.

4. Even though social loafing is quite common, there are ways to lessen its occurrence. The next time you have a group project of some sort, keep in mind some of the tips for reducing social loafing as discussed in your text.

5. Since we often have to make presentations or performances to others, try to use the research on social facilitation to *your* advantage by noting when and how to maximize your performance.

Revisit points #3 and 4 by thinking about previous or current group situations involving conflict or social loafing that you've experienced. To what degree where the techniques outlined in your text helpful in dealing with these problems or issues?

Internet Sites:

http://www.vcu.edu/hasweb/group/gdynamic.htm: The Group Dynamics Resource Page developed by Donelson Forsyth. Excellent set of links to information and illustrations of group dynamics and to group dynamics activities on the Web. See particularly the link to activities from Forsyth's own *Group Dynamics* text.

http://www.vcu.edu/hasweb/group/trip.htm: Information on Triplett's first social psychology experiment and the work on social facilitation that followed.

http://serendip.brynmawr.edu/playground/pd.html: Gold coin version of prisoner's dilemma.

http://www.miskatonic.org/pd.html. Standard version of prisoner's dilemma. Also see *http://www.miskatonic.org/pd-resources.html,* an attached page with more resources and links about the prisoner's dilemma listed.

http://orgs.bloomu.edu/values/DillemaStires.htm. Summary of the commons dilemma including some brief suggestions on solutions.

http://www.uiowa.edu/~grpproc: This website will connect you to the Center for the Study of Group Processes in the Sociology Department at the University of Iowa, Iowa City.

Crossword Puzzle

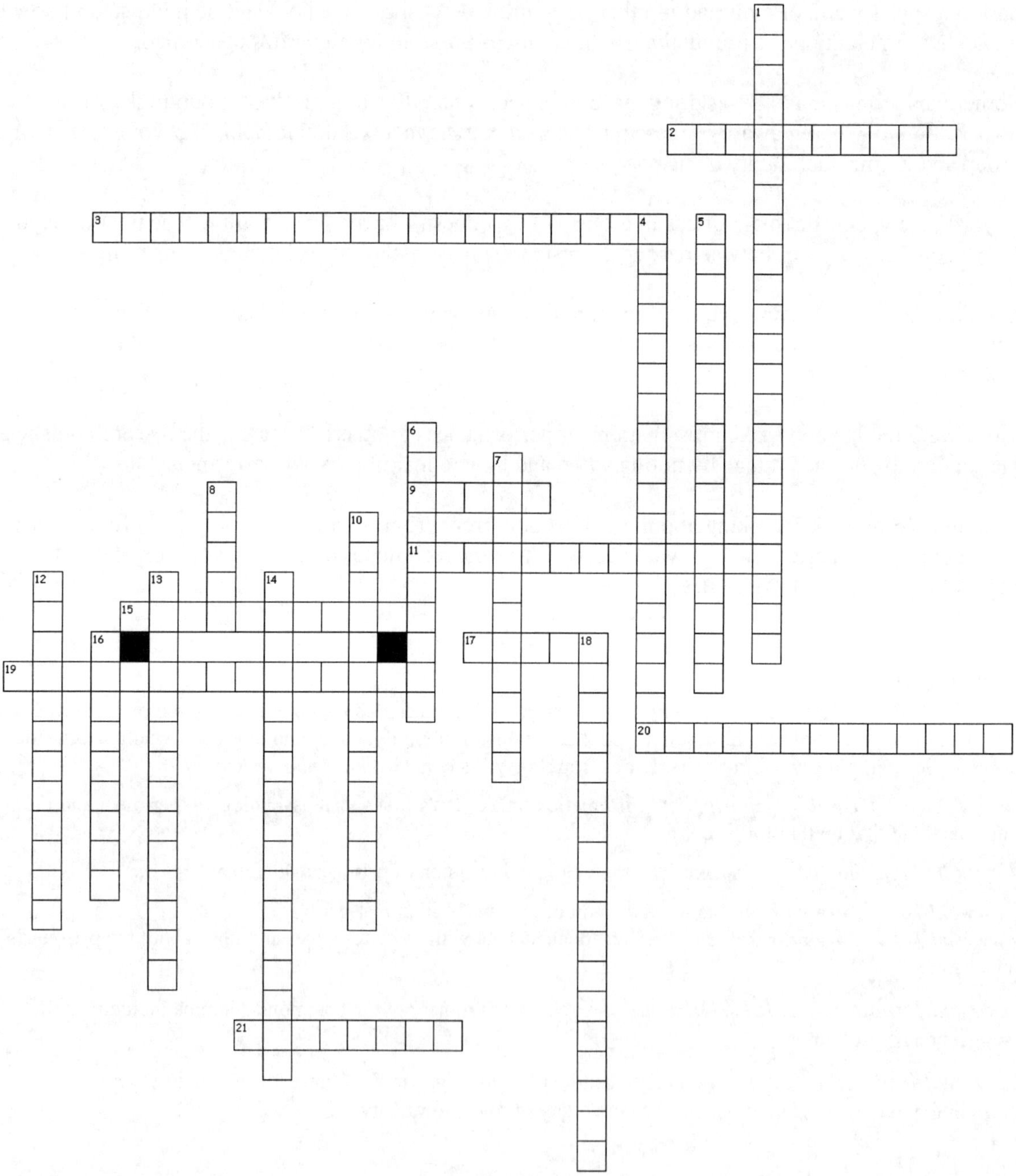

GROUPS AND INDIVIDUALS

Across

2. group assuming that their decisions are not wrong
3. fairness
9. behaviors for people in certain positions
11. group product is the sum
15. groups working together
17. rules within a group
19. reduced social identity
20. reduction of motivation when in a group
21. incompatibility in a group

Down

1. concern of being evaluated
4. mutual group goals
5. improving quality of group decisions
6. negotiation
7. giving back
8. collection of persons bonded together
10. integrating information to choose course of action
12. tightness of a group
13. increasing individual gains by behavior
14. group shifting toward extreme position
16. perception of group as coherent entity
18. performance effected by others

Created by Puzzlemaker at DiscoverySchool.com
http://school.discovery.com/

Modules A and B

SOCIAL PSYCHOLOGY IN ACTION: APPLICATIONS TO LAW, HEALTH, WORK SETTINGS, AND ENTREPRENEURSHIP

Before You Read . . .

Modules A and B look at how social psychological research has been applied to four "real world" areas: law, health, work settings and entrepreneurship. In Module A you will first consider some central issues to forensic psychology, which has to do with the psychological study of legal issues. For instance, you'll have a good understanding of why sometimes the outcome of a trial is greatly determined by what happens *before* the trial ever begins. You'll also understand why eyewitness testimony is often faulty and how it can be improved. A discussion of how the central participants of a trial (i.e., judges, attorneys, jurors, and defendants) help to shape the verdict will also featured. After that, you'll be exposed to the fascinating and ever-developing field of health psychology. As part of this discussion, you'll find out about the factors that shape our responses to health-related information and how to deal with the harmful effects of stress and obesity. In Module B, you will consider the field of industrial/organizational psychology and entrepreneurship. You will learn that industrial/organizational psychology examines the psychology of organizations and the workplace. Topics such as job satisfaction, why we show helpful behaviors at work, and various styles and characteristics of leadership will be discussed. And finally, you will be introduced to the social psychology of entrepreneurship and why some entrepreneurs are just more successful than others.

The Objectives of Module A and B

After reading the two modules, you should be able to:

- Identify and contrast the issues studied by a legal, health, and industrial-organizational psychologist.
- Outline the effects that police procedures (including interrogations leading to the "recovery" of repressed memories) and the media may have on the general impact of a trial before it begins.
- Consider why eyewitness testimony is often faulty and identify ways to improve such recall.
- Consider how certain tactics and behaviors by attorneys and judges may influence a jury.
- Identify some of the key characteristics of defendants and jurors that help to predict how a juror

may vote in a court case.

- Discuss how we may respond to health-related information.
- Provide an overview of the physical and psychological consequences of stress.
- Contrast the disease-prone personality with the self-healing personality.
- Answer the question, "Can a happy person reduce the odds of catching a cold?"
- Describe how increased fitness, positive emotions and regulatory control, and social support can help individuals cope with stress.
- Understand the social and situational factors that contribute to obesity.
- Contrast some of the key organizational and personal factors that seem to predict job satisfaction.
- Define what is meant by "organizational citizenship behavior" and why it occurs.
- Discuss the great person theory of leadership and identify some of the key characteristics of leaders.
- Contrast the two basic dimensions of leader behavior.
- Compare and contrast the following leadership styles: transformational, democratic, autocratic, laissez-faire, and transactional.
- Understand the role that social, cognitive and personal factors play in encouraging individuals to become an entrepreneur.
- List factors that increase the likelihood that an individual will be a successful entrepreneur.

SOCIAL PSYCHOLOGY IN ACTION

As You Read . . .

Important Terms to Know... Below are a list of some of the key terms and concepts from this chapter. Make flashcards in order to enhance your recall ability of these terms. Refer to the definitions that are either in boldface or in the margins of this chapter for help. You may also want to include additional terms from this chapter as you deem necessary.

Forensic psychology	Repressed memory/psychogenic amnesia	Eyewitness testimony and factors that influence its accuracy
Blank-lineup control	Voir dire	Leading questions
Need for cognition	Examples of juror characteristics	Health psychology
Positively vs. negatively framed message	Unrealistic optimism/optimistic bias	Social-image concern
Stress	Coping	Psychoneuroimmunology
Secretory immunoglobulin A	Disease-prone vs. self-healing personality	Fitness and obesity
Emotion- vs. problem-solving coping	Regulatory control	Social support
Industrial/organizational psychology	Job satisfaction	Organizational commitment
Core self-evaluations	Affective temperament	Organizational citizenship behavior
Leadership	The great person theory	The traits of leaders
The Big Five dimensions of personality	Initiating structure	Consideration
Transformational leaders and their characteristics	The three leadership styles identified by Lewin and colleagues	Transactional leaders
Mental contamination	Inquisitorial approach	Adversarial approach
Hassles scale	Nonjudgmental social support	Perfectionism

Module A

Social Psychology and the Legal System

➢ Before the Trial Begins: Effects of Police Interrogation

1. In your own words, discuss the issues considered by a "forensic psychologist."

2. How do detectives go about the interrogation process?

3. When we try to remember any event or past experience, the result is ______________________________

   ____.

4. When telling their stories to the police, suspects and witnesses have three expectations about the police officers' expectations. Name these!

5. Explain what is meant by a "repressed memory" and "psychogenic amnesia." Do you think we can ever truly forget an event?

6. Even though most crime rates have dropped in the United.States, people still claim great concern about being a victim of crime. What might account for this fear?

7. Summarize what typically occurs when a criminal case receives a lot of pretrial publicity.

➢ Eyewitnesses: Are They as Accurate as We'd Like to Believe?

1. It's debate time again! Listed below are a series of points. Your job is to refute these points by offering your own counterpoint.

Point: *Eyewitness testimony is fairly accurate.*

Counterpoint:

Point: *Eyewitness testimony is only inaccurate is when a person has a reason to lie.*

Counterpoint:

Point: *There are very few factors that influence eyewitness accuracy.*

Counterpoint:

Point: *Experienced police officers can easily identify a suspect accused of committing a crime caught on videotape.*

Counterpoint:

Point: *There simply is nothing that can be done about increasing the accuracy of eyewitness testimony.*

Counterpoint:

➢ Key Participants in a Trial: Effects of Attorneys, Defendants, and Jurors

1. Explain the voir dire procedure.

2. Define a "leading question" and when these are allowed to be asked. In reality though, does this always happen the way it should according to the law?

3. A juror with ______________________________________ may *not* always follow a judge's orders to ignore certain parts of courtroom testimony.

4. Discuss how jurors tend to respond when they believe that the judge feels a defendant is guilty versus innocent.

5. Create a list of key juror and defendant characteristics and the impact these have on the verdict.

Juror or Defendant Characteristic?	Description of Characteristic	Impact on Verdict

Social Psychology and Personal Health

1. Health psychology is ____

____.

2 Match it! Match each phrase, word, or sentence on the left side of the page with an identifying concept on the right side of the page. Note that each item on the right should be used *only once.*

___1. Concerns about what others think may color processing of health information	A. positively framed message
___2. Effective in motivating detection behavior message	B. negatively framed message
___3. Associated with ignoring health messages	C. social-image concern
___4. Effective in motivating preventive behavior	D. optimistic bias

➢ Stress: Its Causes, Effects, and Control

1. In your own words, what does it mean to "cope with stress?"

2. Complete this chart by listing: a) events that could cause stress, b) the psychological effects of stress, and c) the physiological consequences of stress.

Stressful events	Psychological effects	Physiological effects

3. Compare and contrast the differences between the self-healing and disease-prone personality.

➢ Coping with Stress

1. Suppose Steve is so stressed about his work that he feels like he is the target for criticism from his boss at any moment as depicted in the picture below. Outline ways he can cope with his stress by discussing the role of increased fitness, emotion- and problem-focused coping, social support, and any other ways that may be beneficial to reducing his (or your) stress level.

➢ Personal Characteristics and Health: Hostility, Perfectionism, and Socioeconomic Status

1. Briefly describe three personal characteristics that can lead to increased stress.

Beyond the Headlines: Sick of the Sniffles? Put on a Happy Face

➢ Can Being A Happy Person Reduce the Odds of Catching a Cold?

1. Summarize some of the research evidence that suggests that having a happy personality can reduce the likelihood of catching a cold.

➢ The Rising Tide of Obesity: A Social-Psychological Perspective

1. Describe some of the social and situational factors that contribute to obesity.

2. List three tactics to turn the tide on unhealthy eating habits.

Module B

Work-Related Attitudes: The Nature and Effects of Job Satisfaction

1. Discuss the issues of concern to an industrial/organizational psychologist.

2. List some organizational and personal factors related to job satisfaction.

3. Why do your text authors conclude "some individuals have a tendency to express either relatively high or relatively low levels of job satisfaction *no matter where they work*?"

Beyond the Headlines: As Social Psychologists See It

➢ When Employees No Longer Care: Effects of Low Job Satisfaction

1. Describe some of the tactics and software that are available to employees so it appears that they are working hard when they are actually not.

➢ The Nature of Prosocial Behavior at Work: Some Basic Forms

1. What is "organizational citizenship behavior."

2. List some factors that influence organizational citizenship behavior.

➢ Leadership: Influence in Group Settings

1. What is the great person theory of leadership? What characteristics do leaders possess? Which of these are the *most* important?

2. List the Big Five dimensions of personality and explain what each of these dimensions has to do with leadership.

3. Complete the following chart by listing the key characteristics associated with an initiating structure, consideration, and transformational leadership.

Initiating structure	Consideration	Transformational leadership

The Social Psychology of Entrepreneurship

➤ Why Do Some Persons Become Entrepreneurs? The Role of Social, Cognitive, and Personal Factors

1. Briefly describe the effect of modeling or observational learning on becoming an entrepreneur.

2. List three personality factors and two cognitive factors that influence an individual's desire to become an entrepreneur.

After You Read . . . Practice Tests

Practice Test 1

The applied psychological area that focuses on legal issues is known as
   a. forensic psychology.
   b. industrial-organizational psychology.
   c. environmental psychology.
   d. community psychology.

2. Police detectives appear to be
   a. chiefly concerned with gathering facts.
   b. chiefly concerned with obtaining a confession.
   c. equally concerned with gathering facts and obtaining a confession.
   d. divided about whether it is more important to gather facts or obtain a confession.

3. Memories for ____ events tend to ____ like a recorder.
   a. all; function
   b. all; not function
   c. select; function
   d. select; not function

4.____ memory purportedly occurs in the aftermath of a traumatic event, whereby an individual has no recollections of the event.
   a. Suppressed
   b. Recovered
   c. Repressed
   d. Flashbulb

5. In recent years, there has been an increase in the
   a. overall crime rate.
   b. violent crime rate.
   c. the number of car thefts.
   d. rate of murders by teenagers.

6. People who make eyewitness identification errors tend to be ____.
   a. elderly
   b. well-meaning
   c. dishonest
   d. overly hostile to the prosecution or the defense

7. Cross-race bias refers to the tendency for
   a. white juries to convict an African-American defendant.
   b. eyewitnesses to identify individuals of their own race fairly well.
   c. eyewitnesses to identify individuals of another race.
   d. verdicts to be perceived more fairly if the judge and attorneys are of different races.

8. All of the following techniques can be employed by police investigators in order to obtain accurate eyewitness testimony, *except*
   a. presenting pictures of the crime scene and victim before an identification is made.
   b. showing the lineup one person at a time, rather than as a group.
   c. providing positive feedback to an eyewitness while he or she is giving information.
   d. encouraging witnesses to give their first impressions.

9. Male and female jurors often show the greatest differences with respect to their
   a. evaluations of physical attractive defendants.
   b. support for life without parole.
   c. approach to cross-racial problems.
   d. tendency to vote "guilty" in rape and child abuse cases.

10. Al, a juror in a criminal case, believes that in some respects, the defendant is also a victim and thus, shouldn't be found guilty. He appears to possess the juror characteristic known as
   a. a leniency bias.
   b. attributional complexity.
   c. an entity theorist.
   d. epistemic understanding.

Practice Test 2

1. The study of the effects of psychological factors in the development, prevention, and treatment of physical illness is called
   a. medical psychology.
   b. physiological psychology.
   c. Health psychology.
   d. Clinical psychology

2. In the United States death rates have declined for all of the following conditions, *except*
   a. AIDS.
   b. cancer.
   c. Heart disease.
   d. stroke

3.Positively framed message is to negatively framed message as
   a. preventive is to detection.
   b. detection is to preventive.
   c. helpful is to harmful.
   d. harmful is to helpful.

4. A possible reason why African Americans tend to have higher blood pressure than European Americans may be due to
   a. genetic differences.
   b. stereotype threat.
   c. the use of poor coping strategies.
   d. reasons that researchers still cannot explain.

5. Josie is feeling a great amount of stress given that tomorrow is her physics final. As such, the presence of *secretory immunoglobin A* should ____ at this point and will ____ once Josie is done with her final.
   a. decrease; remain low
   b. increase; remain high
   c. decrease; increase
   d. increase; decrease

6. All of the following characteristics are associated with a self-healing personality, *except*
   a. having accessible attitudes.
   b. a belief in a just world.
   c. an internal locus of control.
   d. perfectionism.

7. Suppose Michael begins to engage in regular exercise and this results in increased fitness. Of the following outcomes, the one that is *least* likely to occur is
   a. an increased sense of well-being.
   b. an increased feeling of self-efficacy.
   c. a perception of being able to handle stress.
   d. a sense of disillusionment that he probably won't be able to keep up his exercise routine.

8. If Janice wants to decrease her negative emotions and increase her positive ones, then she should *not*
   a. engage in counterfactual thinking.
   b. use humor to cope.
   c. seek comfort in religion.
   d. try to think optimistically during negative events.

9. The hypothesis that pets can lower blood pressure and decrease anxiety
   a. has been disproven.
   b. is partially accurate.
   c. has been verified.
   d. has not yet been tested.

10. Social support is
    a. universally helpful.
    b. usually helpful, but not always.
    c. rarely helpful because those who need it most usually don't ask for it.
    d. only helpful for women.

Practice Test 3

1. Attitudes toward one's company are known as
   a. job satisfaction.
   b. organizational commitment.
   c. organizational citizenship behavior.
   d. career happiness.

2. A personal factor related to job satisfaction is
   a. seniority.
   b. liking one's boss.
   c. a perception that reward systems are fair.
   d. when employees are underloaded with work.

3. The relationship between job satisfaction and task performance is ____.
   a. not significant.
   b. relatively weak.
   c. (surprisingly) inversely related.
   d. extremely strong.

4. An example of ____ would be helping others who have a heavy workload.
   a. affective temperament
   b. transformational leadership
   c. consideration
   d. organizational citizenship behavior

5. A key premise behind the great person theory of leadership is that great leaders are
   a. made, not born.
   b. incapable of being truly understood.
   c. quite different from most others in terms of the traits they possess.
   d. greatly flawed in their personal life.

6. ____ is considered to be one of the Big Five dimensions of personality.
   a. Conscientiousness
   b. Consciousness
   c. Kindness
   d. Psychoticism

7. Leaders who are ____ on the dimension of initiating structure tend to be considered with production and leaders who are ____ on the dimension of consideration tend to unconcerned with people.
   a. high; high
   b. low; low
   c. high; low
   d. low; high

8. Suppose Peter is viewed by his followers as a transformational leader in that he is a charismatic role model. As such, this example highlights the importance of ____ in transformational leadership.
   a. intellectual stimulation
   b. inspirational motivation
   c. individual consideration
   d. idealized influence

9. According to Lewin and colleagues (1939), a(n) ____ leadership style is ideal since it encourages a high level of productivity and cooperation among group members.
   a. transformational
   b. transactional
   c. democratic
   d. autocratic

10. Leaders who are high in charisma tend to be well suited for environments that are
    a. stable and predictable.
    b. chaotic and rapidly changing.
    c. stable or chaotic.
    d. not in the "for-profit" business sector.

Comprehensive Test

(NOTE: Items 1-15 are multiple-choice questions and items 16-23 are true-false questions.)

1. Media information influences the public
   a. in surprisingly few instances.
   b. when negative aspects of the suspect are mentioned.
   c. when positive aspects of the suspect are mentioned.
   d. by making it favorable to the defense argument.

2. Wells and Luus (1990) argue that a police lineup is analogous to a
   a. social psychology experiment.
   b. beauty contest.
   c. wrestling match.
   d. game show.

3. In terms of their ability to select jurors favorable to their side, attorneys are
   a. better than non-attorneys.
   b. uniformly skilled.
   c. uniformly dismal.
   d. no better than college students in doing so.

4. In American courtrooms, leading questions are ____.
   a. never permitted
   b. permitted when the witness is first examined
   c. permitted upon cross-examination
   d. permitted throughout any trial

5. Jurors who are ____ tend to comply selectively with instructions about inadmissibility.
   a. extraverted
   b. high in the need for cognition
   c. low in the need for cognition
   d. low in agreeableness

6. ____ is associated with ignoring various health messages.
   a. Optimism
   b. Unrealistic optimism
   c. Pessimism
   d. Unrealistic pessimism

7. Suppose you're at a party and someone you don't know well says, "Here's some beer—just to let you know, I took a swig from that cup." Based on this information only, you'll likely drink that beer if you have
   a. alcohol myopia.
   b. an optimism bias.
   c. a low social image concern.
   d. a high social image concern.

8. ____ refers to how we deal with threats and their emotional consequences.
   a. Stress
   b. Coping
   c. Psychological response
   d. Psychoneurimmunology

9. Suppose George, who was a pessimist, had an untimely death at age forty due to a heart attack. In terms of understanding why George died relatively early, his pessimism
   a. definitely played no role whatsoever.
   b. definitely caused his heart attack.
   c. may have served as a contributing factor.
   d. probably made him feel angry and anxious while he was alive, but it likely didn't contribute to his heart attack.

10. Holly tends to respond to stress with intensely negative emotions and tends to be sick a great deal. Based on this information, Holly probably exhibits a
    a. Type A behavior pattern.
    b. disease-prone personality.
    c. low social image concern.
    d. high level of psychoneuroimmunology.

11. Industrial-organizational psychology is a branch of
    a. business dominated by psychology.
    b. psychology that dominates the mindset of major corporate businesses.
    c. law that specializes in psychological matters.
    d. psychology that studies behavior in work settings.

12. In terms of its impact on job satisfaction, genetics
    a. plays a very insignificant role.
    b. plays a very important role such that some people will have high or low levels of job satisfaction, no matter where they work.
    c. only predicts what our professions will be and not our levels of job satisfaction.
    d. has not been considered yet as a potential factor related to job satisfaction.

13. All of the following factors may explain why a person engages in various forms of OCB, *except*
    a. a narrow perception of the roles of one's job.
    b. job loyalty.
    c. a hope to be rewarded for such behavior.
    d. feelings of perceived justice.

14. The single most important characteristic of leaders is
    a. motivation.
    b. drive.
    c. flexibility.
    d. self-confidence.

15. All of the following leadership styles were identified by Lewin and colleagues (1939), *except*
    a. transactional.
    b. autocratic.
    c. democratic.
    d. laissez-faire.

Questions 16-23 are True/False Questions

16. Even though social support may make a person feel good, it does *not* help individuals cope with an illness.

17. Being high in self-critical perfectionism can lead to positive outcomes such as improved performance.

18. In the United States 65% of all adults are obese.

19. The stated purpose of voir dire is to ensure that fair and impartial jurors are selected.

20. A defendant's race rarely figures into a jury's final verdict.

21. Some individuals may show the same level of job satisfaction regardless of where they work.

22. A worker's trust in their boss and company is unrelated to their organizational citizenship behavior.

23. Most individuals are quite wary and distrustful of charismatic leaders.

Short Answer/Essay Questions

1. **Eyewitness Testimony**
   Briefly identify two or three ways to increase and improve eyewitness accuracy.

2. **The Impact of Stress**
   Provide at least two examples of how stress can directly cause physical illness.

3. **Social Support**
   Explain why social support can sometimes provide more harm than good to an individual.

4. **Organizational Citizenship Behavior (OCB)**
   How is the issue of perceived justice relevant to the occurrence of OCB?

5. **Leadership Styles**
   Discuss how important it is to have a charismatic leader during stable versus changing times or environments.

6. **Entrepreneurs**
   Discuss some of the contributing factors that create a successful entrepreneur.

When You Have Finished . . .

Applications of Forensic, Health, and Workplace Psychology to Your Life

Any time social psychologists try to *apply* their findings, this has an inherent value and relevance to our everyday lives.

1. Since we all must encounter stress at varying levels and times in our lives, we need to find ways to effectively cope with it.

2. If you ever witness a crime, become a crime victim, or serve as a juror, having an awareness of the psychology of the legal system might allow for you to provide the most objective information possible.

3. By understanding the factors that influence job satisfaction, we are in a better position to maximize our satisfaction with our chosen job or career.

4. By understanding patterns of leadership, you'll have a better understanding of how your boss operates—or, if you're in a leadership position, you'll be aware of what makes an effective leader.

5. By understanding some of the social factors that contribute to obesity, we will be in a better position by having more knowledge about how to counteract these factors and change the tide on the growing rate of obesity.

With respect to point #1, consider some of the suggestions outlined in your text as to how to manage and cope with stress (e.g., increased fitness and social support). The next time you find yourself in a stressful situation, try one or more of these techniques and keep a diary of some sort to note the effectiveness of these techniques in combating stress. Were some techniques more effective than others? Which ones? Were certain techniques effective under certain conditions only? If so, how?

Internet Sites:

http://www.rdc.ab.ca/scottpsych/website/frames/stress.htm: Good links to online stress and coping inventories.

http://www.vanderbilt.edu/nursing/kwallston/mhlcscales.htm:. Multidimensional Health Locus of Control (MHLC) Scales developed by Kenneth A. Wallston.

http://userpage.fu-berlin.de/~health/selfscal.htm: Schwarzer's Generalized Perceived Self-Efficacy Scale: "In contrast to other scales that were designed to assess optimism, this one explicitly refers to personal agency, i.e., the belief that one's actions are responsible for successful outcomes." Site also has a proactive attitude scale.

http://www3.health-center.com/mentalhealth/stress/relief/support.htm.:General interest article discussing four kinds of social support.

http://www.the-stress-site.com/Article%20Type%20A%20personality%20test.htm: A Type-A personality inventory based on Rosenman's work.

http://www.the-stress-site.com/stress.htm: Excellent resource for general information on stress, its consequences, and stress reduction techniques.

http://www.eyewitnessid.com/: A forensic expert's site giving examples of cases of mistaken eyewitness identification.

http://www.pbs.org/wgbh/pages/frontline/shows/dna/: Site for the PBS program *What Jennifer Saw* (on the Ronald Cotton case discussed in the text). Includes an interview with Elizabeth Loftus, a demonstration lineup, and an article by Gary Wells on reevaluating police procedures.

http://www.seweb.uci.edu/faculty/loftus: Elizabeth Loftus' site has several of her articles and a *Psychology Today* article about her work online.

http://www.uchastings.edu/plri/spr96tex/jurysiz.htm:. Summarizes research on jury size.

http://www.bucket-o-brains.com/surveys/trial_fw/: An online jury study.

http://luna.cas.usf.edu/~ruva/Psychology_Law.htm: Contains links to information about organizations, training, and careers in psychology and law.

http://www.siop.org: Website for the Society of Industrial/Organizational Psychologists.

Crossword Puzzle

Across

1. trying to be perfect
7. studies psychological variables and health
9. evidence given by people who have witnessed a crime

10. people who start new businesses
12. making it look like you are working hard
13. memories that we never experienced
14. leaders who use rewards and punishment
15. abbreviation for prosocial behavior at work
16. emotional resources from others
17. attitude toward your job

Down

2. not being able to ignore emotion generating information
3. charismatic leaders
4. biased questions
5. response to threatening events
6. lineup of innocent suspects
8. a theory that great leaders have special traits
11. minor annoyances

Created by Puzzlemaker at DiscoverySchool.com

APPENDIX

CHAPTER ANSWERS: "AFTER YOU READ…" PRACTICE TESTS SHORT ANSWER/ESSAY QUESTIONS AND CROSSWORD PUZZLE

Chapter 1

Item Number	Practice Test 1	Practice Test 2	Practice Test 3	Comprehensive Test
1	B	D	A	A
2	A	A	C	C
3	D	C	B	C
4	A	B	B	C
5	A	A	C	C
6	C	B	D	B
7	C	D	D	D
8	C	D	A	B
9	D	C	C	D
10	A	C	C	B
11				C
12				C
13				A
14				D
15				D
16				F
17		*Correct Responses to*		T
18		*Short Answer/Essay Questions*		T
19		↓		F
20				T
21				T
22				T
23				T

CHAPTER ANSWERS

1. The four most important core values to a scientific field are: accuracy, objectivity, skepticism, and open-mindedness.

2. The three basic processes of evolution are: variation, inheritance, and selection. Variation refers to the fact that organisms belonging to a given species vary in many different ways. Inheritance pertains to how these variations are passed from one generation to the next through complex mechanisms. Selection refers to the fact that some of these variations give individuals an "edge" in terms of reproduction.

3. Based on this negative correlation coefficient value of -.43, the more a person argues with his or her friend (on average), the number of colds a person reports (on average per year) decreases. Obviously, causality cannot be determined given the correlational nature of this study.

4. The independent variable would be the issue that the subjects wrote about (i.e., either the benefits or drawbacks to their relationship or what they ate for breakfast); the dependent variable would be the subject's blood pressure.

5. Deception is often used in social psychological research since participants' behavior might be altered if they knew the true purposes of a study; thus, valid information about social behavior or thought wouldn't be gained. Two problems associated with deception are harm to the subjects or a negative attitude about (social) psychology and research. In order to minimize these problems, social psychologists should never try to use deception to persuade individuals to participate in studies. They should also try to use informed consent and debriefing in all studies.

6. In order to determine whether the results of a research project are real or due to chance, social psychologists use inferential statistics. If the chances are small that the research results occurred by chance (less than 5 times in 100), the results are described as significant.

Crossword Puzzle Answer Key

Across

1. unconscious self-enhancement = **implicit egotism**
4. asking a large number of questions = **survey method**
6. generalizing findings = **external validity**
7. core value of the field = **accuracy**
9. extraneous variable = **confound**
10. likelihood of obtaining the observed findings by chance = **significant**
11. a mental picture of who we would like to be = **ideal self**
13. area in social psychology that studies biological bases of social processes = **socialneuroscience**
14. unintended researcher effects = **experimenter effects**
15. unverified prediction = **hypothesis**
17. withholding information = **deception**
20. technique for studying social behavior = **systematic observation**
21. observing behavior in natural settings = **naturalistic observation**

Down
1. factor systematically varied = **independent variable**
2. understanding cultural and ethnic factors that influence social behavior = **multicultural perspective**
3. many combined studies = **meta analysis**
5. equal chance of being exposed = **random assignment**
8. giving participants information prior to the study = **informed consent**
12. two related variables = **correlation**
16. behavior of others in social settings = **social psychology**
18. full description of purpose of study = **debriefing**
19. aspect of behavior studied = **dependent variable**

Chapter 2

Item Number	Practice Test 1	Practice Test 2	Practice Test 3	Comprehensive Test
1	C	B	C	D
2	B	B	C	A
3	C	A	C	B
4	A	B	B	C
5	B	C	C	C
6	A	B	D	C
7	D	D	D	C
8	C	D	C	A
9	D	B	C	A
10	D	A	B	B
11				D
12				A
13				B
14				B
15				B
16				T
17		*Correct Responses to*		T
18		*Short Answer/Essay Questions*		F
19				F
20		↓		F
21				T
22				T
23				T

CHAPTER ANSWERS

1. There is no simple answer to this question; it depends on the measure of memory employed. In general, people report information consistent with their schemas, but, in fact, information inconsistent with schemas may be strongly present in memory, too.

2. The representativeness heuristic is a strategy for making judgments based on the extent to which current stimuli or events resemble other stimuli or categories; the availability heuristic is used to make judgments on the basis of how easily specific kinds of information can be brought to mind.

3. A life example of priming would be after watching a scary movie you tend to be more cognizant of shadows and dark corners and interpret these cues as scary.

4. Due to the negativity bias, where we have a greater sensitivity to negative than positive information, you would likely recognize the threatening face first.

5. The three principles of magical thinking are as follows: The law of contagion holds that when two objects touch, these pass properties to one another, and the effects of that contact may last well beyond the end of contact between these. The law of similarity suggests that things that resemble one another share basic properties. The third principle suggests that one's thoughts can influence the physical world in a manner not governed by the laws of physics.

6. Affect can influence cognition in terms of its impact on memory. For instance, what we remember while in a given mood may be determined, in part, by what we learned when previously in that mood (mood-dependent memory). Our current moods—particularly if we are in a happy mood—can increase creativity since being in a happy mood activates a wider range of ideas. Also, information that evokes affective reactions may be processed differently than other kinds of information and thus, it may be impossible to ignore or disregard (mental contamination).

Crossword Puzzle Answer Key

<u>Across</u>

1. optimistic predictions = **planning fallacy**
3. predictions that make themselves come true = **self-fulfilling prophecy**
4. what might have been = **counterfactual thinking**
9. unwanted thoughts returning = **rebound effect**
10. schemas remain unchanged = **perseverance effect**
11. using numbers as a starting point = **anchoring**
12. heuristic relying on ease of instance brought to mind = **availability heuristic**
13. preventing thoughts = **thought suppression**
14. increased availability of information = **priming**
15. automatic thought = **automatic processing**
16. ability to process is exceeded = **information overload**
17. brain part responsible for evaluative judgments = **amygdala**
18. mental frameworks = **schemas**
19. trepidation = **bracing for the worst**

Down
2. sensitivity toward negative information = **negativity bias**
5. anchoring = **adjustment**
6. feelings and mood = **affect**
7. simple rules = **heuristics**
8. how affect influences social thought = **affect infusion model**
9. current stimuli resemble other stimuli = **representativeness**

Chapter 3

Item Number	Practice Test 1	Practice Test 2	Practice Test 3	Comprehensive Test
1	A	D	D	D
2	C	D	C	C
3	B	B	C	A
4	C	A	B	D
5	C	B	C	B
6	A	D	B	C
7	B	D	D	A
8	D	B	C	A
9	C	A	B	B
10	B	C	A	D
11				B
12				A
13				A
14				C
15				D
16				F
17		*Correct Responses to*		F
18		*Short Answer/Essay Questions*		F
19		↓		T
20				T
21				F
22				F
23				T

1. Three nonverbal cues related to deception are: microexpressions, interchannel discrepancies, and exaggerated facial expressions.

2. Research has shown that women are superior to men on decoding nonverbal behavior and sending nonverbal behavior.

3. We would tend to conclude that this person is generally a loud and inconsiderate person, according to Jones and Davis' theory. The reason is that it represents freely chosen behavior that is not social desirable and it yields distinctive, noncommon effects.

4. Clearly, this represents a very unfortunate and difficult situation. Since this person is your friend, you will likely want the most favorable outcome for her. As such, you should tell your friend that if she intends to confront her boss about this, it is very likely that she'll been seen by others as a "chronic complainer."

5. An exemplar is a concrete example of behavior that others have performed and is consistent with a given trait. An abstraction is a mental summary of someone that has been gleaned from repeated observations of their behavior.

6. The most commonly used tactic of other-enhancement is flattery (i.e., statements that praise the target person). A couple of additional tactics would include expressing agreement with the target person's views and doing small favors for him or her.

Crossword Puzzle Answer Key

Across

3. a central trait= **warm**
5. understanding others = **social perception**
7. transferred feelings = **emotional contagion**
10. others behavior due to dispositions = **correspondence bias**
11. nonspoken language = **nonverbal behavior**
16. influenced Asch's work = **Gestalt psychologists**
17. aspects of speech = **linguistic style**
18. lick upward but kick downward = **slime effect**
19. situational attribution = **external attribution**
20. dispositional attribution = **internal attribution**
21. attribute our behavior to the situation = **actor observer bias**
22. attribution researcher = **Kelley**

Down
1. nonverbal researcher = **Ekman**
2. producing favorable impressions = **impression management**
4. beliefs about traits = **implicit personality theory**
6. fleeting facial expressions = **microexpressions**
8. first cause as unlikely = **discounting**
9. steadily gazing = **staring**
12. effects caused by one factor but not others = **noncommon effects**
13. a piece of information that Kelley says we use = **distinctiveness**
14. cause of others' behavior = **attribution**
15. cues provided by others' bodies = **body language**

Chapter 4

Item Number	Practice Test 1	Practice Test 2	Practice Test 3	Comprehensive Test
1	B	B	AC	A
2	C	B	B	B
3	A	D	C	A
4	A	B	B	D
5	B	D	D	B
6	A	A	C	D
7	B	C	A	C
8	C	A	A	A
9	D	C	D	A
10	B	B	C	D
11				A
12				B
13				C
14				B
15				C
16				F
17		*Correct Responses to*		F
18		*Short Answer/Essay Questions*		T
19				F
20		↓		F
21				T
22				F
23				F

1. Unlike classical conditioning, exposure to stimuli is below an individual's threshold of conscious awareness with respect to subliminal conditioning.

2. Attitudes serve at least five key functions: organizing and interpreting social information (knowledge), expressing our central values or beliefs (self-expression or self-identity), maintaining or

enhancing our feelings of self-worth (self-esteem), helping people protect themselves from unwanted information about themselves (ego-defensive), and to make a good impression on others (impression motivation).

3. An event activates an attitude that influences our perceptions about the attitude object. Simultaneously, our knowledge of various social norms is activated. These factors shape our definition of the event and this perception, in turn, influences our behavior.

4. You should take a two-sided approach where both sides of the argument will be presented.

5. Dissonance can be used to generate hypocrisy. However, if you truly are going to be able to help your friend, he must publicly advocate the wearing of seat belts, must be induced to think about his own failures to wear his own seat belt in the past, and must be given access to direct means to reduce his dissonance.

6. Fear appeals are most effective for trivial illnesses. An example might be using fear appeal to increase tooth brushing compliance.

Crossword Puzzle Answer Key

Across

1. efforts to change others attitudes = **persuasion**
3. basic form of learning = **classical conditioning**
5. process of comparing ourselves to others = **social comparison**
6. advance knowledge = **forewarning**
7. resistance to persuasion = **reactance**
11. systematic attitude change = **central route**
17. behavior and attitude inconsistent = **cognitive dissonance**
18. evaluations of the social world = **attitude**
19. a technique for reducing dissonance = **trivalization**
20. say one thing do another = **hypocrisy**
21. learning from others = **social learning**
22. overestimate media impact underestimate self's impact = **third person effect**

Down

2. stimuli that are below conscious awareness = **subliminal conditioning**
4. processing information using mental shortcuts = **heuristic processing**
8. extension of the theory of reasoned action = **theory of planned behavior**
9. careful consideration of ideas = **systematic processing**
10. positive and negative evaluations of the same attitude object = **attitude ambivalence**
12. induced to say something inconsistent with true attitudes = **forced compliance**
13. expectations about how people will behave = **social norms**
14. learning from observation =**observational learning**
15. change in attitude due to peripheral cues = **peripheral route**
16. learning from reinforcement = **instrumental conditioning**

Chapter 5

Item Number	Practice Test 1	Practice Test 2	Practice Test 3	Comprehensive Test
1	D	D	C	D
2	C	C	B	B
3	B	B	B	A
4	B	A	C	D
5	D	B	D	D
6	A	C	A	D
7	C	A	D	A
8	D	B	D	B
9	A	A	A	D
10	B	D	B	B
11				C
12				A
13				B
14				C
15				B
16				F
17		*Correct Responses to*		T
18		*Short Answer/Essay Questions*		T
19				F
20		↓		T
21				T
22				T
23				T

1. Males and females describe themselves on dimensions involving concepts such as open- or broad-mindedness *and* passion and romance. However, women (unlike men) tend to have the negative schema of embarrassed/conservative that suggests anxiety and guilt in response to sex. Men often show a schema based on traits pertaining to power and aggression.

2. You make an upward social comparison when you're comparing yourself to someone who's better off than you with respect to a certain attribute. Comparing yourself to a stranger tends to not effect self-esteem since it simply isn't important to you. You might feel depressed and have lowered self-esteem if you compare yourself with someone in your in-group, though; basically, such a comparison suggests that you're not measuring up to your peers. However, comparing yourself with a close other will likely produce an assimilation effect and thus, increase your self-esteem.

3. Janet appears to be a high self-monitor.

4. A stereotype threat can occur when people believe that they might be judged in light of a negative steretoype about their group, (e.g., being very tall or very short).

Crossword Puzzle Answer Key

Across

1. comparing to someone less than self = **downward social comparison**
3. being derogated = **black sheep effect**
5. judged in light of a negative stereotype about your group = **stereotype threat**
6. images of future self = **possible selves**
7. anxiety about dying = **existential terror**
9. monitoring behavior = **self monitoring**
11. application of universal rules = **justice ethic**
14. belief one can achieve a goal = **self efficacy**
15. self is separate from environment = **subjective self awareness**
16. justice and ethics orientation = **care ethic**
17. collectivistic cultures self-concept = **interdependent self concept**
18. Festinger's theory = **social comparison theory**
19. how self-concept is organized = **self complexity**
20. making others like us = **ingratiation**
21. confronting own death = **terror management theory**

Down

2. comparisons between groups = **intergroup comparisons**
4. rate yourself above average = **above average effect**
8. concept in individualistic cultures = **independent self concept**
10. orientation toward self = **self reference effect**
12. attitude toward self = **self esteem**
13. social identities in conflict = **identity interference**

Chapter 6

Item Number	Practice Test 1	Practice Test 2	Practice Test 3	Comprehensive Test
1	C	C	C	C
2	B	C	D	C
3	A	D	B	A
4	C	A	B	A
5	B	D	A	B
6	D	B	C	D
7	C	A	C	D
8	B	B	D	B
9	A	C	B	B
10	C	C	C	A
11				C
12				B
13				C
14				B
15				D
16				T
17		*Correct Responses to*		FT
18		*Short Answer/Essay Questions*		F
19				T
20		↓		T
21				F
22				T
23				F

[continued on next page]

1. Prejudice is a negative *attitude* toward the members of some group, whereas discrimination is a negative *action or behavior* toward the groups that are the targets of prejudice.

2. Realistic conflict theory postulates that prejudice often stems from direct competition between various social groups over scarce and valued resources. However, consistent with the hatred shown by Osama bin Laden and his followers, competition doesn't have to be real or direct to start this process. These individuals view the United States as a direct threat to their religion and culture—so, their end result is to demonize the United States and to try to destroy it as shown by the tragic events of September 11, 2001.

3. We have a great deal of experience with members of our own group, so we're exposed to more variation within this group; typically, we have much less interactions with out-group members and likewise, we observe less variation within such groups.

4. Stereotype threat is a concern on the part of persons who are the target of stereotype that they'll be evaluated in terms of this stereotype. An example of empirical evidence in support of this phenomenon is that black undergraduates performed more poorly on a difficult cognitive task when

their race was made salient and they believed that poor performance would confirm the cultural stereotype that blacks are less intelligent than whites; these effects didn't occur when race wasn't made salient.

5. Collective guilt is the emotion that can be experienced when people are confronted with the harmful actions done by their ingroup against an outgroup. Strategies to deal with this guilt include minimizing the harm done and the severity of the harm done.

Crossword Puzzle Answer Key

Across

8. stereotypes about females or males = **gender stereotypes**
12. prejudice based on gender = **sexism**
14. theory that direct competition creates prejudice = **realistic conflict theory**
15. dividing into categories = **social categorization**
16. shifts in boundaries between groups = **recategorization**
17. prejudice acquired through experience = **social learning**
18. makes ones self-esteem in jeopardy = **threat**
19. being seen as having worth = **respect**
20. stimulus makes accessible information = **priming**
21. the group that you do not belong to = **outgroup**
22. a subset of the group not consistent= **subtype**

Down

1. self-serving attributional bias at the group level = **ultimate attribution error**
2. perception of association between two variables = **illusory correlation**
3. group guilt = **collective guilt**
4. goals achieved by group cooperation = **superordinate goals**
5. prevents females from getting to the top = **glass ceiling**
6. contact reduces prejudice = **contact hypothesis**
7. subtle beliefs of superiority = **modern racism**
9. negative behavior toward members = **discrimination**
10. the group you belong to = **ingroup**
11. hiring based on group membership = **tokenism**
13. beliefs about individuals = **stereotypes**
23. priming measures racial attitudes = **bonafidepipeline**

Chapter 7

Item Number	Practice Test 1	Practice Test 2	Practice Test 3	Comprehensive Test
1	D	A	C	C
2	B	B	B	C
3	A	B	C	D
4	B	C	C	D
5	B	A	A	D
6	C	D	D	A
7	C	C	D	A
8	A	D	B	B
9	B	B	D	B
10	D	C	A	B
11				A
12				C
13				B
14				D
15				B
16				T
17				T
18				F
19				F
20				T
21				F
22				F
23				T

Correct Responses to Short Answer/Essay Questions ↓

1. Some examples of how repeated exposures and proximity function in natural settings include evidence that students are more likely to become acquainted or friends if they sit next to each other in class. It is plausible that attraction could cause proximity or that some third variable could cause both. However, there is empirical evidence showing that when students are randomly assigned to apartments in a college setting, proximity continues to play a key role in attraction. Thus, it is still accurate to conclude that proximity causes liking even in natural settings.

2. The need for affiliation is a basic motive to seek and maintain interpersonal relationships. Some people prefer to be alone most, some, or hardly any of the time—this pertains to their relatively stable disposition or traits. However, certain settings or situations (e.g., having surgery, experiencing a disaster) may motivate an individual to seek out others—this pertains to the temporary states of this need.

3. Physical attractiveness is often viewed as a sign of health, youth, and fertility—particularly in women.

4. They will be in a state of imbalance and can restore balance by either changing or the other's attitudes, misperceiving the degree of dissimilarity, or (in a worst case scenario) simply deciding not to like each other.

5. The repulsion hypothesis is that attraction isn't increased by similar attitudes but only decreased by dissimilar ones. This hypothesis is inaccurate in its prediction that similarity is not relevant to attraction—clearly it is. However, it did contain a partial truth in the sense that we tend to like those we meet until we discover too many areas of dissimilarity.

Crossword Puzzle Answer Key

Across
4. formulations of Heider and Newcomb = **balance theory**
6. emotional state = **affect**
12. Rosenbaum's proposal = **repulsion hypothesis**

Down
1. repeated exposure effect = **mere exposure effect**
2. individuals who share same attitudes = **attitude similarity**
3. beautiful = **physical attractiveness**
5. worry about one's physical characteristics = **appearance anxiety**
7. a person's attitude about another = **interpersonal attraction**
8. characteristics increasing reproductive success = **adaptive response**
9. closeness of two individuals = proximity
10. mere exposure effect = **repeated exposure effect**
11. motive to seek interpersonal relationships = **need for affiliation**

Chapter 8

Item Number	Practice Test 1	Practice Test 2	Practice Test 3	Comprehensive Test
1	D	D	A	C
2	A	D	B	A
3	C	C	B	D
4	D	D	C	A
5	B	C	B	D
6	B	C	D	D
7	A	A	D	C
8	D	D	B	B
9	A	B	A	D
10	B (	C	B	C
11				A
12				C
13				A
14				A
15				B
16				F
17				T
18				T
19				F
20				F
21				T
22				T
23				F

Correct Responses to Short Answer/Essay Questions

↓

1. Chris appears to have a dismissing attachment style.

2. Two external factors that can create loneliness are moving to a new location and social rejection--when another individual has no interest in establishing a relationship with you. The two primary interventions for loneliness are cognitive therapy and social skills training. Cognitive therapy teaches individuals to disrupt the pattern of negative self-evaluations and to encourage new positive cognitions about the self. Since so many lonely people have poor social skills, social skills training allows individuals to learn how to successfully interact with others.

3. Bret appears to be feeling passionate love.

4. Those with an unrestricted sociosexual orientation tend to be male and often feel that members of the opposite sex are sought simply as sex partners without any need for closeness or emotional bonding. Those with a restricted sociosexual orientation tend to be female and believe that a sexual relationship is acceptable only when accompanied by affection and tenderness.

4. Overall, companionate love (e.g., sharing activities, working together, laughing) appears to be the key ingredient for a successful marriage. However, women also show even greater happiness in the marriage if they continue to feel a sense of passionate love as well.

Crossword Puzzle Answer Key

<u>Across</u>

7. socially rejecting another = **social rejection**
9. benevolent acts in a relationship = **communal behavior**
10. unreciprocated love = **unrequited love**
11. ________similarity = **assumed**
12. one's attitude about oneself = **self esteem**
13. face is symmetrical = **bilateral symmetry**
14. different styles of attachment = **attachment style**

<u>Down</u>

1. love based on friendship = **companionate love**
2. complete ideal love = **consummate love**
3. two people spend a lot of time together = **close friendship**
4. sexual excitement = **passion**
5. unrealistic response to another person = **passionate love**
6. Sternberg's theory = **triangular model of love**
7. Self-love = **narcissism**

Chapter 9

Item Number	Practice Test 1	Practice Test 2	Practice Test 3	Comprehensive Test
1	B	D	A	A
2	D	D	D	A
3	D	A	C	D
4	C	B	B	A
5	D	C	B	D
6	D	D	C	D
7	A	B	B	D
8	A	A	A	B
9	D	A	C	C
10	B	D	D	B
11				C
12				B
13				A
14				C
15				C
16				T
17				F
18				F
19				F
20				F
21				F
22				F
23				F

1. Jorge is conforming due to informational and normative social influence.

2. The three key factors are: the minority view must be consistent, the minority shouldn't appear rigid or dogmatic, and their views should be consistent with the general social climate.

3. This is an example of lowballing.

Crossword Puzzle Answer Key

Across

5. unpopular compliance tactic = **pressuring**
7. basis of foot-in-the-door = **consistency**
10. alter behavior or attitude = **social influence**
15. changing the deal at the last minute = **lowball**
16. key to milgram study = **gradual escalation**
18. conformity researcher = **asch**
19. obedience researcher = **milgram**
20. harming the innocent = **destructive obedience**
21. time is running out = **scarcity**
23. tactic based on friendship = **ingratiation**

Down

1. degree of attraction = **cohesiveness**
2. five-hundred dollar fine = **explicit social norm**
3. percent of obedient people in Milgram study = **sixty five percent**
4. what is commonly done = **descriptive norms**
6. basis of that's not all = **reciprocity**
8. ordering behavior = **obedience**
9. large then small request = **door-in-the-face**
11. small then large request = **foot-in-the-door**
12. influence researcher = **cialdini**
13. compliance professionals = **salespeople**
14. tactic to sweeten the deal = **that's not all**
17. normative behavior = **comformity**
22. saying yes to requests = **compliance**

Chapter 10

Item Number	Practice Test 1	Practice Test 2	Practice Test 3	Comprehensive Test
1	C	B	C	A
2	C	C	A	A
3	C	B	A	A
4	C	D	D	B
5	A	B	D	C
6	B	A	B	B
7	C	A	A	A
8	D	D	D	C
9	A	A	A	C
10	B	C	C	D
11				B
12				C
13				D
14				C
15				D
16				T
17		*Correct Responses to*		F
18		*Short Answer/Essay Questions*		T
19		↓		T
20				F
21				F
22				T
23				F

1. In order for a bystander to engage in helping behavior, he or she must do all of the following behaviors in the following order: attend to the situation, interpret the situation as an emergency, assume responsibility for taking action, have the knowledge, skills, or training to provide help, and decide to engage in helping behavior. If *any* of these stages are not followed through, help will not be given.

2. Some shows and characters, such as *Sesame Street*, have clear prosocial models where children are taught the values of kindness and helping behavior; these shows really do appear to increase children's prosocial behavior. However, violent media (such as violent games like "Street Fighter") tend to decrease prosocial behavior. More research needs to be conducted with respect to characters and shows like *The Simpsons* that feature models that aren't violent yet are unconcerned with the plight of others; the text authors conclude that such shows and characters likely have a negative effect on children and their likelihood of showing prosocial behavior.

3. Regardless of whether an emergency is ambiguous, people who are in a good mood don't like to engage in behaviors that could threaten that mood. As such, if they perceive such a threat, they likely will not help.

4. Generativity is an adult's concern for and commitment to the well-being of future generations. Thus, by volunteering, an adult may feel as though he or she is allowing for the development of a better society.

4. In general, this model predicts that you would be most likely to help a close biological relative—particularly to younger fertile relatives (especially women) since they are the key to reproductive success.

Crossword Puzzle Answer Key

<u>**Across**</u>

1. courageous actions = **heroism**
4. one individual is helped when a large group is in need = **selective altruism**
6. concern with one's personal needs = **egoism**
7. unselfish behavior = **altruism**
9. cooperative behavior among strangers = **reciprocal altruism**
10. motivation to appear moral = **moral hypocrisy**
11. kin selection = **inclusive fitness**
12. imitation = **mimicry**
13. inclusive fitness = **kin selection**
14. help effected by the number of bystanders present = **bystander effect**
15. concern for future generations = **generativity**

<u>**Down**</u>

2. decrease in helping behavior by thinking about being in a group = **implicit bystander effect**
3. responsibility of bystanders is shared = **diffusion of responsibility**
4. egoism = **self interest**
5. putting yourself in others shoes = **empathy**
8. motivation to be moral = **moral integrity**

Chapter 11

Item Number	Practice Test 1	Practice Test 2	Practice Test 3	Comprehensive Test
1	C	A	D	C
2	A	B	D	C
3	B	B	C	A
4	C	D	B	B
5	C	C	A	C
6	D	C	D	A
7	A	B	C	D
8	B	B	B	D
9	B	B	B	D
10	D	A	A	C
11				B
12				C
13				C
14				B
15				A
16				T
17		*Correct Responses to*		F
18		*Short Answer/Essay Questions*		T
19				F
20		↓		F
21				F
22				F
23				F

1. The two main categories of GAAM are input variables (such as some kind of attack from another person or the presence of cues associated with aggression) and individual differences (such as specific skills related to aggression or certain values about violence).

2. The Type A behavior pattern consists of high levels of competitiveness, time urgency, and hostility.

3. Low aggressors become more aggressive when intoxicated and high aggressors become slightly less aggressive when intoxicated.

4. The three main categories of aggression in the workplace are: expressions of hostility (e.g., behaviors that are primarily verbal or symbolic in nature), obstructionism (e.g., behaviors designed to impede the target's performance), and overt aggression (e.g., physical assault, theft).

5. Pete is using the incompatible response technique. He should use this with care since it sometimes backfires when the target person is very angry—but if a person isn't already enraged, it can be an effective way to reduce or prevent aggression or anger. So again, it may work—it all depends on how enraged Josh feels.

Crossword Puzzle Answer Key

Across

2. theories suggesting that aggression stems from external conditions = **drive theories**
4. actions that trigger aggression = **provocation**
9. reconciliation = **forgiveness**
10. goal to be aggressive to obtain something of value = **instrumental aggression**
11. behavior with goal of harming another = **aggression**
12. expressing angry impulses = **catharsis**
13. culture where norms say aggression is ok to defend one's honor = **culture of honor**

Down

1. violence in the workplace = **workplace violence**
3. depictions of violent actions in the media = **media violence**
5. aversive consequences delivered = **punishment**
6. a behavior pattern of absence of Type A patterns = **TypeB**
7. a behavior pattern of competitiveness = **TypeA**
8. target person is assaulted repeatedly = **bullying**

Chapter 12

Item Number	Practice Test 1	Practice Test 2	Practice Test 3	Comprehensive Test
1	A	D	D	C
2	B	D	A	A
3	D	B	B	C
4	A	A	B	C
5	C	D	B	C
6	C	C	C	C
7	A	A	A	B
8	D	C	C	A
9	A	A	C	A
10	B	A	C	A
11				A
12				D
13				B
14				D
15				D
16				T
17				F
18				T
19				T
20				F
21				F
22				F
23				F

Correct Responses to Short Answer/Essay Questions

↓

1. Groups function due to the presence of roles, status, norms, and cohesiveness. Roles allow individuals to know their specific duties within the group. Status enables the development of leaders through the importance of position and rank. Norms provide the general rules for how a group should behave. Cohesiveness pertains to a variety of factors that encourage the group to stay together.

2. Expectancy-valence theory suggests that individuals will work hard on a given task only to the extent that the following conditions exist: (1) They believe that working hard will lead to better performance (expectancy), (2) they believe that better performance will be recognized and rewarded (instrumentality), and (3) the rewards obtained are ones they value and desire (valence).

3. A major social factor that creates conflict is faulty attributions; these are errors concerning the causes behind others' behavior. Another factor is faulty communication, whereby communication is relayed in a manner that angers or annoys a person even if that was not the intention; in this respect, destructive criticism leaves the recipient hungry for revenge. A third social cause of conflict involves the tendency to perceive our own views as objective and as reflecting reality, but those of others are biased by their ideology.

4. This example illustrates distributive justice.

5. Social decision schemes are rules relating to the initial distribution of members' views to final group decisions. The majority-wins rule suggests that the group often opts for whatever position is initially supported by most of its members. The truth-wins rule suggests that the correct decision will ultimately be accepted as its correctness is recognized by more and more members. The first-shift rule is the tendency for groups to adopt a decision consistent with the direction of the first shift in opinion shown by any member.

Crossword Puzzle Answer Key

Across

2. group assuming that their decisions are not wrong = **groupthink**
3. fairness = **distributive fairness**
9. behaviors for people in certain positions = **roles**
11. group product is the sum = **additive tasks**
15. groups working together = **cooperation**
17. rules within a group = **norms**
19. reduced social identity = **deindividuation**
20. reduction of motivation when in a group = **social loafing**
21. incompatibility in a group = **conflict**

Down

1. concern of being evaluated = **evaluation apprehension**
4. mutual group goals = **superordinate goals**
5. improving quality of group decisions = **authenticdissent**
6. negotiation = **bargaining**

7. giving back = **reciprocity**
8. collection of persons bonded together = **group**
10. integrating information to choose course of action = **decision making**
12. tightness of a group = **cohesiveness**
13. increasing individual gains by behavior = **social dilemmas**
14. group shifting toward extreme position = **group polarization**
16. perception of group as coherent entity = **entiavity**
18. performance effected by others = **social facilitation**

Modules A and B

Item Number	Practice Test 1	Practice Test 2	Practice Test 3	Comprehensive Test
1	A	C	B	B
2	D	A	A	A
3	B	A	B	D
4	C	B	D	C
5	D	C	C	B
6	B	D	A	B
7	B	D	C	D
8	C	B	D	B
9	D	C	C	C
10	A	B	B	B
11				D
12				B
13				A
14				C
15				A
16				T
17		*Correct Responses to*		F
18		*Short Answer/Essay Questions* ↓		T
19				T
20				F
21				T
22				F
23				F

1. Eyewitness testimony can be improved through a blank-lineup control, which is a procedure in which a witness views a police lineup that doesn't include a suspect. If a witness doesn't identify a suspect, this increases confidence in their testimony; however, if he or she identifies an innocent person, they're told of the mistake and cautioned to be more careful. Either way, this increases accuracy.

Also, encouraging witnesses to give first impressions and to show the lineup one person at a time, rather than as a group enhances eyewitness testimony.

2. Direct and indirect effects of stress each lead to an increase in illness. The indirect effects occur when the negative emotional effects of stress interfere with health-related behavior, such as eating a balanced diet or scheduling a physical examination. The direct physical effects of stress involves the delay of healing process in wounds and negative effects on the endocrine and immune system.

3. Awkward attempts to provide comfort can make things worse; some examples include minimizing the problem, suggesting that the problem is due to the stressed person's fault, and bumbling efforts to help.

4. When individuals feel that they're being treated fairly by their organization, they're more likely to engage in citizenship behavior than when they feel that they're being treated unfairly. In other words, why go that extra mile to help out your organization if your organization doesn't treat you with some degree of equity and fairness?

5. Charisma doesn't appear to matter in stable, unchanging environments. However, in a rapidly changing, chaotic environment, companies who had high charisma leaders outperformed those with low charisma leaders.

Crossword Puzzle Answer Key

Across

1. trying to be perfect = **perfectionism**
7. studies psychological variables and health = **health psychology**
9. evidence given by people who have witnessed a crime = **eyewitness testimony**
10. people who start new businesses = **entrepreneurs**
12. making it look like you are working hard = **shirking**
13. memories that we never experienced = **false memories**
14. leaders who use rewards and punishment = **transactional**
15. abbreviation for prosocial behavior at work = **OCB**
16. emotional resources from others = **social support**
17. attitude toward your job = **job satisfaction**

Down

2. not being able to ignore emotion generating information = **mental contamination**
3. charismatic leaders = **transformational**
4. biased questions = **leading questions**
5. response to threatening events = **stress**
6. lineup of innocent suspects = **blank lineup**
8. a theory that great leaders have special traits = **great person theory**
11. minor annoyances = **hassles**

NOTES

NOTES

NOTES

NOTES

NOTES

NOTES

NOTES

NOTES

NOTES

NOTES